Like a Bride Adorned

Emory Studies in Early Christianity

Original cover design by Gina M. Tansley
(adapted from Rick A. Robbins, Mixed Media, 1981)

The cover design introduces an environment for disciplined creativity. The seven squares superimposed over one another represent multiple arenas for programmatic research, analysis, and interpretation. The area in the center, common to all the arena, is like the area that provides the unity for a volume in the series. The small square in the center of the squares denotes a paragraph, page, or other unit of text. The two lines that extend out from the small square, perpendicular to one another, create an opening to territory not covered by any of the multiple squares. These lines have the potential to create yet another square of the same or different size that would be a new arena for research, analysis, and interpretation.

EMORY STUDIES
IN EARLY CHRISTIANITY

Volumes in this series investigate early Christian literature in the context of Mediterranean literature, religion, society, and culture. The authors use interdisciplinary methods informed by social, rhetorical, literary, and anthropological approaches to move beyond limits within traditional literary-historical investigations. The studies presuppose that Christianity began as a Jewish movement in various geographical, political, economic, and social locations in the Greco-Roman World.

1. David B. Gowler, *Host, Guest, Enemy and Friend: Portraits of the Pharisees in Luke and Acts,* 1991.
2. *H. Wayne Merritt, *In Word and Deed: Moral Integrity in Paul,* 1993.
3. *Vernon K. Robbins, *New Boundaries in Old Territory: Form and Social Rhetoric in Mark,* 1994. Edited and introduced by David B. Gowler.
4. Jan Botha, *Subject to Whose Authority?: Multiple Readings of Romans 13,* 1994.
5. Kjell Arne Morland, *The Rhetoric of Curse in Galatians: Paul Confronts a Different Gospel,* 1995.
6. Peder Borgen, Vernon K. Robbins, and David B. Gowler, eds., *Recruitment, Conquest and Conflict: Strategies in Judaism, Early Christianity, and the Greco-Roman World,* 1998.
7. Mark D. Given, *Paul's True Rhetoric: Ambiguity, Cunning, and Deception in Greece and Rome,* 2001.
8. Anders Eriksson, Thomas H. Olbricht, and Walter Ubelacker, eds., *Rhetorical Argumentation in Biblical Texts: Essays from the Lund 2000 Conference,* 2002.
9. James D. Hester and J. David Hester (Amador), eds., *Rhetorics and Hermeneutics: Wilhelm Wuellner and His Influence at the Close of the Century,* 2004.

* The second and third volumes were published by and are available from Peter Lang Publishing, Inc., 272 Seventh Avenue, 28th Floor, New York, NY 10001-6708; (212) 647-7700; FAX (212) 647-7707; customer service (800) 770-5264, (212) 647-7706; www.peterlang.com.

All other volumes are available through T & T Clark International.

Like a Bride Adorned

Reading Metaphor in John's Apocalypse

Lynn R. Huber

T & T CLARK INTERNATIONAL
A Continuum imprint
NEW YORK • LONDON

T & T Clark International
80 Maiden Lane, New York, NY 10038

T & T Clark International
The Tower building, 11 York Road, London SE1 7NX

T & T Clark International is a Continuum imprint

Library of Congress Cataloging-in-Publication Data

Huber, Lynn R.
Like a bride adorned : reading metaphor in John's Apocalypse / Lynn R. Huber.
p. cm. – (Emory studies in early Christianity)
Includes bibliographical references and index.
ISBN-13: 978-0-567-02674-3 (pbk. : alk. paper)
ISBN-10: 0-567-02674-4 (pbk. : alk. paper)
1. Bible. N.T. Revelation–Criticism, interpretation, etc. 2. Jerusalem in the Bible. 3. Metaphor in the Bible. I. Title. II. Series.

BS2825.6.J4H83 2007
228'.06–dc22

Printed in the United States of America

07 08 09 10 11 10 9 8 7 6 5 4 3 2 1

CONTENTS

ACKNOWLEDGMENTS

I am grateful to the many people who have assisted and encouraged me in this project. While I experienced no shortage of sound advice, the project's shortcomings are solely my own. First of all, I must thank my advisor, Gail R. O'Day. Her guidance and kindness, inside and outside of the academic setting, have been invaluable. She allowed me the opportunity to develop a dissertation project that reflected my varied interests, and she has helped me see it through to completion as a published work. I am especially grateful for her editorial eye and her sharp sense of humor. In addition, Alan Cienki, Luke Timothy Johnson, and Vernon K. Robbins each played an important role in the envisioning of this project. Luke was a particularly helpful source of support during some difficult times, and Vernon deserves a special word of thanks for his willingness to work with me on publishing this manuscript. Kathleen O'Conner at Columbia Seminary in Decatur, Georgia, also played a role as a reader of the dissertation manuscript. I have been fortunate to have a number of friends and colleagues from Emory University who have been and continue to be important conversation partners, including Kent L. Brintnall, Juan Hernandez Jr., Susan Hylen, and Robert H. Von Thaden Jr. Most importantly, my family has been incredibly supportive throughout this experience, although it took me a long way from our home in Portland, Oregon. I must especially thank my father, Archie Huber. He has encouraged me to pursue my goals and dreams, no matter where they take me. This book is dedicated to him and to the memory of my mother, Ruth G. Huber.

CHAPTER ONE

Reading through the "Veil of Obscurity": Interpreting Revelation's Imagistic Language

The story of the interpretation of the Book of Revelation begins in the earliest centuries of the church's life. As early as the third century, readers debated how to interpret Revelation and whether or not it was even worth interpreting.[1] One of the primary things prompting this debate was the symbolic or imagistic nature of this text. As the narrative account of a mystical vision, which includes a trip into the heavenly realm to view future events, Revelation consists of countless fantastic images. These images—multiwinged beasts, scarlet dragons, and furious angels, among other things—are simply not part of the day-to-day reality experienced by humans. As a result, interpreters have continually struggled with how to understand these images: Are they to be understood literally, read symbolically, or do they function as some sort of code? To this day, readers have not reached a consensus regarding the method for interpreting the various images recorded in John's Revelation.

One of the first writers to comment on the general sense of ambivalence concerning how to approach the text of Revelation was Dionysius of Alexandria, a third-century bishop. Even though Dionysius's own writings on Revelation are no longer extant, the church historian Eusebius records some of Dionysius's discussion. Notably, Dionysius refers to interpreters who rejected the Book of Revelation:

> Some before us have set aside and rejected the book altogether, criticizing it chapter by chapter, and pronouncing it without sense or argument, and maintaining that the title is fraudulent. For they say that it is not the work of John, nor is it a Revelation, because it is covered thickly and densely by a veil of obscurity. (Eusebius, *Historia ecclesiastica* 3.25 [Lake])

Approaching the text from a literal perspective, these interpreters found Revelation confusing and consequently meaningless.[2] Dionysius, however,

---

[1] The Muratorian canon (ca. 170–190 C.E.) does not include Revelation in its list of books suited for the church. In his *Ecclesiastical History* (ca. 260–340 C.E.), Eusebius notes that some accepted Revelation into the canon, while others rejected it (*Historia ecclestiastica* 3.25).

[2] Dionysius also refers to Cerinthus, a second-century Gnostic, who read Revelation from

takes a much different approach to the text. Admitting that he does not necessarily comprehend Revelation, Dionysius suggests that the text contains "deeper" and "more wonderful" meanings—meanings that cannot be accessed through literal interpretation of the images (Eusebius, *Historia ecclesiastica* 3.25). The meaning of Revelation is not to be found on the surface of the text, but the meaning of the text lies embedded within its images. As a result, instead of rejecting the text because of its imagistic and enigmatic nature, Dionysius proclaims, "And I do not reject what I cannot comprehend, but rather wonder because I do not understand it" (*Hist. eccl.* 3.25). Above all, Dionysius implies, the elusive nature of Revelation's imagistic language, the fact that Revelation's meaning lies not on the surface but within the depths of the text, makes the text fascinating and compelling.

As Dionysius's account suggests, for centuries readers have attempted to find a meaningful interpretation of John's visionary account. In the first half of this chapter, I will explore some of the predominant ways in which interpreters have approached the text of Revelation and have dealt with the imagistic nature of the text. Specifically, I will explore how representative interpreters understand and approach the images and figures within the text. In the second part of this chapter, I turn the discussion to some of the ways in which modern interpreters have addressed Revelation's nuptial imagery.[3] Situated near the end of the narrative, in chaps. 19 and 21, Revelation's nuptial imagery provides a focal point for understanding how the text's imagistic language has been understood more generally. Recognizing that Revelation's nuptial imagery draws on prophetic traditions depicting Jerusalem/Zion as a woman, interpreters have been quick to make facile connections between Revelation's image of the bride and the church, instead of exploring how these images function to shape the audience's thought.

---

a literal perspective. Unlike other interpreters, Cerinthus did not reject Revelation; rather, he expected that the faithful would soon enjoy the millennial wedding banquet (Rev 19:9; Eusebius, *Hist. eccl.* 3:28).

[3] This discussion does not strictly follow the typical categories scholar use to map out the history of scholarship on Revelation: the church- or world-historical approach, the spiritual (nonhistorical) approach, the end-historical approach, and the contemporary-historical (preterist) approach. Scholars differ over both the names of these categories and how they are divided. These particular category headings come from M. Eugene Boring, *Revelation* (IBC; Louisville, Ky.: John Knox Press, 1989), 47–51. These categories, which often overlap with one another, primarily focus on how interpreters relate the text to history (Elisabeth Schüssler Fiorenza, *The Book of Revelation: Justice and Judgment*, 2nd ed. [Minneapolis: Fortress Press, 1998], 35ff.). The focus of the following discussion is how interpreters deal with Revelation's imagistic language. Thus, while the following analysis often intersects with these categories, they are secondary to the discussion of how imagistic language is approached.

Revelation: "The Things That Must Happen Soon"

Dionysius maintains that Revelation's meaning is most likely embedded within the images of the text, which makes a surface or literal interpretation inadequate. While some early Christian interpreters agree with Dionysius, many others reject this perspective. Many of Dionysius's predecessors and contemporaries, at least those whose works are extant, read Revelation, or significant parts of Revelation, as a generally accurate account of imminent future events—"the things which must happen soon" (Rev 1:1). These interpreters are often described as "church-historical," since they read the text as describing events that will take place within the history of the church.[4] Until the time of Augustine, this approach stands as the dominant scholarly method of interpreting Revelation.[5]

Writing at the end of the second century, Irenaeus provides one of the earliest extant examples of interpreters who approach Revelation from a church-historical perspective. Although Irenaeus does not appear to have written a commentary on Revelation, he briefly offers his opinion regarding the proper method for interpreting this text. Confronting those who deny the resurrection of the flesh, in the fifth book of *Against Heresies*, Irenaeus denounces attempts at reading Revelation, as well as other apocalyptic and prophetic texts, allegorically (*Adversus Haereses* 5.351). Allegorical interpretation is unnecessary because Revelation describes events and entities that are "steadfast, and true, and substantial" (*Haer.* 5.35.2). The images within the text refer to or describe physical realities. If the text is true, as Scripture is assumed to be and as Revelation claims to be (Rev 21:5, 6), then the things described in the text will eventually come to fruition and be experienced.

Irenaeus's description of the new Jerusalem, which draws on Revelation 21, reflects his claim that the text should not be read allegorically. Irenaeus maintains that John's description of the new Jerusalem descending

---

[4] Modern scholars typically label Irenaeus and other early church-historical interpreters as "chiliasts" or "millennialists," although they did not refer to themselves with these labels. The first known use of the label "chiliasts" occurs in Augustine's *City of God* 20.7. In using this label, Augustine denounces these interpreters, with whom he once associated. Similarly, the term "millennialist" is a later label, which emphasizes the fact that many of the future historical interpreters were concerned with the thousand-year reign described in Rev 20:1–6. One must be careful, however, about implying that these early interpreters were somehow obsessed solely with this text; for, the use of this text typically happens within a context in which the interpreter argues for a fleshly resurrection. The interpreters often called "chiliasts" or "millennialists" were not necessarily interested in this text in and of itself; rather, they used this text as one way of supporting a larger concern.

[5] Bernard McGinn, *The Calabrian Abbot: Joachim of Fiore in the History of Western Thought* (New York: Macmillan, 1985), 77f.

from heaven describes an actual and substantial future kingdom of God. Humans who are righteous will "truly dwell in the city of God" (*Haer.* 5.35.2). The inhabitants of this city will actually partake in the wedding feast to which they have been invited (Rev 19:9; *Haer.* 5.36.2). For Irenaeus, there is no reason to assume that the words and images of the text do not describe material aspects of the "real world" or the future "real world."[6]

While some scholars may describe Irenaeus's interpretive method as "literal," this designation is somewhat misleading. Few interpreters of Revelation, even those denouncing "allegorical" readings, actually read or advocate reading the entire text literally. One of Irenaeus's fellow interpreters, Tertullian, demonstrates this interpretive flexibility in his treatise *On the Resurrection of the Flesh,* written around the turn of the third century. Like Irenaeus, Tertullian criticizes those who deny a future physical resurrection of the dead. In so doing, Tertullian delves into a discussion of figurative versus literal language. Tertullian claims that those who deny a fleshly resurrection, as described in Revelation as well as in other Christian texts, do so because they interpret all prophetic statements allegorically or figuratively. They assume that prophetic writers speak almost entirely in figures of speech; thus, they interpret all of the prophetic texts allegorically or according to a spiritual, that is nonphysical, sense. In contrast, Tertullian denies that the prophetic Scriptures, including Revelation, are comprised entirely of figurative language. Instead, these texts make use of both literal and figurative language, figurative language occurring "occasionally" in certain portions of prophetic texts (*De resurrectione carnis* 19–20). In this way, Tertullian recognizes the impossibility of thoroughly literal interpretations of texts such as Revelation, since these authors do employ figurative language.

Tertullian offers some examples, including one from Revelation, of how one might go about interpreting figurative language. Since he is concerned with defending the idea of a physical resurrection, he naturally chooses what he believes to be a figurative image relating to flesh:

> We have also in the Scriptures *robes* mentioned as allegorizing the hope of the flesh. Thus in the Revelation of John it is said: "These are they which have not defiled their clothes with women,"— indicating, of course, virgins. . . . Therefore they shall be "clothed in white raiment," that is, in the bright beauty of the unwedded flesh. (*Res.* xxvi [Holmes]; cf. Rev 3:4; 14:4)

For Tertullian, the image of robes or garments clearly signifies flesh. Depending on how the image is qualified, it can refer to virginal flesh or

[6] The language of "real world" in terms of propositional language comes from Boring, *Revelation,* 51.

nonvirginal flesh. Tertullian continues by referencing other scriptural passages that similarly include the image of a garment or robe, suggesting that in these instances the image also refers to flesh. The image of a garment signifies, in codelike fashion, the concept of flesh. This approach to imagistic or figurative language is clearly not literal, since Tertullian does not assert that the image of a garment signifies only a garment. It can be said, however, that he interprets Revelation's images from a literal perspective. Tertullian's method of interpretation seemingly assumes a basic premise of literal or propositional language—that a signifier within a text exists in a one-to-one relationship with a signified.[7]

Although he does not include a discussion of how he understands figurative language, in the fifth book of *Against Heresies* Irenaeus approaches the images or symbols of Revelation in a manner similar to that of Tertullian. It is instructive to look at Irenaeus's discussion of the meaning of the number 666 in Rev 13:18. Recognizing that, through gematria, this number can equal a number of different names, Irenaeus resists the tendency to pinpoint a name that corresponds to this number. While Irenaeus remains chary about drawing conclusions regarding 666, he does suggest that the number refers to a single historical referent. The name of this figure, however, has simply been suppressed by the Holy Spirit (*Haer.* 5.30.3). Thus, even though Irenaeus recognizes the complexity of this numerical image, he implies that the image refers to a single historical referent.

In Irenaeus and Tertullian, the images in the texts are read as describing material substances and not, primarily, spiritual realities. Although this approach tends to favor reading texts literally, there is the acknowledgment that the text may contain figurative language; yet figurative language still describes realities external to the text.

Reading Revelation "Spiritually": Augustine and His Legacy

As we saw with Dionysius, some of the early interpreters of Revelation adopted a nonliteral, or an allegorical, approach to Revelation.[8] It was not until the beginning of the fifth century, however, with the work of Augustine of Hippo, that this way of interpreting Revelation became the predominant approach to the text's imagistic language. Even though Augustine

---

[7] Raymond W. Gibbs, *The Poetics of Mind: Figurative Thought, Language, and Understanding* (Cambridge: Cambridge University Press, 1994), 60–63.

[8] One important advocate of reading prophetic literature, including Revelation, spiritually was Origen. However, while Origen intended to write a commentary on Revelation, he apparently never completed this project. Consequently, we know very little about Origen's approach to Revelation, except that he claims that the book of Revelation is a book of "deep obscurity" which contains "unspeakable mysteries." Origen, *On First Principles*, trans. G. W. Butterworth (New York: Harper & Row, 1966; repr., Gloucester, Mass.: Peter Smith, 1973), 4.2.3.

did not write a commentary on the Book of Revelation, his "spiritual" reading of Revelation generally shaped the way scholars approached the text for the next nine centuries.[9]

While Augustine's treatment of Revelation is found primarily in his *magnum opus City of God* (ca. 413–426 C.E.), to understand his interpretive method it is necessary to look at his earlier work *De doctrina christiana* (*On Christian Teaching,* ca. 387 C.E.). In this work Augustine discusses the nature of language, including figurative language. His understanding of figurative or imagistic language rests on the supposition that words function as signs that generally represent or point to objects and events (*Doctr. chr.* 1.2).[10] As will be discussed in the next chapter, signs or words can be either proper or figurative. A sign is proper if it points out the object or event which it was presumably designed to point out. A sign is figurative if it is used to refer to something other than it was intended. Figurative language entails the "incorrect" use of a word, since it is used in a way that defies conventional usage.

Given the reality of figurative language, an interpreter must not simply equate particular words with the realities they ordinarily represent. This, according to Augustine in *City of God*, is the mistake of those whom he calls the "chiliasts," referring to church-historical interpreters of Revelation (*De civitate Dei* 20.7). Instead of assuming that the language of Revelation always points to its conventional meaning, in some cases it is necessary to determine "the hidden kernel of meaning" within the sign (*Doctr. chr.* 3.12.18).

In *City of God,* Augustine reveals the kernel of meaning hidden in the images of Revelation 20 and 21. Reading Rev 20:1–6 as a description of an actual thousand-year reign of Christ on earth, the chiliast interpreters turn this text into "ridiculous fables" (*Civ.* 20.7). Not only do these interpreters believe that the millennial kingdom includes the physical resurrection of Christian martyrs, but they emphasize the material abundance of this kingdom. They depict a time of "most unrestrained material feasts, in which there will be so much to eat and drink that not only will those supplies keep within no bounds of moderation but will also exceed the limits even of incredibility" (*Civ.* 20.7 [Bettenson]). For Augustine, this interpretation of Revelation fails to recognize the figurative nature of the text; for it depicts God's saints in a manner contrary to principles outlined elsewhere in Scripture.

---

[9] It is generally acknowledged that Augustine drew his method of interpreting the Apocalypse from Tyconius, a fourth-century Donatist, whose commentary on Revelation is no longer extant. Since Tyconius's works are available only through reconstructions drawing on other texts, I have chosen to focus on Augustine's understanding of Revelation. For a general introduction to Tyconius and his view of the Apocalypse, see McGinn, *The Calabrian Abbot,* 80–84.

[10] John M. Rist suggests that Augustine's own understanding of language actually reflects a number of influences, including Stoic views of language and rhetorical practices. See Rist, *Augustine: Ancient Thought Baptized* (Cambridge: Cambridge University Press, 1994), 23ff.

In contrast to the chiliasts, Augustine suggests that the image of the thousand-year reign refers to either the final period of the world's history or the wholeness of the world's history. While Augustine does not conclude with a single meaning, he clearly indicates that the image should not be read literally as referring to an actual thousand years, but should be read as pointing to a spiritual truth. Augustine does not limit his discussion of Revelation to this single image, but he continues to read the rest of Revelation 20 from a spiritual perspective. Augustine suggests that the image of the new Jerusalem descending from heaven, described in Revelation 21, should be read spiritually. This image represents the church, those individuals who understand themselves as citizens of the "city of God" rather than the "city of the world." It is described as "descending" because it has been coming down from heaven, from God, since its beginning into the period of the present age (*Civ.* 20.17). Revelation is referring not to a physical city that will descend from heaven in the future; rather, the image of the new Jerusalem points to a spiritual, or nonphysical, reality that exists in the past, present, and future.

While Augustine offers a different reading of Revelation than either Irenaeus or Tertullian, he actually expresses and operates with a similar view of language. Both Augustine and those whom he calls chiliasts approach the language of Revelation primarily in terms of propositional language, as signs that point to singular referents. While the chiliasts, or church-historical interpreters, read Revelation's language as referring to actual physical referents, Augustine reads the images of the text as figurative language that points to spiritual realities. Augustine approaches the images in Revelation as signs that point to or refer to "things," even though they do so indirectly and point to spiritual things or realities. While the actual words of a text may appear to describe a future kingdom which is substantial, as figurative signs these words refer indirectly to something other than a physical future kingdom.

Augustine's spiritual interpretation of Revelation provides one of the dominant interpretive approaches for subsequent scholarly interpretations of Revelation. Although there continued to be advocates of church-historical interpretation throughout the church of the Middle Ages, scholarly interpreters, such as the Venerable Bede, Ambrose Autpert, and Beatus of Liébana, continued to emphasize a spiritual interpretation of Revelation's images. As Bernard McGinn explains, "The dominant tendency in the interpretation of the Apocalypse since the end of the fourth century had been an individualizing and moralizing approach that, following the authority of Tyconius and Saint Augustine, had used John's imagery to describe the soul's warfare against vice."[11]

---

[11] Bernard McGinn, *Apocalyptic Spirituality: Treatises and Letters of Lactantius, Adso of Mon-*

Joachim of Fiore: Reading Revelation through the Mind's Eye

At the end of the twelfth century, the Italian abbot Joachim of Fiore (ca. 1132–1202) introduced a popular alternative to the "spiritual" interpretation of Revelation's imagistic language. The complexity of Joachim's approach to Revelation made it difficult for subsequent interpreters to understand and execute. As a result, Joachim's works fostered an extreme turn back to the chiliast view held by some of Revelation's earliest interpreters. Thus, while Joachim approached Revelation with a fairly sophisticated understanding of symbols and figurative language, his work eventually led to reading Revelation as a blueprint for all of history.

Although Joachim writes little about his own life, he does reveal that his view of Scripture, especially John's Apocalypse, comes to him through visionary experiences:

> Having gone through the preceding verses of the Book of Revelation to this place (Rev 1:10), I experienced such great difficulty and mental constraint beyond the ordinary that it was like feeling the stone that closed the tomb opposed to me. . . . About the middle of the night's silence, as I think, the hour when it is thought that our lion of the tribe of Judah rose from the dead, as I was meditating, suddenly something of the fullness of this book and of the entire agreement of the Old and the New Testaments was perceived by a clarity of understanding in my mind's eye. (Joachim, *Expositio in Apocalypsim* 39v)[12]

As this quotation suggests, Joachim's understanding of Revelation is closely bound up with his concept of the relationship between the two Testaments. When Joachim wrote his commentary on the Apocalypse, *Expositio in Apocalypsim*, it is likely that he simultaneously composed two other major works addressing the relationship between the Old and New Testaments, *Liber Concordiae* (*Book of Concordance*) and *Psalterium decem chordarum* (*The Ten-Chorded Psalter*).[13]

Living during a time marked by political instability, ecclesial conflicts, and economic woes, Joachim was fascinated by the connections between Scripture and human history.[14] One of the looming questions for medieval scholars was the relationship between humanity's historical time and God's divine plan: Were they now living within a space after the completed "Sec-

---

tier-En-Der, Joachim of Fiore, The Franciscan Spirituals, Savonarola (Classics of Western Spirituality; Mahwah, N.J.: Paulist Press, 1979), 101.

[12] Translated by Bernard McGinn, *Visions of the End: Apocalyptic Traditions in the Middle Ages*, 2nd ed. (New York: Columbia University Press, 1998), 130.

[13] Delno C. West, "Introduction," in *Joachim of Fiore in Christian Thought: Essays on the Influence of the Calabrian Prophet* (New York: Burt Franklin, 1975), iii.

[14] West, "Introduction," ii.

ond Dispensation" of God, were things progressing within the "Second Dispensation," or were things generally decaying before some great renewal? As Marjorie Reeves explains, "The problem for medieval thinkers was how to relate the moving moments of this time-process in which they were caught to the unchanging eternal pattern of reality which was the ground of their faith. They did this by means of images."[15] Through images, such as the image of history as a pilgrimage, medieval thinkers found a variety of ways to conceptualize and understand their own experience of history in relation to their thoughts about God's plan for history. It is in this context of using images to think about history and its relationship to God that Joachim's interpretations of Revelation are best addressed. For Joachim, Revelation provides the images that draw together and elucidate past, present, and future history.

As the final book in the Christian canon, Joachim understands Revelation to be "the key of things past, the knowledge of things to come; the opening of what is sealed, the uncovering of what is hidden" (Joachim, *Expositio* 3r).[16] In a view that grows out of his visionary experience, Joachim finds that the images of Revelation provide the means for conceptualizing and understanding the structure and significance of both the first and second *status* of history (described in the Old and New Testaments respectively), as well as their relation to a coming third *status* of history (the time of the Spirit).[17] Believing that he is living at the cusp between the second and third *status*, Joachim reads the bulk of Revelation as describing past and present history—the first and second *status*. Joachim, however, does not read Revelation simply as a linear description of historical events. Since the first and second *status* share a certain concord, Revelation draws the events of the two *status* together, revealing their relationship. For example,

---

[15] Marjorie Reeves, *Joachim of Fiore and the Prophetic Future: Medieval Study in Historical Thinking*, rev. ed. (Gloucestershire: Sutton, 1999), 1. Reeves notes that Anselm of Havelberg and Rupert of Deutz, both writing in the first half of the twelfth century, also grappled with the meaning of history and its relationship to God's plan for the future. However, neither of these scholars investigated the relation of history to the coming age in as thorough a manner as Joachim. Reeves, *Joachim of Fiore*, 2.

[16] Translated by McGinn, *The Calabrian Abbot*, 147.

[17] Many medieval biblical scholars, drawing on ancient views, operate with the assumption that the two Dispensations of God, represented by and in the Old and New Testaments, embrace parallel persons and events. Often this relationship is understood in terms of *allegoria* (allegory). Specific persons and objects in the Old Testament are understood to be *like* aspects of the New Testament. Joachim suggests that the two Dispensations also possess *concordia* (concordance or agreement). Each of the Testaments reveal histories (*status*) that are fundamentally related to each other. That is to say, not only are certain persons and events described in the Old Testament parallel to those described in the New Testament, but the very structure of the first and second *status* are parallel. See McGinn, *Apocalyptic Spirituality*, 122.

Joachim highlights the image of the seven seals as describing especially the past and present *status*. He does this by reading the actual seals on the scroll, described in 5:1, as representing the seven periods of Old Testament history, while reading the *opening* of these seals relating directly to seven periods of the church.[18] Joachim's interpretation of the seal imagery suggests that he is not simply proposing the existence of two parallel histories, but he sees the events of the second *status* as ensuing out of and augmenting the events of the first *status*. The image of the seven seals does not function as a rigid template into which the events of history are forced. Instead, Joachim uses Revelation's imagery as a way of thinking about history and its relation to the future.

Joachim's use of imagery as a way of conceptualizing abstract ideas, particularly the progression of history, is evident in his many *figurae*. These are illustrations or diagrams nestled within Joachim's scriptural exposition and subsequently collected into a volume comprised entirely of figures, *Liber figurarum*.[19] The presence of these illustrations, as Reeves and Beatrice Hirsch-Reich demonstrate in their study of Joachim's illustrations, witness to the fact that Joachim had a visual imagination and approached the biblical texts with "the eyes of the mind" (*oculi mentis*).[20]

A number of Joachim's illustrations, drawing pon Revelation's own imagery, relate directly to his interpretation. Most obvious are Joachim's illustrations of Revelation's seven-headed dragon, which is described in Revelation 12 and 17. Following the text of Revelation, which describes the heads as kings (Rev 17:10), Joachim identifies the heads as seven tyrants who persecute the church during the second *status*.[21] These tyrants include Herod, who persecuted the Jews, Nero, Constantius II,[22] Muhammad, Masemoth,[23] and Saladin. The seventh head remains unnamed in this illustration and is identified only as a future *Antichristus*.[24] While other interpreters

---

[18] Reeves, *Joachim of Fiore*, 8; Joachim, *Expositio* 3v.

[19] Marjorie Reeves and Beatrice Hirsch-Reich, *The Figurae of Joachim of Fiore* (Oxford: Clarendon Press, 1972). The authorship of *Liber Figurarum* is not certain, since there are a number of works, including illustrations, spuriously attributed to Joachim. As the illustrations of the *Liber Figurarum* are generally more detailed and complex than those found within Joachim's three major works, it is often argued that these illustrations may have been expanded and compiled by a disciple of Joachim. Whether or not this text was created by the hand of Joachim, Reeves and Hirsch-Reich argue that the illustrations reflect and draw together many of the ideas that originally ensue from the "kaleidoscopic imagination" of Joachim himself (Reeves and Hirsch-Reich, *The Figurae*, 95).

[20] Reeves and Hirsch-Reich, *The Figurae*, 20; e.g., Joachim, *Expositio* 36r.

[21] McGinn, *Apocalyptic*, 136.

[22] Constantius was an Arian emperor from 337–361 C.E.; McGinn, *Apocalyptic*, 294.

[23] While it is unclear, this name may refer to a North African Moorish ruler. McGinn, *Apocalyptic*, 294

[24] McGinn, *Apocalyptic*, 136.

might stop at the point in identifying the different heads, Joachim allows the image of the dragon as a whole to evoke additional ideas. For example, in his illustration Joachim draws a large tail on the dragon. In his notations around the image of the tail, he suggests that it represents the final Antichrist. The illustration helps elucidate the text of Revelation, which suggests that besides the seven heads, the beast itself "is an eighth and it belongs to the seven" (Rev 17:11b). Joachim associates this eighth Antichrist with the commander of Gog, who is mentioned in Revelation 20, and suggests that he will come during the third *status*.[25] Joachim's illustration suggests, moreover, that this final Antichrist, the commander of Gog, is part of the same beast as the Antichrists before him. In this way, the image of the dragon allows Joachim to illustrate, literally, not only the identity of the Antichrists, those who persecute the church within the second *status*, but also to illustrate the relationship between these persecutors and the one who will come in the third *status*. While this does not exhaust Joachim's reflection on the image of the seven-headed dragon, it does begin to convey the way in which Joachim uses the images of Revelation to conceptualize history.

Joachim's interpretation of Revelation reveals a complex understanding of images and imagistic language.[26] Joachim naturally turns both to images and imagistic language in order to express difficult and even paradoxical concepts. For Joachim, symbolic language communicates ideas that are essentially inexpressible in literal or propositional language. This understanding of imagistic language involves approaching the images of the text as tools for understanding and expressing difficult concepts, including how particular concepts relate to one another. This approach to Revelation's images differs significantly from that of Irenaeus and Tertullian, as well as of Augustine. Whereas they tend to treat the images of Revelation as propositional language, in which the words of the text function as signs pointing to singular realities, Joachim understands figurative language as expressing complex networks of concepts.

Another significant way in which Joachim differs from spiritual interpreters, notably Augustine, is his tendency to make connections between Revelation and history. Bernard McGinn comments, "In this Joachim stands in resolute, if silent, opposition to Augustine."[27] Augustine and other "spiritual" interpreters chafed at the idea that Revelation described, in any way, actual historical events. In contrast to this, Joachim's interest in the rela-

---

[25] Ibid., 140.

[26] Bernard McGinn, "Symbolism in the Thought of Joachim of Fiore," in *Prophecy and Millenarianism: Essays in Honour of Marjorie Reeves*, ed. Ann Williams (Essex: Longman, 1980), 145–64.

[27] McGinn, *The Calabrian Abbot*, 151.

tionship between Scripture and human history sometimes leads him to make close connections between Revelation's images and historical personages and events, even though this is not necessarily representative of his overall approach to Revelation's images. It is this aspect of Joachim's work, however, that his disciples adopt and expand.[28]

Joachim's ideas continued to spread throughout medieval Europe after his death in 1202. A number of subsequent works were attributed to Joachim, including commentaries on Jeremiah (ca. 1240) and Isaiah (ca. 1260) and at least one collection of spurious illustrations, which Marjorie Reeves and Beatrice Hirsch-Reich call the *Praemissiones*.[29] For the most part, the authors of these spurious works, as well as many other writers following after Joachim, misunderstood Joachim's ideas and failed to retain the complexity of his interpretations. They did this by primarily emphasizing Joachim's connections between Revelation and history. One example of the tendency to emphasize historical connections is seen in the writing of Gerardo of Borgo San Donnino. In his *Introduction to the Eternal Gospel* (1254), which was condemned by the church in 1255, Gerardo attempts to summarize Joachim's three major works. In so doing, Gerardo pinpoints the beginning of the third *status*, claiming that it will begin in 1260, with the end of the church. Further, Gerardo predicts that the writings of Joachim, which he describes as the "Eternal Gospel," will completely supersede both the Old and New Testaments.[30]

Not only did Joachim's disciples use his ideas and methods of interpretation to try to determine the date of the third *status*, but they also used his works to identify the Antichrist. In the *Commentary on Jeremiah*, for instance, Emperor Frederick II and his successor are described as the horned beasts of Revelation. This type of interpretation was adopted by Pope Gregory II who, in a 1239 letter, also described Frederick II as the beast of Revelation 13:

> The beast filled with the names of blasphemy has risen up from the sea. With the feet of a bear, a mouth like a lion, and the rest of his limbs like a leopard, in his rage he has opened his mouth to blaspheme the divine name. . . . Cease to be surprised that he who now arises to destroy the name of the Lord from

[28] McGinn, *Visions of the End*, 159.

[29] Reeves and Hirsch-Reich, *The Figurae*, 275ff. They explain that while the illustrations illustrate many of Joachim's own ideas, in some places the author clearly misunderstands Joachim. Interestingly, the sixteenth-century editors of works attributed to Joachim believed that this collection of illustrations exemplified the thought of Joachim. See Reeves and Hirsch-Reich, *The Figurae*, 296.

[30] Given that Gerardo's work was condemned, there are no extant copies of his work. The primary source for his ideas is *The Protocol of Anagni*, which includes the particularly offensive elements of Gerardo's text. See McGinn, *Visions of the End*, 165; cf. Reeves, *Joachim of Fiore*, 33.

> the earth directs an injurious sword against us. Rather, so that you may be able to resist his lies with open truth and to confute his fallacies with pure argument, carefully consider the beginning, middle, and end of this beast Frederick called emperor. . . .[31]

Not to be outdone, Frederick II offers a retort in which he compares the pope to the great dragon of Revelation 12 and the angel of the abyss described in Revelation 16![32] Although Joachim is much more careful about making connections between the images of Revelation and historical figures and events, his work ignited a growing tendency to use the text as a key to predicting and interpreting historical events. This mode of interpretation is often called "world-historical," because the text of Revelation is understood to relate to events of world history, including political events. Even more so than interpreters in the ancient church-historical approach, these interpreters read the images of Revelation as a coded description of past, present, and future events. Almost every aspect of the text is treated as a reference to particular historical entities and events.

The interpretations of Joachim demonstrate the creative potential that exists within Revelation's images. Joachim appropriates the images from Revelation and develops new ideas while working within the structures of the imagery. Joachim envisions Revelation along with John, finding new ways of understanding these images as they unfold. In contrast, the disciples of Joachim demonstrate the ease with which well-meaning interpreters can fall into reading Revelation as a code.

Reading Revelation after Joachim

The scholarly struggle over how to approach Revelation's imagistic language continued. As the timetables for the end of the world were proven wrong and identifications between images in the text and historical figures seemed more and more driven by polemics, scholars began to search for other ways to understand the images in the text. Many scholars turned to reading the text as a reflection of past history and not as a map of future history. This approach manifests itself in two different, yet related, ways. First, during the seventeenth century some scholars, often called "preterists," began to approach Revelation as containing prophecies about history, although they understood that these prophecies had been fulfilled prior to the time of Constantine. As early as 1614, the Jesuit interpreter Luis de Alcazar began reading Revelation as a description of prophecies already fulfilled. Alcazar advocated reading Revelation 12–19 as John's predictions

---

31 McGinn, *Visions of the End*, 173–74.

32 Ibid., 174–75.

about the foundation and growth of the Christian church.[33] Soon this method of reading Revelation's images was appropriated by a number of notable Protestant scholars, including Hugo Grotius (1644).[34]

While Alcazar and his contemporaries were offering their interpretations during the seventeenth century, preterist interpretation truly began to spread during the eighteenth century.[35] With the growing influence of rationalist thought on biblical studies in the late-eighteenth and nineteenth centuries, however, many scholars were wary of addressing Revelation in terms of predictions. Consequently, an interpretive shift takes place during this period. The images of Revelation began to be read primarily as references to aspects of the author's context.[36] Believing that Revelation's author, John, writes during a time of persecution, crisis, or perceived crisis, these interpreters suggest that the author employs traditional images as a way of describing his own context. Through the manipulation of symbols, the author critiques the dominant culture, typically understood as the Roman Empire.[37] This approach, often called the *zeitgeschichtliche* or "contemporary-historical" approach has persisted in a variety of guises as one of the dominant scholarly approaches to Revelation.[38] This kind of refer-

---

[33] Arthur W. Wainwright, *Mysterious Apocalypse: Interpreting the Book of Revelation* (Nashville: Abingdon Press, 1993), 63; Otto Böcher, *Die Johannesapokalypse* (Erträge der Forschung; Darmstadt: Wissenschaftliche Buchgesellschaft, 1975), 2.

[34] Böcher, *Die Johannesapokalypse*, 2.

[35] Böcher notes that in the late eighteenth century two influential New Testament scholars, Johann Salomo Semler (1725–1791) and Johann Gottfried Herder (1744–1803) embrace the contemporary-historical method of interpreting Revelation (*Die Johannesapokalypse*, 2–3).

[36] Wainwright, *Mysterious Apocalypse*, 108ff.; Böcher, *Die Johannesapokalypse*, 6f.

[37] Not all contemporary-historical interpreters have read Revelation as a response to Roman persecution of Christians. Wainwright notes, for example, that some of the early contemporary-historical critics read the text as describing the fate of Jerusalem leading up to the destruction of the Temple in 70 C.E. (*Mysterious Apocalypse*, 125ff.).

[38] The nineteenth-century German scholar Friedrich Lücke, whose edition on Revelation was originally published in 1832, stands as one of the early advocates of the contemporary-historical approach (*Versuch einer Vollständigen Einleitung in die Offenbarung des Johannes*, 2nd ed. [Bonn: Eduard Weber, 1852]; Böcher, *Die Johannesapokalypse*, 7). Lücke's work is truly groundbreaking since he is one of the first interpreters to recognize the similarities between Revelation and other so-called apocalyptic literature, including Daniel and Ezekiel. In so doing, Lücke recognizes that many apocalyptic texts include the description of past events in prophetic terms. That is, apocalyptic texts contain "predictions" of events that have happened in the past, a phenomenon often called *ex eventu* prophecy. Lücke brings this understanding of apocalyptic texts to bear on Revelation, suggesting that John describes events that are happening within his own context and events that he truly believes will happen imminently. More specifically, John describes the reign of Christ within the context of the Roman Empire, which John depicts as an anti-Christian world power.

Although Lücke's work on Revelation is massive, he does not offer a traditional commentary on the text of Revelation. In his 1862 commentary on Revelation, Friedrich Bleek approaches the text and its images from a perspective similar to that of Lücke (*Vorlesungen*

ential reading, which dominates in the modern period, is best illustrated by looking at one image system. In this case, we will explore interpretations of Revelation's nuptial imagery. In so doing we will focus on ways these interpretive tendencies shape the reading of Revelation's nuptial imagery.

Narrowing the Focus: Modern Critical Readings of Revelation's Nuptial Imagery

John's description of the new Jerusalem descending "prepared as a bride adorned for her husband" is arguably one of the most compelling images in Revelation, even though its mention is relatively brief. Introduced in the final chapters of the text (19:7–9 and 21:1–4, 9–11), the nuptial imagery is located at the culmination of the text. This suggests its rhetorical importance.[39] The rhetorical importance of this imagery is also suggested by its structural pairing with the image of the great prostitute, described in chaps. 17 and 18—an image that receives a great deal of attention in the text.[40] The importance of Revelation's nuptial imagery also stems from its connection to the image of the new Jerusalem, which is one of the final images used to characterize the community of those who follow God and the Lamb.

In spite of the rhetorical significance of nuptial imagery in Revelation, there have been few significant scholarly studies devoted solely to Revelation's nuptial imagery.[41] Discussions of this imagery occur in a number of related contexts: (1) history-of-religions studies focusing on the mythic backgrounds of Revelation; (2) full-scale commentaries on Revelation that generally note the Jewish and early Christian "backgrounds" of the nuptial imagery; (3) literary-functional readings of Revelation that address the nuptial imagery as a rhetorical device related to the image of the great prosti-

---

über die Apokalypse [Berlin: Georg Reimer, 1862]; see also Böcher, *Die Johannesapokalypse,* 7; Wainwright, *Mysterious Apocalypse,* 128). Like his contemporary, Bleek reads Revelation as primarily functioning as a critique of the Roman Empire, including a prediction of its imminent demise (*Vorlesungen,* 325ff.). Each aspect of John's image points to a referent in his historical milieu. In this way, the images of the text function as coded references to aspects of John's first-century context.

[39] Rhetorically, things that come at the end of the text are particularly significant, as they are likely to be remembered more readily than things coming at the beginning or in the middle of a text.

[40] The fact that the images of the great prostitute and the bride are parallel is suggested by, among other things, the uniting of the images within the hymn in 19:1–8. For a thorough discussion of the parallel nature of these image, see Barbara R. Rossing, *The Choice Between Two Cities: Whore, Bride, and Empire in the Apocalypse* (Harrisburg, Penn.: Trinity Press, 1999).

[41] While there are no major scholarly discussions dealing specifically with Revelation's nuptial imagery, there are a few monographs devoted to the study of nuptial imagery across different aspects of the Christian tradition. See, for example, Richard A. Batey, *New Testament Nuptial Imagery* (Leiden: E. J. Brill, 1971).

tute; (4) feminist-critical readings of Revelation that seek to expose the ways in which gender functions within the text. In the following pages, we will examine representatives of these different approaches to Revelation's nuptial imagery. This analysis is not specifically intended to identify the failures of these different approaches; rather, by examining previous scholarship on the text at hand we can hopefully gain a "thick" understanding of the imagery.

The Myth behind the Marriage: Revelation's Nuptial Imagery as Ancient Myth

While critical scholarship on Revelation predates the late-nineteenth and twentieth centuries, the work of Hermann Gunkel and Wilhelm Bousset marks a radical turn in Revelation scholarship.[42] Part of the *religionsgeschichtliche Schule,* the history-of-religions school, Gunkel and Bousset read the imagistic language of Revelation in relation to the ancient myths that were circulating during the first century. The claims of some of today's most influential contemporary scholars on Revelation, including Adela Yarbro Collins, develop out of the insights of Gunkel and Bousset.

Gunkel presents the history-of-religions method of interpretation as a desirable alternative to traditional interpretive approaches to Revelation, especially the contemporary-historical method of interpretation.[43] Inter-

---

[42] R. H. Charles, *Studies in the Apocalypse*, 2nd ed. (Edinburgh: T & T Clark, 1915), 75ff. Pinpointing a starting point for critical scholarship on Revelation is nearly impossible. As early as the third century C.E., scholars were questioning the authorship and authority of this text. Notably, Dionysius, a bishop in Alexandria, rejected Johannine authorship on the basis of Revelation's linguistic style. This is reported by Eusebius in *Hist. eccl.* 3.25–28.

It is possible to argue that the beginning of modern criticism of Revelation arises out of mid-seventeenth century and preterist interpretation. As scholars became increasingly dissatisfied with reading Revelation as a prediction of future events, they began to search for other ways to understand the images in the text. In particular, the preterists advocated reading Revelation in relation to past history. The text contained prophecies about history; however, they believed these prophecies to have been fulfilled prior to the time of Constantine. This method of interpretation begins as early as 1614 with the Jesuit interpreter Luis de Alcazar. Soon this method of reading Revelation's images was appropriated by a number of notable Protestant scholars, including Hugo Grotius (1644). While Alcazar and his contemporaries were offering their interpretations during the seventeenth century, preterist interpretation truly began to spread during the eighteenth century (Wainwright, *Mysterious Apocalypse*, 63; and Böcher *Die Johannesapokalypse*, 2).

[43] Hermann Gunkel, *Schöpfung und Chaos in Urzeit und Endzeit: Eine religionsgeschichtliche Untersuchung über Gen 1 und Ap Joh 12,* 2nd rev. ed. (Göttingen: Vandenhoeck & Ruprecht, 1921), 202ff. See also idem, *Zum religionsgeschichtlichen Verständnis des Neuen Testaments*, 3rd ed. (Göttingen: Vandenhoeck & Ruprecht, 1930). For a general introduction into the *religionsgeschichtliche Schule*, see Werner Kümmel, *The New Testament: The History of the Investigation of Its Problems*, trans. S. McLean Gilmour and Howard C. Kee (Nashville: Abingdon Press, 1972), 245ff.

preters reading Revelation from the contemporary-historical perspective understand the images as references, possibly encoded, to specific aspects of the author's context.[44] This approach, Gunkel argues in *Schöpfung und Chaos in Urzeit und Endzeit* (1895), fails to recognize the traditional nature of much of the material found in Revelation. Looking at the myths of the ancient Near East, certain images and narrative units of Revelation clearly have long histories prior to their incorporation into this particular text. These images and stories are versions of myths that humans have used for centuries to understand abstract concepts, including, as the title of Gunkel's work suggests, the concepts of "creation" and "chaos." By the time the author of Revelation encounters these traditions, many of which developed within a Babylonian setting, they had already been appropriated and altered by a variety of cultural communities. The mythological language of Revelation does not function so much as a coded description of events occurring around the author of Revelation but to describe the deeper concepts with which humanity grapples.[45]

Both Gunkel and Bousset highlight Revelation 12, which depicts a cosmic battle between a woman and a dragon, as especially reflective of ancient mythic traditions. Noting that this narrative has no direct precedent in Jewish literature, Gunkel claims that chap. 12 is the *pièce de résistance* of Revelation's appropriation of Asian mythical elements.[46] Gunkel argues that this text reflects, in particular, the ancient Babylonian creation myths about Marduk and Tiamat. In this tradition the world is created through Marduk's defeat of the great chaos-monster, Tiamat. building on the work of Gunkel, in his commentary on Revelation (1896), Bousset explores a variety of different mythological antecedents to chap. 12, including Greek myths about Apollo and his mother Leto and the Egyptian legend of Isis and Osiris.[47] In his analysis of the text in relationship to these other myths, Bousset concludes, against Gunkel, that the similarities of these myths suggest the existence of an international mythic narrative describing a sun god who overcomes the power of evil. John, the author of Revelation, then transforms this general myth into a symbolic representation of the victory of Christ over Satan.[48]

Gunkel maintains that the structure of this myth, whether it is specifically Babylonian or a more universally known myth,[49] extends into the final chapters of Revelation, including the nuptial imagery in chaps. 19 and 21.

---

[44] Wainwright, *Mysterious Apocalypse*, 108ff; Böcher, *Die Johannesapokalypse*, 6f.

[45] Gunkel, *Schöpfung*, 202ff.; Böcher, *Die Johannesapokalypse*, 13f.

[46] Gunkel, *Zum religionsgeschichtlichen Verständnis*, 54.

[47] Wilhelm Bousset, *Die Offenbarung Johannis,* 2nd ed. (Göttingen: Vandenhoeck & Ruprecht, 1906), 405ff.

[48] Bousset, *Die Offenbarung Johannis*, 411.

[49] In his later work, Gunkel interacts with the work of other scholars, including Bousset, who posits a universal myth underlying Revelation (*Zum religionsgeschichtlichen Verständnis*, 55).

Gunkel notes that various ancient myths, including the myth of Marduk, depict a divine wedding along with the god's conquest of his foes. Gunkel explains that the importance of this myth is underscored by the fact that it was reenacted annually in ancient Babylon. Every spring, the divine wedding was celebrated, suggesting that wedding image was associated with fertility and prosperity.[50] Placed within the context of Revelation, the divine wedding, as a symbol of fertility, is the culmination of the Messiah's victory over chaos and evil. Fertility and prosperity can only come about after the divinity brings order. Gunkel does not suggest that the woman clothed in the sun, as described in chap. 12, and the bride of the Lamb are the same figure; however, the episodes need to be read in light of each other.

Another influential scholar employing the history-of-religions method is Ernst Lohmeyer, whose commentary on Revelation was first published in 1926 as a part of the German series Handbuch zum Neuen Testament.[51] Addressing the nuptial imagery of Revelation 19, Lohmeyer recognizes that the author actually weaves together a number of different traditions, including OT images that depict God as the husband of Israel. This allusion to the prophetic traditions does not explain the specific reference to the wedding banquet in Revelation 19. For this specific image, Lohmeyer looks to other texts that depict Jesus as a bridegroom and the parables that describe a king preparing a wedding banquet for his son. These texts draw on a source apart from the OT tradition—namely, ancient redeemer myths.[52] In these traditions a heavenly/divine redeemer figure marries and subsequently enjoys a wedding feast after having conquered the forces of chaos. This myth provides the structure for Revelation 12, as well as the text's nuptial imagery.[53]

Furthermore, Lohmeyer notes that John also draws on some noncanonical Jewish traditions. Specifically, he notes the pseudepigraphal *Odes of Solomon*, which depicts the one who conquers as marrying the city or land that is saved.[54] Drawing together this variety of traditions, Lohmeyer suggests that the nuptial imagery of Revelation 19 and 21 communicates the story of a cosmic redeemer who is united in marriage to the land or city that he saves.[55] In this way, the marriage image is indicative of the entire salvific or redemptive act. Furthermore, read in relation to the image of the great prostitute Babylon, depicted in Revelation 17–18, the nuptial

---

[50] Ibid., 58–59.

[51] Ernst Lohmeyer, *Die Offenbarung des Johannes,* 2nd ed. (HNT; Tübingen: J. C. B. Mohr, 1953).

[52] Ibid., 154.

[53] Ibid., 97.

[54] Lohmeyer quotes *Odes of Solomon* 38:11, which describes evil powers imitating good in the context of wedding feast. See Lohmeyer, *Die Offenbarung des Johannes*, 155.

[55] Lohmeyer, *Die Offenbarung des Johannes*, 155.

imagery fulfills a polemical purpose. The city worthy to be the divine Redeemer's bride is the new Jerusalem and not Babylon.[56]

The work of the history-of-religions scholars begins to shed light on the text of Revelation, including its nuptial imagery. Reading the text through the lens of ancient myth, these interpreters suggest some of the possible allusions conveyed through the image of the bride and the wedding feast in Revelation 19 and 21. According to their analysis, the image of a divine wedding alludes to some important mythic concepts within the ancient milieu—fertility, prosperity, redemption. The pairing of the wedding imagery with the imagery of the divine warrior also conveys that these positive values come only through the defeat of chaos.

The history-of-religions interpreters also highlight the importance of reading Revelation's nuptial imagery in relation to the mythic narrative of chap. 12. Interestingly, this claim is not made on the basis that both units of texts include feminine images.

While these turn-of-the-century scholars contribute to our understanding of Revelation's nuptial imagery, their work does have at least one serious drawback. In his study of the heavenly Jerusalem imagery, J. A. du Rand observes that the history-of-religions approach fails to grasp the function of the city imagery within the text.[57] The same can be said with regard to the history-of-religions treatment of the text's nuptial imagery. While these scholars note important parallel traditions and begin to suggest possible ideas communicated through this imagery, only Lohmeyer touches on the issue of how the nuptial imagery functions within the overall text. Lohmeyer's suggestion about the polemical function of the nuptial imagery, however, is brief, and fails to explore possible ways in which the image functions in a more constructive manner.

The work of these early history-of-religions scholars continues to influence modern scholarship on Revelation. Adela Yarbro Collins embraces the history-of-religions sensibilities while exploring the ways in which the text of Revelation may have functioned within its first-century setting.[58] Yarbro Collins uses the history-of-religions method to illuminate the feminine symbols used in Revelation.[59] These feminine symbols include the Bride of the Lamb, the Woman Clothed in the Sun (chap. 12), and the Great Prostitute (chaps. 17 and 18).

---

[56] Ibid.

[57] J. A. du Rand, "The Imagery of the Heavenly Jerusalem (Rev 21:9–22:5)," *Neot* 22 (1988): 67.

[58] Adela Yarbro Collins, *The Combat Myth in the Book Revelation* (HDR 9; Missoula, Mont.: Scholars Press, 1976); and "Feminine Symbolism in the Book of Revelation," *BibInt* 1 (1993): 20–33.

[59] Yarbro Collins engages in a Jungian analysis of the symbols as well. In the following we will examine her appropriation of the history-of-religions method, because the Jungian

Like the history-of-religions scholars who precede her, Yarbro Collins reads Revelation in relation to ancient myths, particularly the paradigmatic combat myth observed by Gunkel and Bousset. This myth, she explains, depicts a cosmic battle for universal kingship; however, it is often used to express the "the basic conflicts in human life and nature."[60] Through this myth the author and audience grapple with fundamental issues such as the human struggle with chaos, sterility, and death. The myth resolves this tension by depicting the defeat of the symbolic representation of chaos, usually a dragon. At the resolution of the conflict, there is typically a sacred marriage in which the hero unites with a feminine figure, often a goddess. This marriage suggests the fulfillment or completion of the divine creation.[61]

It is within the context of this combat myth that the wedding of the Lamb described in Revelation is understood, although Yarbro Collins argues that the text has also been shaped by Hebrew Bible prophetic traditions that depict Israel as God's wife, namely, Isaiah 54. The prophetic depiction of a community as a feminine figure who is united to the deity is merged with the mythic tradition of the sacred marriage. Yarbro Collins implies that instead of portraying a marriage of the hero, the Lamb, to a feminine divinity figure, the author of Revelation draws on prophetic traditions to suggest that the community of the faithful is the hero's marriage partner.[62] Interpreted within the context of traditions about the sacred marriage, this suggests that the uniting of the community of the faithful to the deity is the culmination of creation and the end of chaos.

Yarbro Collins asserts that the inclusion of this feminine symbol, as well as the more obviously goddesslike figure of the Woman Clothed in the Sun (chap. 12), indicates that Revelation's author "was forced to come to terms

---

perspective on the text offered by Yarbro Collins has not been widely adopted. See Yarbro Collins, "Feminine Symbolism," 27–33.

[60] Yarbro Collins, "Feminine Symbolism," 23.

[61] Yarbro Collins explores the function of the combat myth in Revelation in more detail in her book *Crisis and Catharsis*, published in 1984. In this work, Yarbro Collins argues that the author of Revelation uses these ancient myths in an effort to create a cathartic experience for his audience. Written within a context of perceived crisis, in which the churches of Asia Minor understand themselves to be in conflict with the dominant culture, Revelation allows its audience to experience God's victory over evil. The text appropriates the classic myths about the defeat of chaos and evil to describe the divine control over the dominant culture, which is believed to be at odds with God's purposes. In this way, the text provides the audience an opportunity for a cathartic release of its psychological tension. Unfortunately, however, *Combat and Catharsis* does not include a specific discussion of how Revelation's nuptial imagery functions as part of the text's attempt at inducing catharsis, even though this would be an interesting line of analysis (*Crisis and Catharsis: The Power of the Apocalypse* [Philadelphia: Westminster Press, 1984]).

[62] Yarbro Collins, "Feminine Symbolism" 25.

with the feminine aspect of the divine."[63] The inclusion of these figures, which bear a striking resemblance to ancient goddesses (e.g., Isis and Leto), implies that the author was consciously or unconsciously reacting to the variety of goddess traditions prevalent within the milieu of first-century Asia Minor. Although it is possible to interpret this as an act of "relativizing" goddess traditions, Yarbro Collins interprets it more positively:

> The fulfillment of God's creation and God's interaction with humanity cannot be described in purely abstract terms or in metaphors that are only masculine. Both the masculine and the feminine are needed to express the richness, complexity, and vitality of the created world in its fulfillment. . . . Because of the present crisis, which John implied was about to intensify, the ideal was to renounce sexual relations and to prepare for the end. At the same time, as one of the fundamental characteristics of God's good creation, sexuality is a symbol of the new creation, of wholeness, of the time of salvation.[64]

For Yarbro Collins, the image of the wedding of the Lamb can be interpreted in positive terms, as it utilizes a feminine symbol to characterize the heavenly world, God's ideal community, and God's interaction with the earthly world. She also recognizes, however, the problematic nature of this imagery for modern interpreters, as it depicts the feminine only in relation to masculine images, which fails to do justice to the reality of actual gender.[65]

Utilizing methods developed by history-of-religions scholars, Yarbro Collins begins to explore possible functions of the combat myth, including its traditional feminine imagery, in Revelation. While she does not fully explore the text's nuptial imagery, she does begin to raise important questions about this imagery: How does the nuptial imagery combine OT traditions with other ancient mythic traditions? What is the relationship between Revelation's feminine images and the goddess traditions prevalent in first-century Asia Minor? And, what are the ideological implications of Revelation's feminine images, especially as they are read and appropriated by women interpreters? These questions reflect Yarbro Collins's move toward reading Revelation's feminine imagery in ways that capture the richness of the imagery. In her work, she refuses to reduce the imagery to coded descriptions. Instead, she employs the history-of-religions method to explore how the images function within the context of Revelation's narrative.

---

[63] Ibid., 24.

[64] Ibid., 25.

[65] Ibid., 33.

Another recent work that builds on the observations of history-of-religions scholarship is Bruce Malina's *The New Jerusalem in the Revelation of John: The City as a Symbol of Life with God*. Although he characterizes his work as social-scientific, he readily acknowledges his indebtedness to the observations of history-of-religions scholars, including Franz Boll, whose work *Aus der Offenbarung Johannis: Hellenistische Studien zum Weltbild der Apokalypse* was published in 1914.[66] Along with Boll, Malina contends that Revelation is typical of ancient astrological and astronomical reports.[67] As such, the text of Revelation is not to be taken allegorically or metaphorically; instead the text recounts John's encounter with a variety of celestial entities and phenomena while being in an altered state of consciousness. This is not to suggest that the stars have no significance in relation to earthly events. In fact, the celestial visions provide insights into earthly events and how humans should live.[68]

As an astronomical/astrological report, many of the images within the text of Revelation describe constellations, which were understood as corresponding to specific celestial deities and powers. Malina observes that the image of the Lamb, as described by John, closely resembles descriptions of the constellation Aries, the Ram. The first sign of the zodiac, Aries, functions as the beginning and head of the cosmos. In addition, Malina explains, "Among the learned of antiquity, it was common belief that when the cosmic Lamb reached its original position, that is, the sky location it occupied as it issued from the hands of God the creator, then the sky and earth would be renewed, made new."[69] The celestial Lamb, or Aries, brings about the renewal of the cosmos. In his analysis, Malina suggests that the author of Revelation understands this Lamb, Aries, in relation to the Lamb of God, the risen Christ, of the Christian tradition.

Similarly, John's reference to the impending marriage of the Lamb (19:7–9), according to Malina's analysis, refers to an upcoming celestial event. There was, according to some other ancient texts, a constellation known as the Wedding of the Gods. Malina suggests, however, that since Revelation describes something that is not yet extant but about to occur, the text is not referring to this particular constellation. Instead, he argues, the concept of marriage describes the conjunction of two distinct constellations.[70] In the case of Revelation, the author withholds the identity of the

---

[66] Bruce J. Malina, *The New Jerusalem in the Revelation of John: The City as Symbol of Life with God* (Collegeville, Minn.: Liturgical Press, 2000). See also Malina's earlier article, "How a Cosmic Lamb Marries: The Image of the Wedding of the Lamb (Rev 19:7ff.)," *BTB* 28 (1998): 75–83.

[67] Malina, *New Jerusalem*, 16–27.

[68] Ibid., 19.

[69] Ibid., 68.

[70] Ibid., 73.

celestial bride until chap. 21. It is not until this later chapter that John reveals that the Bride of the Lamb is actually a "sky city" that is the home of God. Within an altered state, John catches a glimpse of the abode of God, which is the seat of God's power.[71] The marriage that John describes is the merging of Aries and God's celestial city.

Even though John devotes a great deal of his text to describing events and entities that exist in the sky, Malina argues that John's description of celestial phenomena has significance for his earthly audience. John's "reading of the sky" communicates a message to his fellow believers.[72] This message, among other things, communicates that God's presence with the faithful is inaugurated in the merging of these celestial entities.[73] Revelation's nuptial imagery signals a future celestial event which is a hopeful event for John's fellow believers.

Arguing in favor of reading the text as ancient astronomy/astrology, Malina explicitly rejects allegorical or metaphorical interpretations. Instead of operating with the assumption that the signifiers in the text refer to other ideas/things, Malina asserts that interpreters should read John's description of celestial events as actual celestial events:

> John the seer can and must be taken at his word. If he says that he was in the sky and looked around, he obviously believed that he was in the sky and looked around. He was neither fabricating fiction nor composing midrash. What he saw is what he said he saw, not an allegory for something else.[74]

While Malina's desire to take John at his word is admirable, it is also questionable to deny the text any sort of meaning beyond the literal. Malina himself does not consistently maintain such a position, as is seen in his description of the "marriage" of two constellations. In this instance, John clearly uses metaphorical or allegorical language, that of marriage, even if it does describe the conjunction of two celestial entities. In fact, Malina implies that while on one level Revelation describes celestial events, on another level the text communicates a message about how the followers of the resurrected Jesus are to live on earth. The meaning of the text, even for Malina, cannot be restricted to a literal meaning. Rather, even if one agrees with Malina that John the Seer's writings are astronomical/astrological in nature, Revelation is still about much more than astronomical predictions.

Through reading Revelation within the context of ancient mythology, history-of-religions scholars and their methodological progeny demonstrate the universal character of many of Revelation's images and narratives. They

---

[71] Ibid., 54–62.

[72] Malina, "How a Cosmic Lamb Marries," 76.

[73] Malina, *New Jerusalem*, 76.

[74] Ibid., 16.

bring to light the fact that symbols and mythological narratives are remarkably fluid and adaptable to different contexts. Through the use of imagistic language, an author is able to demonstrate the ways in which abstract and universal concepts such as good and evil relate to particular events and individuals, such as Christ. Further, even when used in a particular context, these traditional images seemingly convey a wealth of allusions, stemming from the earlier usage of these images. In this way, the history-of-religions approach to Revelation generally results in expanding the possible meanings of Revelation's images.[75]

Exploring the Bride's Prophetic Heritage

The history-of-religions focus on the "pagan" mythic traditions that influence Revelation has been criticized by some interpreters, especially those who want to emphasize the relation between Revelation and its Jewish antecedents. Writing shortly after Gunkel and Bousset, E.-B. Allo explicitly criticizes the history-of-religions scholars who attempt to relate John's nuptial imagery, as well as the traditions in Revelation 12, to the Marduk tradition or the gnostic marriage tradition. He challenges the supposition that these ancient traditions provide a more likely background for Revelation than OT traditions. Instead, Revelation's nuptial imagery reflects the prophetic, psalmic, and wisdom traditions of the OT,[76] as well as early Christian traditions depicting Christ as the bridegroom.[77]

---

[75] The history-of-religions focus on the mythic traditions that stand behind the text encouraged the search for actual textual traditions and sources upon which John may have drawn, as well as the investigation into the possibility of editorial additions to the text. While history-of-religions scholars, such as Gunkel and Bousset, engage in this type of project in conjunction with their overarching interests, the search for Revelation's textual sources becomes a central aim for others. The detailed commentary of R. H. Charles, which was completed over a span of twenty-five years, provides the classic example of this approach to biblical texts—the source-critical method. Charles clearly acknowledges the symbolic nature of Revelation and, more specifically, the traditional character of the text's symbolism. In light of the claims and methods of the history-of-religions approach to Revelation, which focuses on the mythic origins of Revelation's images, as well as apparent inconsistencies within the text, Charles wrestles with the issue of which parts of the text actually reflect the author's work. He undertakes the arduous task of determining which parts of the text most likely reflect John the Seer's religious experience or vision. This involves establishing a direct connection between the imagery of Revelation and the supposed context of the Seer. Thus, Charles ends the second volume of his commentary with his version of the "original" text of Revelation (*A Critical and Exegetical Commentary on the Revelation of St. John*, 2 vols. (New York: Charles Scribner's Sons, 1920).

[76] E.-B. Allo, *L'Apocalypse*, 4th ed. (ÉBib; Paris: J. Gabalda, 1933), 334–36.

[77] Many scholars note the use of nuptial imagery in the Gospels as a possible parallel to or source of the use of this imagery in Revelation. This is particularly highlighted by L. A. Vos in his work on the relation between Revelation and the Synoptic Gospels (*The Synoptic Traditions in the Apocalypse* [Kampen: Kok, 1965], 165–68, 174).

Allo is not alone in favoring Jewish, especially OT, and early Christian traditions as the background for Revelation and its nuptial imagery. The tendency to address Revelation's nuptial imagery in relation to its OT antecedents, especially the prophetic traditions, was the dominant approach to this imagery in twentieth-century scholarship. Many of the modern full-treatment critical commentaries on Revelation, as well as numerous articles and monographs, embrace this approach. These scholars, including George B. Caird, Gregory K. Beale, and others, often note the parallels between Revelation's nuptial imagery and the prophetic traditions that depict Israel/Jerusalem as the bride of Yahweh (e.g., Ezekiel 16; Hosea 1–2; Isaiah 61:10) and the wedding banquet imagery of the Gospels (e.g., Matt 22:1–14; 25:1–13; Luke 14:15–24).

In the brief introduction to his commentary on Revelation,[78] Caird notes that while John's original audience would have been well versed in the symbolism of Revelation, the modern reader is faced with the issue of "how far to take this picture language literally and how far to take it figuratively."[79] With this understanding, Caird approaches John's metaphor by highlighting the various sources from which John derives this imagery. This reflects the common assumption that contemporaneous texts use images in similar fashions.

Even though Caird depicts John as a "master of his medium and not its slave,"[80] he approaches Revelation's nuptial imagery by untangling the various aspects of the image. Stating that "the bride is the church," Caird notes the meanings of particular parts of the metaphor complex.[81] For instance, the bride's clean garments, mentioned in Rev 19:7, are a symbol

[78] George B. Caird, *The Revelation of St. John* (BNTC; Peabody, Mass.: Hendrickson, 1966). Caird names Austin Farrer as an important influence on his reading of Revelation. Reacting against the source-critical perspective of scholars such as R. H. Charles, Farrer engages in one of the first scholarly attempts to read the Apocalypse as a conscious and careful literary creation of John. One of the strengths of Farrer's work is the recognition of the depth of human imagination and its capacity for metaphor; however, Farrer's analysis of Revelation's imagery is labyrinthine and often misguided. While he does not focus on Revelation's nuptial imagery, Farrer maintains that the nuptial imagery of Revelation 19 represents the feast of Purim and the story of Esther. Reading the nuptial imagery in relation to the preceding harlot imagery, this imagery supposedly represents the characters of Esther (the bride) and Vashti (the harlot). Fortunately, while Caird draws on Farrer's appreciation of John's artistry, he offers a more sustainable treatment of the text. See Austin Farrer, *A Rebirth of Images: The Making of St. John's Apocalypse* (Boston: Beacon Press, 1949). Note, in particular, Kenneth Burke's introduction to the paperback edition of this text in which he offers an apt description of *A Rebirth of Images*: "A commentator may seem quite clear if he simply says that the use of imagery in Revelation is 'liquid,' and lets it go at that. But it's a bitter fact about the hard lot of the critic or exegete that, once he tries to work out the laws of such liquidity, things are much tougher for both writer and reader" (1).

[79] Caird, *The Revelation of St. John*, 6–7.

[80] Ibid., 234.

[81] Ibid.

for sanctity, and the wedding dress points to the bride's readiness. Caird pulls apart the different pieces of John's nuptial image, pinpointing the singular meaning of each individual element. While rightly acknowledging the various pieces of John's metaphorical complex, Caird continues the pattern of equating these pieces with literal or propositional claims.

Caird's method of interpreting Revelation's nuptial imagery generally corresponds to the understanding of metaphor elaborated in his later book, *The Language and Imagery of the Bible*.[82] While this work addresses neither nuptial imagery nor specifically metaphor in Revelation, it is worth mentioning here as it outlines a typical view of metaphor that is often implicitly brought to bear on Revelation. In this work, Caird describes metaphor in terms of a dichotomy between literal and nonliteral (often called "figurative") language, and metaphor belongs to the later category.[83] Literal statements are those that are meant to be understood in their "primary, matter-of-fact sense."[84] In contrast, nonliteral statements, or figurative language, seemingly involve statements that say one thing but actually mean another. Even though Caird maintains that metaphor is not the same as code, he intimates that metaphor functions as a complex form of code. While a symbol within a code typically connotes the same idea despite its context, a metaphor can be used to connote different ideas in different contexts.[85] So, while in one context a metaphor communicates one idea, in another context it communicates another idea. Caird's explanation implies that the meaning of metaphors really could be expressed in literal language. As is evident in his commentary on Revelation, Caird's tendency appears to be to translate metaphorical language into propositional claims.

The massive commentaries of David E. Aune and Gregory K. Beale, published in 1998 and 1999 respectively, are two of the most recent critical commentaries on the text of Revelation.[86] Both employ a variety of historical and literary-critical methods in their analysis of Revelation, including its nuptial imagery. Like Caird, but in much more detail, both emphasize the connections between Revelation's nuptial imagery and its Jewish and Christian antecedents. Of the two works, Beale's commentary stands out for the special attention its gives to this imagery.

---

[82] G. B. Caird, *The Language and Imagery of the Bible* (Grand Rapids, Mich.: Eerdmans, 1980). It is important to note the caveat with which Caird begins this text, "This is a book by an amateur, written for amateurs" (ix).

[83] Caird, *The Language and Imagery of the Bible,* 131–97.

[84] Ibid., 133.

[85] Ibid., 148–49.

[86] David Aune, *Revelation*, 3 vols. (WBC 52A-B; Dallas, Tex.: Word, 1997–1998); and Gregory Beale *The Book of Revelation: A Commentary on the Greek Text* (NIGTC; Grand Rapids, Mich.: Eerdmans, 1999).

Beale's treatment of Revelation's nuptial imagery is unique among full-scale commentaries on Revelation. Beale identifies textual and cultural precursors to this metaphorical imagery and explores how different aspects of this imagery function in relation to one another and in relation to the rest of the narrative. Especially notable is Beale's thorough discussion of the meanings communicated through the imagery of the bride's wedding clothes and how this imagery relates to other references to clothing in Revelation. Beale's discussion of this imagery rests on his conclusion that the phrase τὰ δικαιώματα τῶν ἁγίων in 19:8 should be read primarily as an objective genitive. As an objective genitive, the phrase describes *God's* righteous deeds or acts of vindication *on behalf of* the saints, who constitute the bride of the Lamb.[87] Beale comes to this conclusion through an analysis of terms related to δικαιόω ("to declare righteous"), which Revelation typically uses to describe God's just judgments. Beale also supports this reading of the text through his reading of OT antecedents to Revelation's nuptial imagery. In particular, he notes that Isa 61:10, on which Revelation seems to draw, employs the language of adornment to communicate "God's sovereign provision."[88] Even though the Isaiah text, like Revelation 19, uses language to describe the bride's preparation for the wedding, this can occur only because God gives garments to the bride. Beale argues that Rev 21:2 develops the imagery according to this *passive* sense: "the primary point is not that the saints' effort contributes to the acquisition of righteousness. The metaphorical significance is, rather, that God's people are finally entering into the intimate relationship with him that he has initiated."[89] Beale does acknowledge that the phrase τὰ δικαιώματα τῶν ἁγίων "might" also be read as a subjective genitive, describing the saints' righteous or just acts. He emphasizes that this is not, however, the primary meaning.[90]

Beale places his treatment of this particular aspect of Revelation's nuptial imagery in conversation with other scholars, namely, R. H. Mounce, who see this passage as related to the theological issue of "justification," which is typically associated with Pauline theology.[91] Beale writes,

> it would be better to view vv 7–8 as indicating that a transformed life of good works (though certainly not perfection) is not only "the proper response" [quoting Mounce] to justification but a necessary external response or "badge" [again quoting Mounce] required before entrance to the wedding of the Lamb

[87] Beale, *The Book of Revelation*, 936–38.

[88] Ibid., 938.

[89] Ibid., 940.

[90] Ibid., 936–37.

[91] Robert H. Mounce, *The Book of Revelation*, rev. ed. (NICNT; Grand Rapids, Mich: Eerdmans, 1998), 340.

> is granted. Theologically, this would mean that justification is the causal necessary condition for entrance into the eternal kingdom, but good works are a noncausal necessary condition. In this regard, cf. also Rom. 2:6–8; 2 Cor. 11:2.[92]

In this way, Beale's reading of Revelation's nuptial imagery appears to be shaped by a concern for maintaining the theological unity of the NT. This is not to suggest that Beale fails to read this imagery in relation to its function in Revelation, but he privileges one aspect of the imagery over the rest based on this theological concern. The title of his analysis of Rev 19:7–8, "The Wedding Clothes," highlights Beale's privileging of this piece of the metaphorical construction.[93] In chap. 5 I will propose a reading of Revelation's nuptial imagery that embraces all the pieces of this metaphorical construction.

The authors of full-scale commentaries are not alone in reading Revelation's nuptial imagery in light of its Jewish and early Christian antecedents. First, in an article entitled "Transformation of Symbols: The New Jerusalem in Rv 21.1–22.5," Celia Deutsch suggests that Revelation's nuptial imagery reconfigures both biblical and Second Temple traditions.[94] Deutsch's article represents a rare but important attempt at engaging theories of metaphor in order to analyze Revelation's image of the new Jerusalem. Second, Jan Fekkes explores the relationship between Revelation and Isaiah's nuptial imagery in his article "'His Bride Has Prepared Herself': Revelation 16–21 and Isaian Nuptial Imagery."[95] Fekkes's article

---

[92] Beale, *The Book of Revelation,* 935.

[93] Ibid., 934.

[94] Celia Deutsch, "Transformation of Symbols: The New Jerusalem in Rv 21.1–22.5," *ZNW* 78 (1987): 106–26.

[95] Jan Fekkes, "'His Bride Has Prepared Herself': Rev 16–21 and Isaian Nuptial Imagery," *JBL* 109 (1990): 269–87. While the articles by Deutsch and Fekkes are two of the most recent discussions dedicated specifically to Revelation's nuptial imagery, there are other recent works that are important to note. All of these works generally approach the text from the perspective of its OT backgrounds. Édouard Cothenet's article stands out as it compares Pauline and Revelation's use of nuptial imagery ("L'Église, Épouse du Christ [Éph 5; Apoc 19 et 21]," *L'Église dans la Liturgie* [Rome: Edizioni Liturgiche, 1980], 81–106). There are also several articles and essays that address the image of the new Jerusalem as a political image. While these articles may note Revelation's use of the bridal motif, they emphasize the portrayal of the idealized Christian community as a city. See Otto Böcher, "Bürger der Gottesstadt: Kirche in Zeit und Endzeit nach Apk 21f," in *Kirche in Zeit und Endzeit: Aufsätze zur Offenbarung des Johannes* (Neukirchen-Vluyn: Neukirchener Verlag, 1983), 157–67; J. A. Du Rand, "The Imagery of the Heavenly Jerusalem (Revelation 21:9–22:5)." *Neot* 22 (1988): 65–86; Dieter Georgi, "Die Visionen vom himmlischen Jerusalem in Apk 21 und 22," in *Kirche: Festschrift für Günther Bornkamm zum 75. Geburtstag*, ed. Dieter Lührmann and Georg Strecker (Tübingen: J. C. B. Mohr, 1980), 351–72; Klaus Wengst, "Babylon the Great and the New Jerusalem: The Visionary View of Political Reality in the Revelation of John," in *Politics and Theopolitics in the Bible and Postbiblical Literature*, ed. Henning Graf Reventlow, Yair Hoffman, and Benjamin Uffenheimer (Sheffield: JSOT Press, 1994), 189–202.

is important for the critical gaze with which he addresses the use of prophetic antecedents for understanding Revelation's nuptial imagery.

In the introduction to her article, which focuses on the vision of the new Jerusalem in Rev 21:1–22:5, Deutsch highlights the important insights that studies of symbol and myth bring to studying the text of Revelation. Drawing on Claude Lévi-Strauss's discussion of myth and symbol, as well as making reference to Caird's *The Language and Imagery of the Bible* (see above), Deutsch points out that "the trans-temporal nature of myth and symbol allows them to transform themselves to accommodate new experience and shift in community setting."[96] Even though an author uses traditional symbols, the meanings of these symbols are altered through their use in a new context. By making this point, Deutsch seeks to avoid the assumption that the meaning conveyed by Revelation's imagery is identical to the earlier textual traditions on which it draws.

Deutsch's analysis of the new Jerusalem imagery involves exploring how Revelation transforms the traditions of its Jewish milieu. Deutsch observes that the oft-noted use of bridal imagery in Isaiah generally depicts the restoration of Israel. Similarly, Deutsch argues, there are instances from the Second Temple period in which feminine imagery is used to convey the hope of a new Jerusalem (e.g., *4 Ezra* 10:17).[97] These traditions utilize the symbolic language of marriage in order "to make a statement about the quality of the relationship between God and community, whether in the historical or eschatological order. The image of the woman in these materials symbolizes love and intimacy."[98] Deutsch then concludes that Revelation 21, "as in traditional materials," evokes a similar sense of newness, ardor, and fidelity. Instead of examining how Revelation's nuptial imagery might be *transformed* in its new setting, a move suggested by Deutsch's dis-

---

Two recently published dissertations are also important to note. First, Unyong Sim discusses Revelation's heavenly Jerusalem image in relation to ancient cities, including the literary depiction of ideal cities. In so doing, Sim observes that the tradition of personifying the city as a bride has its roots in the OT tradition in which the earthly Jerusalem is described as a woman or as a bride (*Das himmlische Jerusalem in Apk 21,1–22,5 im Kontext biblisch-jüdischer Tradition und antiken Städtebaus* [Trier: Wissenschaftlicher Verlag, 1996]). Second, the recently published dissertation of Pilchan Lee discusses the image of the new Jerusalem in relation to its Jewish antecedents, highlighting the Temple imagery in the text (Lee, *The New Jerusalem in the Book of Revelation: A Study of Revelation 21–22 in the Light of its Background in Jewish Tradition* [Tübingen: Mohr Siebeck, 2001]).

For a discussion of both the Jewish backgrounds and reception history of Revelation's new Jerusalem imagery, especially its utopian element, see Rita Müller-Fieberg, *Das "neue Jerusalem"–Vision für alle Herzen und alle Zeiten? Eine Auslegung von Offb 21,1–22,5 im Kontext von alttesamentlich-frühjüdischer Tradition und literarischer Rezeption* (Bonner Biblische Beiträge; Berlin: Philo, 2003).

[96] Deutsch, "Transformation of Symbols," 108.

[97] Ibid., 108.

[98] Ibid.

cussion of methodology, she falls prey to the tendency to assume that the meaning of Revelation's imagery is equivalent to the original context. Furthermore, Deutsch also fails to explain why the bridal imagery communicates newness, fidelity, etc.[99] While the author of Revelation may actually use the bridal image to convey these qualities, Deutsch offers no explanation as to how the text communicates these ideas. Thus, although her premise maintains that authors alter traditional images when they place them in new contexts, Deutsch fails to demonstrate how this occurs with regard to Revelation's nuptial imagery.

In his article, as well as in his published dissertation,[100] Fekkes both follows the tendency of reading Revelation's nuptial imagery in relation to prophetic traditions and challenges the connections previous scholars have made between Revelation and its antecedent traditions. Fekkes does this by examining "the interrelationship of the three passages that make up the bride construct in Revelation (19:7–9; 21:2; 21:9, 19–21)" and the connections between these texts and Isa 61:10 and 54:11–12.[101]

While scholars have long recognized a relationship between Revelation 19 and 21 and Hebrew Bible prophetic depictions portraying Israel or Jerusalem as the wife of Yahweh, Fekkes argues that they have done so with imprecision. Many scholars fail to distinguish between the various prophetic uses of this personification, including positive and negative depictions of Israel as God's wife. Fekkes argues that Isaiah alone provides the background for Revelation rather than other OT traditions often linked to Revelation, such as Ezekiel and Hosea, because "only Isaiah employs marriage imagery in a consistently positive manner of the future relationship between Yahweh and his faithful remnant symbolized by the personified Zion-Jerusalem."[102] In contrast to scholarly claims that Revelation's nuptial imagery draws on traditions that depict Zion-Jerusalem as the *unfaithful* bride of Yahweh, especially Ezekiel 16, Fekkes maintains that "John is describing the New Jerusalem not with random OT motifs but with prophetic texts specifically concerned with the glorious eschatological Jerusalem."[103] Fekkes begins by exploring possible textual and linguistic similarities between Isa 61:10, in both its Greek and Hebrew forms, and Revelation's nuptial imagery. After noting some "dictional" similarities, Fekkes argues that Revelation 19 also shares some "conceptual similarities" with Isa 61:10. These conceptual correspondences include references to "the clothing of the salvation community collectively" and the garment as a gift from God. Both passages share the metaphorical connection between

[99] Ibid.

[100] Jan Fekkes, *Isaiah and Prophetic Traditions in the Book of Revelation: Visionary Antecedents and their Development* (Sheffield: JSOT Press, 1994).

[101] Fekkes, "His Bride," 269.

[102] Ibid., 272.

[103] Ibid., 273.

clothing and spiritual character and the theme of adornment.[104] On the basis of these similarities, Fekkes maintains that there is a thematic link between the two traditions. He then subsequently interprets Revelation's imagery as equivalent to that of Isaiah 61.[105]

The second half of Fekkes's article proves more provocative; here he uses Revelation's allusions to Isaiah 54 as the grounds for asserting a new reading of Revelation's nuptial imagery. Fekkes suggests that the description of the jewels that adorn the new Jerusalem, as described in chap. 21, should be understood as part of the nuptial imagery. This reading is based on Revelation's supposed dependence on Isaiah 54, which combines the image of Zion as the wife of Yahweh with architectural imagery. This architectural imagery includes depictions of precious stones, on which John, Revelation's author, models his description of the new Jerusalem.[106] In this way, Fekkes allows his analysis of one of Revelation's antecedents to suggest new readings of Revelation itself.

Following the lead of scholars such as Allo and Caird, who argue for Revelation's dependence upon OT traditions, Beale, Deutsch, and Fekkes analyze Revelation's nuptial imagery in relation to its Jewish antecedents. They do this with varying success. Beale stands out among them as he explores the imagery's background traditions with an eye to how this imagery functions within the narrative of Revelation. He resists the assumption that Revelation's nuptial imagery functions in a manner identical to its predecessors. Most disappointing is Deutsch's treatment of Revelation's nuptial imagery. Despite articulating a view of symbolic language that highlights its ability to communicate new ideas and meanings within different contexts, Deutsch assumes that John employs his nuptial imagery in ways identical to earlier traditions. Further, belying her methodological claims, Deutsch's analysis approaches Revelation's nuptial imagery as though the component parts had singular meanings (e.g., a marriage equals intimacy). Finally, while Fekkes's article sometimes adopts a pedantic view of Revelation's use of the prophets of the Hebrew Bible, he does encourage us to read Revelation's bridal imagery in new ways. Fekkes establishes the close relationship between Isaiah's vision of Jerusalem and Revelation 21 to call for a more nuanced view of Revelation's imagistic language.

Marriage as a Literary Construction: Literary-Functional Readings of Revelation's Nuptial Imagery

There has been an ever-increasing tendency in the past twenty-five years to employ literary-critical methods in reading Revelation in order to do jus-

[104] Ibid., 273–74.
[105] Ibid., 287.
[106] Ibid., 284.

tice to its highly imagistic nature. One of the first scholars to engage consciously in a literary-critical interpretation of the Book of Revelation was Paul Minear.[107] In his interpretation, Minear explicitly criticizes the tendency of scholars to treat the images and metaphors of Revelation as code words for historical realities. He finds this tendency to be a "literalism and historicism of the worst sort."[108] In contrast to this, Minear maintains the importance of determining the meaning of the images within their narrative context. While Minear spends very little time addressing John's use of nuptial imagery, he does suggest that this imagery be read in conversation both with the prostitute imagery of chaps. 17 and 18 and with other symbols for the new Jerusalem. Challenging the traditional tendency to equate the harlot image with first-century Rome, Minear quite persuasively argues that the images of harlot and bride depict two possible forms of existence for the Christian community.[109] The community can live in idolatry, as a prostitute, or the community can life in faithfulness to God, as a bride.[110] Moreover, read in conjunction with the other metaphors associated with the new Jerusalem (the holy city, the water of life, the death of death), the bridal image communicates a sense of qualitative newness. Through the complex of metaphors associated with the new Jerusalem, including the nuptial imagery, John communicates the radically new nature of the community that lives in faithfulness to God.

Clearly, Minear's reading of metaphor in Revelation presents a significant stride forward, toward appreciating the complexity of metaphor within narrative texts. He challenges the prevalent method of interpreting metaphor in terms of code, as well as the assumption that metaphors can be reduced to literal truth claims. Instead, he attempts to read Revelation's metaphors in terms of their function within the narrative. Given the groundbreaking nature and the scope of his project, however, Minear addresses this imagery only briefly, focusing more closely on images that tend to dominate the text, such as the prostitute image. Further, while he balks at the tendency to find one-to-one relationships between symbols and their referents, at times his interpretation lapses into this sort of oversimplification. This is seen, for instance, when he notes that the image of the new creation in chap. 21 is the key to understanding the symbols of the

---

[107] Paul Minear, *I Saw a New Earth: An Introduction to the Visions of the Apocalypse* (Washington, D.C.: Corpus Books, 1968). A more recent commentary that offers an explicitly literary-critical reading is David L. Barr, *Tales of the End: A Narrative Commentary on the Book of Revelation* (Santa Rosa, Calif.: Polebridge Press, 1998). In this short commentary, however, Barr does not address John's nuptial imagery.

[108] This quotation refers particularly to the tendency to equate Rome and Babylon, although throughout his text he does repudiate this tendency in general (Minear, *I Saw a New Earth*, 246).

[109] Ibid., 169.

[110] Ibid., 273.

holy city, the bride, the death of death, etc., since all of these images function as symbols of newness.[111] While this simple observation may be true, it provides the extent of Minear's discussion of the function of the bridal imagery in conjunction with other symbols for the new Jerusalem.[112]

Elisabeth Schüssler Fiorenza critiques Minear's approach to "mythopoeic" language in her article "Visionary Rhetoric and Social-Political Situation."[113] She specifically faults Minear, along with French scholar Jacques Ellul,[114] for reducing the symbols of Revelation to philosophical concepts. While Minear objects to the tendency to treat Revelation's images as codes for historical entities, Schüssler Fiorenza maintains that he actually treats the images as codes for archetypes or ontological realities. The images of Revelation's poetic language are still propositional claims. In contrast, Schüssler Fiorenza maintains the importance of recognizing "the ambiguity, openness, and indeterminancy of all literature."[115] The recognition of this indeterminancy allows for a view that poetic language, particularly the language of the Apocalypse, evokes a range of possible meanings rather than defines meaning. For Schüssler Fiorenza, this recognition does not necessarily equal the concession that language, particularly poetic language, can have no particular meaning. However, the possibility of finding a particular range of meaning for mythopoeic language requires attention to the rhetorical situation and function of the language. The question that must be asked is whether a particular interpretation "fits" the rhetorical situation.[116] In order to begin the process of delimiting the meaning potential of Revelation's poetic language, Schüssler Fiorenza advocates reading the text primarily from a social-rhetorical standpoint.[117]

While Schüssler Fiorenza brings this understanding of mythopoeic language to bear on the text of Revelation in her brief commentary *Reve-*

---

[111] Ibid.

[112] In a separate article, Minear addresses the complex city imagery in Revelation, particularly in relation to ecclesiology. While the nuptial imagery is woven together with the city imagery (21:2), Minear does not really address the nuptial imagery. Despite this, the article does offer some important insights into John's use of city imagery. See Paul S. Minear, "Ontology and Ecclesiology in the Apocalypse," *NTS* 13 (1967): 89–105.

[113] Elisabeth Schüssler Fiorenza, "Visionary Rhetoric," in *The Book of Revelation: Justice and Judgment*, 2nd ed. (Minneapolis: Fortress Press, 1998), 181–203. See also eadem, "Introduction: Research Perspectives on the Book of Revelation," in *The Book of Revelation: Justice and Judgment*, 2nd ed. (Minneapolis: Fortress Press, 1998), 21–23.

[114] Jacques Ellul, *Apocalypse: The Book of Revelation*, trans. George W. Schreiner (New York: Seabury, 1977).

[115] Schüssler Fiorenza, "Visionary Rhetoric," 186.

[116] Ibid., 187.

[117] Schüssler Fiorenza is not the only scholar who maintains the necessity of reading Revelation in light of its specific rhetorical situation; however, there is a great deal of debate over the exact nature of this rhetorical situation.

lation: Vision of a Just World, she also addresses the text from a feminist-critical perspective. In doing so, she describes two of the primary ways in which feminist-critical interpreters approach androcentric (male-centered) symbolic language. Many feminist-critical interpreters interpret the symbolism of Revelation from the perspective of linguistic-symbolic determinism. They interpret the androcentric symbolic language of Revelation as if it were part of a closed sex/gender system signifying reality. Masculine-defined symbols are read as referring to actual males, while feminine-defined symbols are read as referring to actual females. For instance, the bride of the Lamb, a feminine-defined symbol, is read as signifying a positive view of male control over the passive and sexually powerless female. While Schüssler Fiorenza recognizes that this sort of interpretation rightly highlights the dominant androcentric perspective in Western culture, she argues that this interpretive method "reinscribes this system as a self-contained totality. Such an interpretation seeks to make readers conscious of internalized male identifications, but it cannot reclaim cultural texts and traditions for women."[118]

In contrast to the above approach, Schüssler Fiorenza advocates a feminist-critical reading of androcentric symbols in line with her understanding of the openness of mythopoeic language. Language and symbols are understood as a "tool that enables readers to negotiate and create meanings in specific contexts and situations."[119] Language is not a closed system in which grammatical gender is necessarily identified with actual gender. It is possible, Schüssler Fiorenza maintains, for grammatically gendered language and symbols to be read in specific linguistic and social contexts as either generic or gender-specific language. Women throughout the centuries have been able to find meaning in and identify with texts, including biblical texts, that are comprised of male-identified language because these female interpreters could identify with the values and visions of these texts. In light of this, while she reserves the right to criticize John's use of gendered images, Schüssler Fiorenza reads the symbols of Revelation, including the explicitly androcentric metaphors, primarily in relation to their literary and rhetorical context.

More specifically, Schüssler Fiorenza reads Revelation's nuptial imagery, as well as the prostitute imagery, in relation to its prophetic backgrounds. Unlike many of her predecessors who focus on the sources of John's imagery, however, Schüssler Fiorenza seems more interested in how the images function within their earlier contexts as a source of comparison for establishing the ways the images function within the rhetorical context of Revelation. Originally the prostitute/bride imagery functioned as a way

[118] Elisabeth Schüssler Fiorenza, *Revelation: Vision of a Just World* (Proclamation Commentaries; Minneapolis: Fortress Press, 1991), 13.

[119] Schüssler Fiorenza, *Revelation*, 13.

of characterizing Israel and other nations. These images were attempts to represent "cities as the places of human culture and political institutions."[120] Similarly, within the context of Revelation the images represent two opposing cities, Rome/Babylon and the new Jerusalem, which are places of human, social, and political community. The bridal imagery functions as a contrast to the image of the great prostitute, which generally depicts Babylon/Rome, "in order to encourage readers to resist the murderous power of Rome."[121] Schüssler Fiorenza notes, however, that even though John uses the prostitute/bride imagery to call his readers to resist the evils of an oppressive social and political power, John's use of this imagery obscures his purpose. By using female-gendered symbolism, John shifts the audience's attention away from his political and religious intentions and toward issues of gender and sexuality: "The alternative between the empire of Babylon and the qualitatively new world of God is changed into the alternative between sexual purity and impurity signified by the metaphors of bride, temptress, wife and harlot."[122]

Schüssler Fiorenza's reading of Revelation's nuptial imagery is another advance in reading the text's metaphorical imagery. While she is particularly concerned with reading the text within its original rhetorical context, she acknowledges the complex nature and function of the text's metaphorical language. In an article dealing with the history of scholarship on Revelation, Schüssler Fiorenza calls others to appreciate the mythopoeic language of the Apocalypse:

> Exegetes and theologians still have to discover what artists have long understood: the strength of the language and composition of Revelation lies not in its theological argumentation or historical information but in its evocative power inviting imaginative participation. The language and narrative flow of Revelation elicit emotions, reactions, and convictions that cannot and should not be fully conceptualized and phrased in propositional-logical language. Since the author does not employ discursive language and logical arguments but speaks in the language of symbol and myth, the often somewhat unsophisticated discussion of the imaginative, mythopoeic language of Revelation needs to be replaced by a literary approach and symbol analysis that would bring out the evocative power and "musicality" of its language, which was written to be read aloud and to be heard.[123]

[120] Ibid., 95–96.

[121] Ibid., 111.

[122] Ibid., 131. Adela Yarbro Collins comes to a similar conclusion in "Feminine Symbolism," 20–33. She suggests that while Revelation makes a positive move in including both masculine and feminine symbols to represent God's salvation and God's interaction with the world, the particular forms of Revelation's feminine symbolism are limited and, in effect, limiting for women.

[123] Schüssler Fiorenza, "Introduction," 22.

In her monograph *The Ladies and the Cities*, Edith McEwan Humphrey investigates the function of the woman/building image in a number of apocalyptic texts, including Revelation, *Joseph and Aseneth, 4 Ezra,* and the *Shepherd of Hermas.* Each of these texts includes and elaborates an image of a woman or women who are transformed into buildings or cities.[124]

Humphrey's driving question revolves around how the image of the woman who is transformed into a building or city (woman/building) functions as a symbol of transformation in apocalyptic texts. She asks this question within the context of the scholarly discussion concerning the genre characteristics of apocalyptic literature. As a result, she focuses on how the woman/building fits into the overall structure of each apocalyptic text.[125]

Since she explores the function of a particular symbol, Humphrey offers a short discussion of the nature of symbols and symbolic language. Following the recent trend in scholarship on Revelation, she emphasizes the polyvalence of the woman/building symbol and apocalyptic symbolism in general. She, like many of her contemporaries, qualifies this claim by asserting that this does not imply that the image can mean anything. In particular, Humphrey notes that the traditional nature of this image actually limits its meaning. In each of the texts she addresses, the woman/building image draws on OT imagery of Jerusalem or Zion. Consequently, she asserts that the use of this image in each text alludes to "the people of God."[126] Moreover, in her conclusion, Humphrey observes that in each text the image relates to similar themes, including the question of identity, humility, and suffering.[127] Even though there are obvious parallels among the texts, she demonstrates that each text presents and uses the image in a different manner. Each author shapes the woman/building to his or her own narrative. By exploring the ways in which a particular image is utilized in different textual contexts, Humphrey demonstrates the paradoxical nature of an image that is both expansive and limited in meaning.

As suggested above, Humphrey focuses on the ways in which the image of the woman/building functions within the unfolding of the overall text. This presents a problem when looking at the Book of Revelation, since its structure is notoriously difficult to map.[128] After working through a variety of ways in which interpreters understand the structure of this text,

---

[124] Edith McEwan Humphrey, *The Ladies and the Cities: Transformation and Apocalyptic Identity in Joseph and Aseneth, 4 Ezra, the Apocalypse and the Shepherd of Hermas* (JSP; Sheffield: Sheffield Academic Press, 1995), 170.

[125] Humphrey, *The Ladies and the Cities,* 19; cf. Martha Himmelfarb, "The Experience of the Visionary and Genre in the Ascension of Isaiah 6–11 and the Apocalypse of Paul," *Semeia* 39 (1986): 91–111.

[126] Humphrey, *The Ladies and the Cities*, 20f.

[127] Ibid., 156ff.

[128] Ibid., 97.

Humphrey notes that most recognize the centrality of chap. 12 and the climactic positioning of chap. 21.[129] In light of this, Humphrey explores the relationship between the image of the woman clothed in the sun, depicted in Revelation 12, and the bride of the Lamb, depicted in Revelation 21.[130] Commentators have long wondered about the connection between these two "positive" feminine images. Humphrey works through the salient arguments both for reading the two images together and for approaching them separately.[131] One of the primary reasons for reading the two images synoptically, according to Humphrey, is the corporate nature of both images. Arguing against Yarbro Collins, who maintains that this woman represents an individual of sorts, Humphrey explains that the reference to the "other offspring" of the woman in chap. 12 conveys the sense of a corporate nature.[132] Finally, she concludes that

> It seems likely that a complete hearing or reading of the Apocalypse at one sitting would call great attention to the reappearance of a positive female figure in ch. 21. Since both figures have obvious corporate association, it seems unlikely that the hearer/reader could be expected to make a fine distinction between two heavenly entities with earthly counterparts.[133]

Humphrey reads the two images in relation to each other, although she is careful not to collapse the two images into a single image. The image of the woman clothed in the sun, according to Humphrey, serves as a sign or portent, as the text suggests, of the coming bride—the new Jerusalem.[134]

Although Humphrey's project involves examining the woman/building image, in her treatment of Revelation she spends little time addressing the details of this particular image. She does not offer a discussion of the woman/building image apart from her discussion of the woman in chap. 12. This makes it difficult to observe how, in fact, the language of the text contributes to the shape of the image.[135] Humphrey also focuses on the

---

[129] Ibid., 103f.

[130] The author of Revelation actually introduces the bridal image in chap. 19; however, Humphrey does not offer an explicit discussion of the image in this chapter. In fact, she only mentions the image in chap. 19 three times (*The Ladies and the Cities*, 108, 109, 114).

[131] Humphrey interacts primarily with Yarbro Collins, who offers a litany of reasons for reading the two images separately. Among other things, Yarbro Collins notes that two figures are simply not described using the same terms and that there is no connection between the woman in chap. 12 and the holy city. See Adela Yarbro Collins, *The Combat Myth in the Book Revelation* (Missoula, Mont.: Scholars Press, 1976).

[132] Humphrey, *The Ladies and the Cities*, 109.

[133] Ibid., 106.

[134] Ibid., 111.

[135] Humphrey's lack of close attention to the language of the image of the woman/building and her emphasis on the structure of the text may stem from her agreement with Ellul's advice, which she quotes, that "It is necessary . . . to go back from the text to the symbol and

woman aspect of the image almost to the exclusion of the building or city aspect of the image. She asserts that the new Jerusalem (building or city) itself encompasses a variety of connotations, but she spends little time exploring these.[136] In the end she simply concludes that the woman/building image conveys a sense of both the continuity and transformation of the people of God.

In *The Choice between Two Cities: Whore, Bride, and Empire in the Apocalypse*, Barbara Rossing offers another perspective on the function and significance of the feminine imagery, specifically the prostitute or whore and the bride, in Revelation.[137] Her work functions, at least in part, as a response to interpreters, such as Tina Pippin (see below), who emphasize the gendered aspect of these images.[138] Rossing suggests that this emphasis on gender may account for how modern readers understand the text, but it ignores ancient readers. Aligning herself with Schüssler Fiorenza's rhetorical approach to the text, Rossing explores how ancient readers may have understood the text's depiction of the prostitute and the bride. In this vein, Rossing reads the Book of Revelation as an example of deliberative rhetoric. The text includes traditional rhetorical strategies to persuade the audience toward right action.[139]

More specifically, Rossing argues that the images of the prostitute and the bride, which are both closely linked with city imagery, function as a "two-women" topos, a stereotyped rhetorical construct. She demonstrates that this topos occurs both in biblical wisdom traditions, notably Proverbs 1–9, and in Greco-Roman sources, particularly in Xenophon's retelling of the choice of Heracles.[140] In this topos two feminine images, one evil and one good, are contrasted as a way of presenting two ethical options: One can either follow Vice, personified as a woman, or Virtue, personified as a woman. This topos also includes the use of some standard rhetorical topics, including descriptions of the women's physical appearance (clothing, bodily traits, etc.).[141] In her analysis of Revelation, Rossing notes some striking parallels between the description of the prostitute in Revelation and the descriptions of the "evil woman" in other texts. She notes, for example, that descriptions of "purple garments" and "gold and jewels" are common elements in the two-women topos.[142]

---

not to study the symbol more than the text." As quoted by Humphrey, *The Ladies and the Cities*, 117.

[136] Humphrey, *The Ladies and the Cities*, 114f.

[137] Barbara R. Rossing, *The Choice between Two Cities: Whore, Bride, and Empire in the Apocalypse* (Harrisburg, Pa.: Trinity Press, 1999).

[138] Ibid., 12f.

[139] Ibid., 14f.

[140] Ibid., 17ff.

[141] Ibid., 38.

[142] Ibid., 78.

Noting that the author of Revelation merges the images of prostitute and bride with images of cities, Rossing suggests that the two-women topos in Revelation actually reflects a more general "two-choices" topos. Drawing on the work of Robert Kraft, Rossing maintains that there is a "basic binary form" that presents an either/or choice between ethical opposites. She explains, "A whole range of biblical and classical texts appeal to the same general two-choice ethical structure, which may have arisen independently in several different forms, and which could be elaborated in a number of possible directions by focusing on ways, women, or other imagery."[143] The "two-women" topos is one particular elaboration upon a more general topos that presents two options for ethical behavior. Thus, Rossing seemingly implies, the fact that the text of Revelation employs the images of the prostitute and the bride, feminine images, is of little consequence, since the images of ways and women were used interchangeably in antiquity.[144]

In her analysis of Revelation, Rossing emphasizes the fact that the author merges the two-women topos with the images of two cities. In so doing, Rossing asserts that the author of Revelation uses this topos primarily as a critique of Rome or the Roman Empire. She suggests that the figure of Babylon signifies Rome: "Revelation's prostitute is the foreign city of Babylon/Rome. The audience is scripted in a male or spectator role, viewing and being warned against the dangerous prostitute Rome who is paraded before them."[145] Furthermore, Rossing notes that the image of the city, which represents Rome, quickly usurps the image of the woman or prostitute: "Riding on the beast of Rome, the prostitute is transformed from an evil-woman seductress figure into a thoroughly political symbol."[146] Rossing essentially argues that the imagery of the evil woman loses its effect as chap. 17 progresses.

Rossing offers an extended discussion of Rev 17:16, which describes the destruction of Babylon: "And the ten horns which you saw, they and the beast will hate the harlot; they will make her desolate and naked, and devour her flesh and burn her up with fire . . ." (Rev 17:16 RSV). Rossing's discussion of this verse serves as a response to feminist-critical interpreters who suggest that this verse describes the rape and torture of woman's body. This discussion is particularly interesting in terms of how Rossing reads the text's imagistic language.[147] Given her claim that the woman imagery of

---

[143] Ibid., 44.

[144] Ibid., 53.

[145] Ibid., 76.

[146] Ibid., 81.

[147] Ibid., 87. Rossing notes Tina Pippin and Marla Selvidge as two feminist scholars who read this verse as describing a sexual murder. See Marla J. Selvidge, "Powerful and Powerless Women in the Apocalypse," *Neot* 26 (1992): 157–67.

chap. 17 completely gives way to the city imagery, Rossing argues that the language of this verse primarily conveys the sense of actions against a city and not a person. She argues, first of all, that ἐρημόω, "to make waste," is used throughout the Hebrew prophets to describe the destruction of cities or lands. Likewise, she notes that classical authors and the Jewish historian Josephus use this verb to describe "the razing, deforestation, and depopulation of conquered landscapes and cities following warfare."[148] Rossing concludes that the phrase should be read as describing the destruction of a city. That which the RSV translates "they will make her desolate" should be read as "they will make it a wasteland."[149] Second, Rossing notes that the language of making Babylon "naked" or "bare" (γυμνός) is ambiguous. While the term can be used to describe the literal or figurative nakedness of a person, it can also be used to describe "cities, kingdoms, landscapes, and objects."[150] Looking to the one other reference to nakedness in Revelation (3:17–18), which is the letter to the church at Laodicia, Rossing concludes that the reference to Babylon's nakedness most likely refers to "economic reversal" and not sexual exposure.[151] For Rossing, the image of Babylon in 17:16 is clearly a city image and not an image of a woman. Interestingly, while Rossing offers an extended discussion of these two phrases, she does not offer a close analysis of the rest of the verse, which reads, "and [they will] devour her [its] flesh and burn her [it] up with fire."[152] It seems that the reference to flesh (σάρξ) may be more difficult to reconcile with the image of a city.

Rossing's treatment of the image of the bride is less detailed than her treatment of the prostitute. This stems partly from the fact that the text spends much less time on this figure; however, it also reflects Rossing's suggestion that the image of the bride functions primarily to complete the two-women topos. The image serves little purpose other than to invoke "recognition of the two-women *topos*."[153] Rossing argues against scholars who suggest that the bride image somehow functions as a figure with which the audience is to identify. Highlighting the macarism in Rev 19:10, "Blessed are those who are invited to the marriage banquet of the Lamb," Rossing asserts that the text places the audience in the role of the guests at the wedding. She comments, "scholars who argue that the bride is the church in this text are faced with the task of explaining how readers can be

---

[148] Rossing, *The Choice between Two Cities*, 90.

[149] Ibid., 87.

[150] Ibid., 92f.

[151] Ibid., 97.

[152] Interestingly, Rossing also tries to mitigate the explicit personification of Babylon in Rev 18:7 (ibid., 126ff.).

[153] Ibid., 141.

both bride and guests in the same scene."[154] Everything about the image of the bride relates to the two-women topos. For instance, her attire is part of the stereotypical portrayal of the "good woman," setting her apart from the "bad woman," Babylon.[155] Finally, as in her discussion of Babylon, Rossing emphasizes the fact that the image of the woman, the bride, is transformed into the image of a city, the new Jerusalem. She offers an interesting discussion of many aspects of the description of this city, although she rarely relates this imagery back to the bridal imagery. For Rossing, the feminine imagery is clearly secondary to the city imagery.[156]

Besides offering a number of exegetical insights, Rossing's study provides an important perspective on Revelation's feminine images by highlighting their rhetorical function. She also reminds us, as does Humphrey, that the feminine images of the whore and bride are closely intertwined with city imagery. Interpreting the feminine images requires attention to the relation between these different images. While making these important contributions, Rossing's suggestion that these feminine images function mainly to invoke the two-ways topos brings her close to treating this rhetorical topos as a stylistic ornament with little impact on textual meaning.[157] Her argument fails to address the impact of the inclusion of this form of the topos in the text, rather than a different form of the topos, such as the "two-ways." She continues this tendency by limiting the possible range of influence the feminine images have within the text. In response to interpreters who have overemphasized gender, Rossing limits the feminine imagery to only a few verses. More specifically, as we saw above, she argues that 17:16 functions as city imagery and not feminine imagery. Not only does she fail to complete this argument, ignoring the last part of the verse, but at times she seems unwilling to allow that the language is polyvalent, simultaneously alluding to both the city and the woman.[158] Rossing's reading at this point borders on approaching the imagistic language of the text as propositional language. Rossing's

[154] Ibid., 140.

[155] Ibid., 142.

[156] Ibid., 144ff.

[157] Schüssler Fiorenza discusses how, in common parlance, the term "rhetoric" often connotes something that is completely stylistic or deceptive and devoid of any content (*The Book of Revelation*, 210).

[158] In her concluding chapter Rossing offers a comment that sounds as if she is more willing to accept the possibility of polyvalence. She writes, "The judgment against Babylon in Rev 17:16 describes the exposé . . . and devastation . . . of the city in imagery that also carries overtones of personal threat against Babylon." However, in a footnote following this sentence she offers an almost contradictory claim: "I argue in chapter 2 that ἐρημόω is a technical term for city destruction, however, and that the use of the verb precludes the reading of Rev 17:16 as the torture of a woman's body . . ." (*The Choice between Two Cities*, 162–63).

tendency to read the imagery as propositional is also seen in her equation of Babylon with the city Rome.[159]

Likewise, Rossing's treatment of the image of the bride downplays the complexity of the image. This is seen primarily in her discussion of the relationship between this image and the audience. As discussed above, she reads the macarism in Rev 19:10 as indicating that the audience represents guests at the wedding. For her, this categorically excludes the possibility that the audience may also identify with the bridal imagery, since it makes little sense for the readers to "be both bride and guests in the same scene."[160] This argument suggests that Rossing expects Revelation's imagistic language to conform to the rules of logic and linear thought. This assumption is problematic, as interpreters throughout history have discovered that the text continually resists such conformity. The fact that the text equates the linen clothing of the bride with "the righteous deeds of the saints" (Rev 19:8) demonstrates that this image, like others within the text, resists the rules of logic and propositional language.[161] As Schüssler Fiorenza notes, the language of Revelation is highly evocative and, consequently, it engages the audience in many different ways.

Unveiling the Bride: A Feminist-Critical Reading

Another contemporary scholar who addresses Revelation's nuptial imagery from a feminist-critical perspective is Tina Pippin.[162] Pippin is explicit regarding her assumptions and methods as a reader. Early in the text, she announces her intention to "play with the polyvalance" of Revelation's symbols.[163] Noting, however, that not all deconstructive readings are created equal, Pippin approaches the text from the perspective of a Marxist feminist. As such, Pippin reads for the "gender codes" in the narrative and in Revelation's symbolic language.[164] In particular, her concern is to demonstrate how these gendered symbols, especially the feminine symbols, expose "the deep misogyny of this vision of the end of the world."[165] In so doing, Pippin observes that in contrast to his depiction of the whore, John depicts

---

[159] Ibid., 62

[160] Ibid., 140.

[161] See also Caird, *The Revelation of Saint John*, 234.

[162] Tina Pippin, *Death and Desire: The Rhetoric of Gender in the Apocalypse of John* (Literary Currents in Biblical Interpretation; Louisville, Ky.: Westminster John Knox Press, 1992). See also the following essays by Pippin: "The Heroine and the Whore: Fantasy and the Female in the Apocalypse of John," *Semeia* 60 (1992): 67–82; and "Eros and the End: Reading for Gender in the Apocalypse of John," *Semeia* 59 (1992): 193–210.

[163] Ibid., 14.

[164] Ibid., 23.

[165] Ibid., 42.

the bride as a passive object. Standing adorned and ready, the bride is an image of male erotic desire.[166] The contrast between the whore, a sexually powerful woman who is destroyed or punished, and the passive bride establishes a problematic dichotomy, for it leaves women readers no real alternative with which to identify: Either experience rape and torture like the whore or be the object of male sexual control like the bride.

Pippin's reading of Revelation's feminine symbolism offers an important perspective on the text. Not only have most interpreters of Revelation failed to address the ways in which gender assumptions contribute to the meaning of Revelation's imagery, but most interpreters have also failed to note the patriarchal assumptions that are communicated when these images are appropriated in modern contexts.[167] In this way, Pippin's reading of Revelation's androcentric imagery provides an important corrective. However, even though she expresses her intention to emphasize the polyvalence of Revelation's symbolic language, this is not always the case. Instead, Pippin often reads the feminine symbols of Revelation within a closed system of language, just as Schüssler Fiorenza observed is often the case. In *Death and Desire,* Revelation's gendered symbols are depicted as signifying actual gender. Female-identified metaphors supposedly reveal the text's options for female existence. This sort of reading forgets that gender-related symbols or metaphors may not necessarily be about gender.[168] As Schüssler Fiorenza points out, this way of reading the feminine images of Revelation actually "literalizes the gender inscriptions of the Apocalypse."[169] By making one-to-one connections between the female-identified metaphors and actual females, a reader risks reducing Revelation's metaphorical language to propositional claims.

This discussion of the modern history of interpretation of Revelation's nuptial imagery has only begun to scratch the surface; it demonstrates the

---

[166] Pippin, *Death and Desire,* 72.

[167] More recently Revelation's imagery has been addressed by feminist interpreters: Susan R. Garrett, "Revelation," in *The Women's Bible Commentary,* ed. Carol A. Newsom and Sharon H. Ringe (Louisville, Ky.: Westminster John Knox Press, 1992); Jane Schaberg, "Response to Tina Pippin, 'Eros and the End,'" *Semeia* 59 (1992): 219–26; Selvidge, "Powerful and Powerless," 157–67; Yarbro Collins, "Feminine Symbolism," 20–33. See also the many feminist-critical interpretations of the harlot/bride imagery in Hebrew prophetic literature. For instance, Cheryl J. Exum, "The Ethics of Biblical Violence Against Women," in *The Bible in Ethics: The Second Sheffield Colloquium,* ed. John W. Rogerson, Margaret Davies, M. Daniel Carroll (Sheffield: Sheffield Academic Press, 1995), 248–71; T. Dorah Setel, "Prophets and Pornography: Female Sexual Imagery in Hosea" in *Feminist Interpretation of the Bible,* ed. Letty M. Russell (Philadelphia: Westminster Press, 1985), 86–95.

[168] Caroline Walker Bynum, "Introduction: The Complexity of Symbols," in *Gender and Religion: On the Complexity of Symbols,* ed. Caroline Walker Bynum, Stevan Harrell, Paula Richman (Boston: Beacon Press, 1986), 2–3. See also Elisabeth Schüssler Fiorenza, *Sharing Her Word: Feminist Biblical Interpretation in Context* (Boston: Beacon Press, 1998), 88ff.

[169] Schüssler Fiorenza, *Sharing Her Word,* 100.

need for approaching John's metaphorical language with a more refined understanding of metaphorical language.[170] While many interpreters have noted Revelation's symbolic language and its poetic images, few have approached the text equipped with an understanding of metaphor or language that does justice to the nature of metaphorical language and, hence, to the biblical texts in which metaphor is found.

[170] Another contemporary scholar who should be mentioned is Eugene Boring, since his commentary includes a discussion of Revelation's "pictorial" language. Unfortunately, Boring's discussion of Revelation's language is problematic. Further, since Boring does not offer an extended treatment of John's nuptial imagery I have chosen to exclude his work from this discussion. See M. Eugene Boring, *Revelation* (IBC; Louisville, Ky.: John Knox Press, 1989).

CHAPTER TWO

KNOWING IS SEEING: Ancient, Medieval, and Modern Theories of Metaphor

As we saw in chap. 1, since the earliest centuries of the church, interpreters have acknowledged the imagistic or metaphorical nature of the Book of Revelation, although they disagree about what this characterization means. This suggests that bringing the insights of metaphor theory to bear on Revelation would be an appropriate and fruitful endeavor, especially contemporary theories of metaphor which emphasize the cognitive nature of this phenomenon. This is not to suggest that scholars have ignored discussions about metaphor in their work on Revelation; rather, there has been little systematic analysis of the metaphorical language in the text. Scholars who have addressed the role of metaphor in Revelation tend to do so in broad strokes.[1] This chapter explores various scholarly discussions about metaphor in order to develop a full picture of the nature and function of figurative language. This survey will facilitate a careful analysis of one set of metaphors within Revelation, its nuptial imagery.

This chapter begins with ancient and medieval discussions of metaphor. First, the ancient and medieval theorists set the terms of the conversation about the nature of metaphor. In particular, Aristotle's view on metaphor provides a starting point for many modern discussions. Second, unlike some modern theories of metaphor, ancient theorists approach metaphor with the assumption that metaphorical language functions persuasively. Metaphor makes it possible for an audience to "see" something in a particular way and in a way that it might not have been seen before.[2]

[1] Most notable is Elisabeth Schüssler Fiorenza, who relates Revelation's evocative and rhetorical power to the text's figurative language. Her important work on the text sets the stage for even closer attention to specific metaphors and figures within the text ("Visionary Rhetoric and Social Political Situation," in *The Book of Revelation: Justice and Judgment*, 2nd ed. [Minneapolis: Fortress Press, 1998], 181–203). See also, for example, David L. Barr, *Tales of the End: A Narrative Commentary on the Book of Revelation* (Santa Rosa, Calif.: Polebridge Press, 1998).

[2] Mark Turner contrasts modern literary theorists and scholars of metaphor to the classical tradition, namely Aristotle, arguing that the former fail to recognize the cognitive aspect of metaphorical language, which is something the classical theorists assume (*Death Is the Mother of Beauty: Mind, Metaphor, Criticism* [Chicago: University of Chicago Press, 1987], 3–9).

This recognition is pertinent for studying Revelation, since Revelation seeks to persuade an audience to accept a very specific view of reality. Third, looking at medieval discussions of metaphor gives us some sense of how metaphor came to be treated as a simple trope which does not contribute to the meaning of a text. This helps explain why many scholars have tended to approach Revelation's metaphorical language as something to be translated into literal claims.

Aristotle: Metaphor and "Bringing Something before the Eyes"

Modern scholars of metaphor often begin with an acknowledgment of Aristotle, because he is one of the first thinkers to offer a detailed study of metaphor. Andrew Ortony writes, "Because rhetoric has been a field of human enquiry for over two millennia, it is not surprising that any serious study of metaphor is almost obliged to start with the works of Aristotle."[3] Unfortunately, some of these "serious studies" use Aristotle's work primarily as a foil for describing the problematic views that seemingly ensue from his writings.[4] Noting the definition of metaphor he offers in *Poetics*, scholars paint Aristotle as the founding father of the somewhat misguided "comparison theory" of metaphor.[5] As we will see, however, Aristotle recognizes that metaphorical language can function as a particularly effective rhetorical tool because of its ability to evoke and enliven mental images.

Before turning to Aristotle's discussion of metaphor in *Poetics*, it is necessary to gain some sense of the way in which he understands language to

---

[3] Andrew Ortony, "Metaphor, Language, and Thought," in *Metaphor and Thought*, ed. Andrew Ortony; 2nd ed. (Cambridge: Cambridge University Press, 1993), 3.

[4] Raymond Gibbs treats Aristotle under the "traditional view" of metaphor, with which he clearly disagrees. Among other things, Gibbs suggests that Aristotle's work leads to the view that metaphor is a deviation of language and, therefore, inferior to literal language (*The Poetics of Mind: Figurative Thought, Language, and Understanding* [Cambridge: Cambridge University Press, 1994], 61, 210–11). Likewise, Max Black suggests that Aristotle has led interpreters down a "blind alley" in which they suppose that metaphorical statements can be replaced by literal translations, an approach Black finds particularly problematic (see below) ("More About Metaphor," in *Metaphor and Thought*, ed. Andrew Ortony; 2nd ed. [Cambridge: Cambridge University Press, 1993], 20–22). Note also George Lakoff's discussion of J. L. Austin. Lakoff faults Austin for treating what Lakoff understands to be metaphor as analogy. In so doing, Lakoff offhandedly suggests that Austin follows Aristotle. This comment reveals Lakoff's assumption that Aristotle operates with a comparison theory of metaphor, a theory that Lakoff argues adamantly against (*Women, Fire and Dangerous Things: What Categories Reveal about the Mind* [Chicago: University of Chicago Press, 1987], 19). For a discussion on the "misreadings" of Aristotle's view of metaphor, see James Edwin Mahon, "Getting Your Sources Right: What Aristotle *Didn't* Say," in *Researching and Applying Metaphor*, ed. Lynne Cameron and Graham Low (Cambridge: Cambridge University Press, 1999), 69–80.

[5] E.g., John R. Searle, "Metaphor," in *Metaphor and Thought*, ed. Andrew Ortony; 2nd ed. (Cambridge: Cambridge University Press, 1993), 89–90. See also George A. Miller, "Images and Models, Similes and Metaphors," in *Metaphor and Thought*, ed. Ortony, 368.

function. Aristotle addresses this topic in *De interpretatione*, explaining that spoken words "are symbols or signs (σύμβολα) of affections or impressions (παθημάτων) of the soul; written words are the signs of words spoken" (*De interp.* 1.5). Words stand for or represent particular mental experiences—experiences of different things or states or realities. As Umberto Eco explains, this implies a twofold function of words: "by uttering a word (or by producing other kinds of signs) one 'means' or 'signifies' a thought, or a passion of the soul, and 'names' or 'refers to' a thing. . . ."[6] Words do more than refer directly to things (which include immaterial as well as material things); words also conjure the human experience or understanding of the thing that is named. In this way a word is not reducible to a singular referent; rather, words point to clusters or networks of associations stemming from human experience. The signs (σημεῖα) assigned to these experiences differ from culture to culture (*De interp.* 1). There is not a necessary or inherent connection between the mental experiences of things and the particular signs assigned to these experiences;[7] however, these signs do generate and shape cognition.

In *Poetics,* Aristotle addresses the nature and function of different types of poetry, including tragic, epic, and comic forms. One element that comprises poetry is style (λέξις), which involves not *what* is said, but *how* it is communicated (*Rhetorica* 3.1.2–3).[8] In his discussion of style, particularly in reference to the nature of nouns, Aristotle offers his oft-quoted definition of metaphor: "Metaphor is the applying (ἐπιφορεῖν, lit., 'bringing to') of a strange term from the genus to species or from the species to the genus or from the species to [another] species according to analogy" (*Poetica* 21.7). Instead of using the conventional or proper term for a particular thing, metaphor involves applying the term of another thing to the object or idea being expressed. Aristotle actually uses metaphorical language to describe this phenomenon. Using the verb "to bring to" (ἐπιφορεῖν), Aristotle depicts metaphor as the act of carrying or bringing an object from one place to another. By using a term (A) other than a conventional term (B) in a particular context, a metaphor brings the meaning of term (A) into an unusual context. Since for Aristotle a word or name refers to more than just the thing in and of itself, with a metaphor the impression or sense of the thing to which term A refers is brought to bear on B or the thing to which B

---

[6] Umberto Eco, "Denotation," in *On the Medieval Theory of Signs,* ed. Umberto Eco and Costantino Marmo (Amsterdam: John Benjamins, 1989), 47.

[7] This view of language stands in contrast to the Stoic claim that words [*logoi*] actually reflect the nature of things and communicate characteristics of those particular things (Martin Irvine, *The Making of Textual Culture: 'Grammatica' and Literary Theory, 350–1100* [Cambridge: Cambridge University Press, 1994], 32–38).

[8] For an updated English translation, see George A. Kennedy, *On Rhetoric: A Theory of Civic Discourse,* trans. and ed. George A. Kennedy (New York: Oxford University Press, 1991).

refers. As a process of transferring terms, metaphor is more complex than a codelike substitution of one word for another.

This process of applying one term to another thing involves a perceived analogy or similarity between the things represented by the terms. The term "A" can be applied to thing "B" based on some similarity between A and B. For example, since both evening and old age come at the end of a delineated period of time (a day and a life respectively), this similarity permits a poet to describe old age as the evening of a life (*Poet.* 21.13–14). The analogy inherent within a metaphor need not reflect an actual analogy between things. This is evident in Aristotle's claim that the successful use of metaphor demands an ability to see (θεωρέω) or perceive the resemblances in different things (*Poet.* 22.17). Through the use of metaphor, the poet communicates this perceived similarity. Although Aristotle suggests that metaphor can be an effective means of communicating in poetry, he calls for moderation in the use of metaphor. One of the fundamental virtues of poetry is clarity, and the overuse of metaphor tends to obscure rather than to clarify (22.11–12).

In his essay on contemporary misreadings of Aristotle's view of metaphor, James Mahon notes that many scholars fail to consider the discussion of metaphor in *On Rhetoric*, and so fail to recognize the complexity of Aristotle's view of metaphor.[9] While discussion of metaphor in *On Rhetoric* reiterates some of the observations of *Poetics* (*Rhet.* 3.1.10, 3.2.5–6), it augments that discussion as well. In particular, its discussion of metaphorical language reflects the overall aim of *On Rhetoric*, which is to discuss and describe rhetoric as the art of persuasion (*Rhet.* 1.2.1). As part of this work Aristotle demonstrates the ways in which metaphorical language functions to persuade an audience—to "move [an] audience from one locus of thought to another. . . ."[10]

Aristotle highlights the positive attributes of metaphorical language as part of his discussion of "clever/urbane and popular expressions" (*Rhet.* 3.10.1). Metaphor and simile, which Aristotle describes as different versions of the same phenomenon, make certain popular sayings particularly effective means of teaching and persuading. Aristotle explains, "Metaphor most brings about learning; for when [Homer] calls old age 'stubble,' he creates understanding and knowledge through the genus, since both old age and stubble are [species of the genus of] things that have lost their bloom" (*Rhet.* 3.10.2–3 [Kennedy]). Aristotle observes that the analogy between stubble and old age reflects their shared genus. By exchanging one for the other,

---

[9] Mahon, "Getting Your Sources Right," 72–73.

[10] Turner, *Death Is the Mother of Beauty*, 3. Turner, unlike some of his contemporaries, highlights Aristotle's understanding of metaphor, suggesting that the ancient philosopher not only recognizes the persuasive aspect of metaphor but also begins to explore the connection between cognition and language.

Homer highlights the aspects of old age which belong to this genus—the aspects of old age which old age shares with stubble. In transferring one word (stubble) to another context or word (old age), the author communicates some very particular ideas about an abstract concept. Aristotle maintains that this is an effective means of communication; for even though the complexity of the idea may not be immediately obvious to the audience, the metaphor communicates a complicated idea in a simple phrase (*Rhet.* 3.10.4).

Aristotle further explains that metaphorical expressions that "bring something before the eyes" (πρὸ ὀμμάτων ποιεῖν) are effective means of communication. These expressions use metaphor in the attempt to signify activity (*Rhet.* 3.10.6, 11.1–2). For example, in the line from Euripides "the Greeks darting forward on their feet," the poet metaphorically uses "darting" to create a verbal image of activity. Likewise, Homer's lines "the arrow flew" and "the spear-point sped eagerly through his breast" effectively use metaphor to create an enlivened image for the audience. Through the use of metaphor an author or speaker is able to animate the lifeless, thereby appealing to the audience's visual imagination. In some sense, the author or speaker communicates to the audience by encouraging it to see things in the same way in which he/she does. On account of this, metaphorical expressions play a useful role in persuasive speaking.

In *Poetics,* Aristotle describes metaphor as transferring the meaning of one word to another context based on some perceived resemblance or similarity between the referents of the two terms. Assuming that words not only name things but that they also conjure the impressions of the thing on the soul, Aristotle implies that metaphor is more than a mere substitution of one name for another (*De interp.* 1.5). Metaphor involves bringing the allusions and experiences of one thing into another context. This is based on some perceived similarities between the two terms within the metaphor. More importantly, as Aristotle explains in *On Rhetoric*, metaphor allows an audience to "see" one thing in terms of another. Through the use of metaphorical language, a speaker can actually bring an idea into the sight of his/her audience, making metaphorical language quite persuasive. By conjuring the impressions of a particular thing or experience through a metaphor, an author makes visible or evident the characteristics of something else, something more abstract.

Metaphor in the Latin Rhetorical Traditions

While Aristotle's understanding of metaphor plays an important role in modern critical theory, the Latin rhetoricians writing centuries after Aristotle play a larger role in shaping the discussion that progresses throughout the Western literary and rhetorical tradition. In the writings of the

Latin rhetoricians we see a tension between two trends: trying to understand the nature of figurative language in general and attempts at delineating different figurative expressions. The latter tendency, in particular, thrives during the Middle Ages in the form of grammatical textbooks and encyclopedias.

There is an important connection between rhetoric and literary criticism or textual interpretation in the ancient tradition. While in the most basic sense the rhetorical handbooks were written to instruct students in the art of constructing and delivering speeches, they also relate to and reflect the ways in which educated individuals approached and understood written texts. In the late classical period especially, the fields of *grammatica*, which included the interpretation of literature, and *rhetorica* as well as *dialecta*, overlapped considerably. In particular, rhetoric and grammar overlapped in their discussion of style, which includes the discussion of figurative language.[11] Therefore, even though the rhetorical texts discuss tropes and figures as part of a larger program of teaching persuasive speech, these texts also reflect the ways in which interpreters read and understood texts.[12]

The Latin rhetorical handbooks provided the foundation of education through the end of late antiquity and into the Middle Ages. Even though in the earliest centuries many philosophers continued a long tradition of criticizing rhetoricians, rhetorical schools served as one of the primary places of education in the ancient world.[13] As a result, these traditions not only influenced early Christian authors, including Augustine (see below), but they contributed to the shape of discourse in the Western tradition.[14] The technical discussion of metaphor, subsumed under the larger category of "figures of speech" developed in the Roman rhetorical tradition, provides one of the standard models for understanding metaphor in the Western literary tradition.

Cicero's name stands out among all other Latin rhetoricians. As one scholar notes, Cicero is "the unquestioned *magister eloquentiae* for the

[11] Irvine, *The Making of Textual Culture*, 7–8.

[12] Kennedy suggests that during the Greco-Roman period there is little or no differentiation between rhetorical theory and literary criticism. Generally, the prescriptive texts of the rhetoricians reflected and provided the framework through which literature was discussed and understood (*A New History of Classical Rhetoric* [Princeton: Princeton University Press, 1994],159).

[13] The tradition of criticizing orators stems back to Plato's *Gorgias* and continues, most notably, in the works of Tacitus. Tacitus's criticism of the rhetorical schools is often thought to describe the general decline of the rhetorical traditions in the second century; however, his criticism also attests to the fact that rhetorical training was still popular during this time period. See Tacitus, *Dialogus de oratoribus* 35.

[14] James J. Murphy, *Rhetoric in the Middle Ages: A History of Rhetorical Theory from St. Augustine to the Renaissance* (Berkeley: University of California Press, 1974), 23.

Middle Ages."[15] His early and unfinished rhetorical handbook, *De inventione* (ca. 92–88 B.C.E.), functioned as one of the standard rhetorical textbooks in the ancient and medieval worlds.[16] *De inventione* lacks a discussion of style (*elocutio*), which would have included a discussion of metaphor. Cicero does offer, however, an interesting explanation of metaphorical language in his later dialogue *De oratore* (ca. 55 B.C.E.). Cicero's comments on metaphor in this work resemble those of Aristotle, including his claims about the ability of metaphorical language to address the senses of the audience.

Unlike later rhetoricians, Cicero addresses the nature of metaphorical language in general and does not make a specific point of differentiating between types of figurative or metaphorical expressions. For example, he does not specifically distinguish between metaphor, simile, and allegory.[17] Instead, Cicero defines metaphorical language in general as involving any occasion in which words are used in a context or way that is not typical or proper. This use is based on some resemblance (*similitudo*) between the thing expressed and the object, word, or idea being communicated or explicated. When a "proper term" simply cannot convey the meaning intended by the speaker, the speaker "borrows" another term to convey his/her idea (*De or.* 3.38.155–56). For instance, using an example that Cicero offers, the term "separation" (*divortium*) can be used metaphorically to describe a relationship between a husband and a wife that has ended (*De or.* 3.40.159). This metaphor is based on some resemblance between the separating of ways or roads and the separating of people in a marriage relationship. While the use of metaphor, such as this example, often functions to fill lexical lacunae, orators continue to use metaphor on account of its "entertaining" or pleasant quality (*De or.* 3.33.152–55).

Cicero, again echoing his Greek forerunner, argues that metaphorical language possesses the capability of making an idea clear to one's audience. First, he explains, through metaphor an orator can use a single word to suggest a larger picture (*De or.* 3.40.160). A single metaphorical word can conjure a wealth of relevant images that add to the meaning of the idea being conveyed. Second, again sounding like Aristotle, Cicero describes metaphor as having "a direct appeal to the senses, especially the sense of sight . . ."

---

[15] Murphy notes that Cicero's works were translated into vernacular languages, including Italian and French. Further, a number of medieval scholars wrote commentaries on the works of Cicero, attesting to the significance of Cicero's works for the Middle Ages. For example, Thierry of Chartres wrote a commentary on *De Inventione* in the twelfth century (Murphy, *Rhetoric in the Middle Ages*, 106).

[16] Kennedy, *A New History of Classical Rhetoric*, 118.

[17] E.g., *De or.* 3.40.161. The text of *De oratore* includes a sentence explaining the difference between a metaphor and simile, which the editor of the text believes to be an interpolation! See Rackham's translation in the Loeb Classical Library of Cicero *De or.* 3.39.157.

(*De or.* 3.40.160–61 [Rackham]). Unlike other types of speech, metaphorical language can make sensible that which is nonsensible or abstract, thereby making the abstract reality more easily known. This is done through a speaker's ability to highlight the resemblances between the abstract and aspects of the sensible world. For example, the metaphorical phrases "the fragrance of good manners" and "the softness of a humane spirit" draw on resemblances between that which can be known through the senses (fragrance and softness) and that which is more abstract (good manners and a humane spirit). In particular, Cicero commends metaphors that rely on the sense of sight, which bring the abstract into the audience's "mental vision" (*De or.* 3.40.161). By making an idea "visible" to one's audience, metaphorical language can be an effective tool in persuasion.

Although Cicero's *De oratore* is not widely referenced in the Middle Ages, a rhetorical handbook erroneously attributed to Cicero, *Rhetorica ad Herennium* (ca. 85–80 B.C.E.), played an important role in medieval education.[18] The treatment of metaphor in this work differs from that in *De oratore*, reflecting the tendency of some Latin rhetoricians to treat style (*elocutio*) in a technical manner.[19] The author of *Ad Herennium* discusses metaphor within his discussion of style as one of over forty different figures of speech. In this way, *Ad Herennium* stands at the beginning of a long tradition of texts that codify figures of speech as the tools used to embellish speech or writing.

According to the author of *Ad Herennium* the style of a speech primarily involves the ways in which and the extent to which an orator embellishes his/her speech (*Ad Her.* 4.1). The grand style of speech involves the most embellishment, while the simple style of speech lacks embellishment in favor of "standard speech" (*Ad Her.* 4.8). Specifically, an orator lends dignity (*dignitas*) to his/her speech through the use of figures of thought and figures of speech. Figures of thought, on the one hand, are the ways in which an orator dignifies his speech through the use of unstated ideas. For example, as a figure of thought, understatement (*diminutio*) involves thinking that a subject exhibits an exceptional advantage, but purposely speaking of it in moderate terms in order to avoid appearing arrogant (*Ad Her.* 4.38). The dignity of the speech is enhanced by the idea "behind" the speech, in this case, the desire not to appear arrogant, and not specifically through the words themselves. On the other hand, figures of speech describe the specific choice and arrangement of words, which in and of themselves lend distinction or dignity to the speech. For instance, among the forty-five figures of speech described in *Ad Herennium* is *epanaphora*, when the same word forms the successive beginnings of a number of

[18] Kennedy, *A New History of Classical Rhetoric*, 121.

[19] Ibid., 125.

phrases, and *antistrophe*, when the last word of successive phrases is repeated. As we see in these two examples, in contrast to figures of thought, figures of speech typically describe the ways in which an orator enhances the "surface" of the text. Figures of speech function as tools for creating variety and embellishing a speech (*Ad Her.* 4.13).

Metaphor (*translatio*) is one of the figures of speech codified in *Ad Herennium*. The author classifies metaphor as one of ten tropes—a subsection of "figures of speech." By definition, a trope is a departure from the ordinary meaning of a word in order to use the word in different sense (*Ad Her.* 4.31). In other words, a trope is a misuse of a word. What makes metaphor unique from other tropes, such as *onomatopoeia* and *metonymy*, for example, is that it requires recognizing some similarity between distinct things: "Metaphor occurs when a word applying to one thing is transferred to another, because the similarity seems to justify this" (*Ad Her.* 4.34). The author of *Ad Herennium* suggests that there are a number of reasons for using metaphor within a speech. While metaphor can be used for the sake of brevity or to avoid using obscenity, the first reason *Ad Herennium* suggests for using metaphor is to create a "vivid mental picture" for the audience (*Ad Her.* 4.34). Overall, however, the author of *Ad Herennium* suggests that metaphor functions simply as one of many devices for making a speech more interesting and possibly more compelling to a speaker's audience (*Ad Her.* 4.34).

While *Ad Herennium* classifies metaphor as a figure of speech, comparisons (*similes*) and simile (*imago*) are classified as figures of thought. This classification is fascinating, because these figures are elsewhere often associated with metaphorical language, as we saw with Aristotle. In fact, the author of *Ad Herennium* observes a connection between comparison and metaphor. Comparison, the author explains, "is a manner of speech that carries over an element of likeness from one thing to a different thing" (*Ad Her.* 4.45 [Caplan]). Comparing two unrelated terms can be used, among other reasons, to clarify a particular idea. Further, when presenting a comparison between two things, an orator may actually use a metaphor or metaphorical language to communicate the basic comparison (*Ad Her.* 4.48). For example, an orator may compare false friends to swallows by using the metaphor "they fly away" to describe their departure (*Ad Her.* 4.48). While the comparison of the friends and swallows lies behind the words of the text, the comparison is not explicitly stated in the speech. The metaphorical use of "fly" communicates the implicit comparison between friends and swallows. Thus, even though *Ad Herennium* relegates metaphor to the figures of speech, it recognizes that metaphor is related to and reflects conceptual comparisons.

Ad Herennium marks the beginning of one of the most prevalent approaches to metaphor in the Western tradition. First, this text reflects a common dichotomy between figures of thought and figures of speech, with metaphor being placed within the latter category. While the author of *Ad Herennium* assumes some connection between metaphor and figures of thought such as comparison, for some subsequent interpreters there is an assumption that figures of speech have little or no connection to the thought that the orator or author communicates. Metaphor, like other figures of speech, is understood primarily as an arrangement of words. Second, *Ad Herennium* reflects the growing tendency to approach metaphor as a trope. This understanding implies, among other things, that there is another "right" or "correct" way to communicate what is communicated through a metaphor. Metaphors have little communicative value other than the variety that they can bring to a speech.

While *Ad Herennium* establishes a precedent for treating metaphor as a trope used for embellishment, it is mistaken to assume that all of the Latin rhetoricians shared the same view of metaphor.[20] In *Institutio oratoria* (ca. 93 C.E.), which also exerted influence during the Middle Ages, Quintilian followed the lead of *Ad Herennium* by classifying metaphor as a trope and treating it within his discussion of style; however, Quintilian's understanding of style lends his discussion of metaphor a certain hue not quite achieved in *Ad Herennium* (*Inst.* 8.6). In some sense, Quintilian's work bridges the gap between the understanding of metaphor that Cicero offers and that of *Ad Herennium*.

Quintilian argues that the element of style (*elocutio*) relates directly to the concepts or ideas communicated in a speech: "For the verb *eloqui* means the production and communication to the audience of all that the speaker has conceived in his mind, and without this power all the preliminary accomplishments of oratory are useless as a sword that is kept permanently concealed within its sheath" (*Inst.* 8.preface.15 [Butler]). Style, the selection and arrangement of words and sentences, communicates the speaker's ways of thinking about his/her topic. Style is not primarily the embellishment of a speech, but it involves attempting to communicate ideas to one's audience so that the audience can be persuaded to conceive of things in the desired manner. As such, style plays an important role in the construction of a speech. Quintilian, however, also cautions his readers to avoid overattention to style, which can diminish the clarity of one's speech—clarity being one of the chief values of rhetoric (*Inst.* 8.2.1, 22).

Quintilian's claim that style and thought are often related extends into his discussion of tropes or figures of speech and figures (*figura*), specifically figures of thought. First of all, Quintilian recognizes that the distinc-

---

[20] *Contra* Murphy, *Rhetoric in the Middle Ages*, 8. While not addressing metaphor in particular, Murphy characterizes the Roman rhetorical tradition, including *ad Herennium* and Quintilian's *Institutio Oratoria* as homogenous.

tion between tropes and other figures of speech is hotly debated; however, he finds the debate trifling:

> This is a subject which has given rise to interminable disputes among the teachers of literature, who have quarreled no less violently with the philosophers than among themselves over the problem of the *genera* and *species* into which *tropes* may be divided, their number and the correct classification. I propose to disregard such quibbles. . . . (*Inst.* 8.6.1–2 [Butler])

Second and more significantly, Quintilian acknowledges that the distinction between figures of speech, including tropes, and figures of thought is problematic. Dismissing the simple separation of thought and speech, Quintilian argues that the use of figures of thought often requires the use of figures of speech, "For the former lies in the conception, the latter in the expression of our thought" (*Inst.* 9.1.16 [Butler]). It is not uncommon for a figure of thought to be expressed in metaphorical language, making the distinction between figures of thought and tropes such as metaphor problematic.

While acknowledging the problems with the category of trope, Quintilian discusses metaphor along with other figures that are considered tropes. Like his predecessors, Quintilian describes metaphor as the transferring of a word's meaning to a different or unusual context. The meaning of a particular word is borrowed by placing that word in a different context (*Inst.* 8.6.4–6). While this can be done for decorative effect, it can also be used to clarify a speaker's idea. Metaphorical language, including metaphors and similes, can contribute to the effectiveness of a speech by bringing something before the "eyes" of the audience (*Inst.* 8.3.72, 81–82).

Although he values clarity in a speech, something which the use of tropes threatens, Quintilian offers a justification of the use of tropes:

> some tropes are employed to help out our meaning and others to adorn our style, that some arise from words used properly and others from words used metaphorically, and that the changes involved concern not merely individual words, but also our thoughts and the structure of our sentences. In view of these facts I regard those writers as mistaken who have held that tropes necessarily involved the substitution of word for word. And I do not ignore the fact that as a rule the tropes employed to express our meaning involve ornament as well, though the converse is not the case, since there are some which are intended solely for the purpose of embellishment. (*Inst.* 8.6.2–3 [Butler])

Distinguishing between tropes used solely for embellishment and tropes that "help out" a speaker's meaning, Quintilian notes that at times tropes are necessary to communicate a particular idea. It is interesting that Quintilian rejects the notion that tropes simply involve the substitution of a word for another word, since this is often how the ancient approach to metaphor is characterized.[21] In contrast to a simple substitution of words, Quintilian implies that the "mis-use" of words in a trope shapes and reflects the meaning of the sentence and the thought as a whole. This claim seemingly reflects Quintilian's suggestion that figures of speech and thought are not easily distinguished.

Cicero, *Ad Herennium*, and Quintilian offer a sense of the variety of approaches to figurative language and specifically metaphor in the Roman rhetorical tradition. These different approaches introduced some patterns that continued into the Middle Ages. First, continuing the trend set by Aristotle, the rhetoricians generally understood metaphor in terms of transferring the meaning of a word to an unusual context. The meaning of the word is "borrowed" by placing it in a new and different setting. Second, in the Roman rhetorical handbooks we begin to see the classification of different types of figurative speech, including metaphor. Related to this trend is the tendency to distinguish between figures of thought and figures of speech. In so doing, metaphor may be relegated to the category of figures of speech, specifically a trope, even though other types of "metaphorical language" may be classified as figures of thought. The project of classifying figures of speech grows as we progress into the Middle Ages. Third, all three of the above rhetoricians seemingly suggest that while figurative language functions as an embellishment of a speech, it also can serve to clarify an argument. In making this latter claim, many of the theorists use the language of sight to describe figurative language and metaphor: Metaphor brings an idea before the eyes of one's audience, making it possible to communicate a difficult idea. This aspect of figurative language, according to some, lends it a definite rhetorical force. At times, however, this function of metaphorical language is lost as theorists emphasized the decorative function.

Augustine and Interpreting the Figurative Language of Scripture

The work of Augustine demonstrates how the rhetorical traditions reflect and shape the practice of textual interpretation. A former teacher of rhetoric,[22] Augustine became one of the most influential interpreters of Scripture in the Christian tradition. Initially, however, his background in rhetoric, especially his familiarity with the eloquent philosophical works of Cicero, led Augustine to despair of the language of Scripture, particularly its obscure figurative language: "For not as when now I speak did I feel

[21] E.g., Paul Ricoeur, *The Rule of Metaphor: Multi-disciplinary Studies of the Creation of Meaning in Language*, trans. R. Czerny with K. McLaughlin and J. Costello (Toronto: University of Toronto Press, 1977), 44–48.

[22] Augustine, *Confessions* 4.4.2.

when I turned towards those Scriptures, but they appeared to me to be unworthy to be compared with the dignity of Tully [Cicero]; for my inflated pride shunned their style, nor could the sharpness of my wit pierce their inner meaning"(*Confessionum libri XIII* 3.5.9 [NPNF[1] 1:72]). Ironically, Augustine later brought the grammatical and rhetorical traditions, which led him to hold the Scriptures in disdain, into conversation with Scripture, using these traditions as tools for interpreting the sacred writings.

In a work that became one of the most influential texts of the Middle Ages, *De doctrina christiana* (ca. 396),[23] Augustine draws together elements of secular thought and teaching, including the study of grammar and rhetorical theory, and the divine Word of God, for the sake of interpreting and proclaiming the latter (*Conf.* 4.1.2). The similarities between Augustine's discussion of language and the Latin scholarly tradition lead contemporary scholars to debate the question of Augustine's indebtedness to his predecessors in the rhetorical tradition, especially Cicero.[24] Clearly, the subject matter of this work, the nature of language and grammar, including the interpretation of texts, reflected some of the central scholarly concerns and questions of his day.[25] Furthermore, Augustine's use of secular or "pagan" scholars "baptized" them into the Christian tradition, and made them acceptable subjects of study for subsequent Christian scholars.[26] This is not a minor point, since this enables the works of Cicero and other Latin scholars to continue to shape the ways in which scholars read and write throughout the Middle Ages.

Although this work functioned, in some sense, as a handbook for Christian scholars, *De doctrina* begins with a discussion more in keeping with ancient philosophical treatments of language than with the technical hand-

---

[23] *De doctrina christiana* was composed in two different stages. The first three books were written about 396 C.E., shortly after Augustine was ordained as the bishop of Hippo. The final book was added in 426 (Irvine, *The Making of Textual Culture*, 178).

[24] Augustine, *On Christian Doctrine*, trans. D. W. Robertson (Upper Saddle River, N.J.: Prentice Hall, 1958). Augustine, in fact, quotes Cicero more than once in this work (4.5.7, 12.27. John M. Rist suggests that Augustine's own understanding of language actually reflects a number of influences, including Stoic views of language and rhetorical practices. See John M. Rist, *Augustine: Ancient Thought Baptized* (Cambridge: Cambridge University Press, 1994), 23ff.

[25] For a discussion of how *De doctrina christiana* resembles and relates to other ancient grammatical texts in particular, see Irvine, *The Making of Textual Culture*, 178–89.

[26] Augustine's *De doctrina christiana* responds to a context of debate over the question of whether or not it was appropriate for Christians to study the works of secular or "pagan" authors. Likewise, Christian scholars argued over the appropriateness of learning and using rhetorical techniques in order to preach the Christian message. Jerome, writing in 384 C.E., captures the sense of this debate in his famous quotation, "What has Horace to do with the Psalter, Virgil with the Gospels, and Cicero with Paul?" See *Select Letters of Jerome* (trans. F. A. Wright (LCL; Cambridge: Harvard University Press, 1933), 22.29.

books discussed above.[27] Augustine begins by exploring the relationship between words and reality or things. This entails a thorough discussion of the nature of words as signs [*signa*] that represent things [*res*] or realities other than themselves. Signs, including both things and words, are the means by which one's mind is directed to other realities (*Doctr. chr.* 1.2). Words are signs par excellence, since they are not things in themselves, but function only in reference to other things.[28] Further, Augustine explains, words are conventional signs. Unlike natural signs (e.g., smoke as a sign of fire or footprints as a sign of an animal), the meaning of a word is a matter of convention, as it is agreed upon by the participants in a culture (*Doctr. chr.* 2.2.3).

As signs, words can be either proper or figurative. On the one hand, a word is proper if it points out the object or event to which it conventionally refers. Modifying an example from Augustine, if the word "cow" is used to represent the four-legged, ruminant animal that is typically referred to as a "cow" in English, then "cow" functions as a proper sign or word. On the other hand, a word is figurative if it is used to refer to something other than it was intended, if it defies conventional usage. If the word "cow" is used to refer to a human individual, then the word "cow" is being used figuratively (*Doctr. chr.* 2.10.15). Figurative language involves the "incorrect" use of a word, since it is used in a way that defies conventional usage. Despite this, in both the proper and figurative usages, signs point to realities beyond themselves.

Most significantly, Augustine explicitly brings this understanding of language to bear on the process of interpreting Scripture, grappling with the issue of how to understand and approach the figurative language of God's Word. In so doing, he presupposes, like other Christian interpreters, that the language of Scripture is qualitatively different from all other forms of human language. First, since God ultimately authors Scripture, the signs of Scripture, *even the figurative signs*, communicate truth. This is different from secular or nonsacred texts, which may communicate ideas and claims that are not truthful. Unlike other texts, even the most obscure images and figures contain some element of God's truth. Second, as a result of divine origin, the signs within Scripture communicate perfectly (*Doctr. chr.* 1.36.41). Naturally, Augustine does not suggest that Scripture is always understood perfectly or properly; rather, incorrect interpretations of Scripture result from the imperfect and fallen nature of the interpreter as well as the polysemous nature of language.[29]

---

[27] Irvine, *The Making of Textual Culture*, 170.

[28] R. A. Markus, "St. Augustine on Signs," *Augustine: A Collection of Critical Essays*, ed. R. A. Markus (Garden City, N.Y.: Anchor Books, 1972), 73.

[29] For a discussion of the relationship between language and the fall in Augustine's writings, see Carol Harrison, *Beauty and Revelation in the Thought of Saint Augustine* (Oxford: Clarendon Press, 1992), 59–67.

The presence of figurative language makes Scripture even more difficult to interpret: "Some of the expressions are so obscure as to shroud the meaning in the thickest darkness" (*Doctr. chr.* 2.6.7 [Robertson]; cf. 2.10.15). In light of this ambiguity, Augustine offers some criteria for interpreting figurative language in Scripture. First of all, he suggests, the "plainer" passages of Scripture should be used to determine the meaning of complex, figurative portions. These straightforward passages communicate all that is necessary for faith and the Christian life; thus, the Christian should study these diligently. Knowledge of these passages helps the interpreter determine the presence of figurative language. If a passage contradicts the idea of God's love and love of neighbor, then one knows it is figurative. Augustine offers even more specific formulations of this interpretive principle. For instance, he suggests, when Scripture seemingly attributes sinful actions to God or saints, such as gluttony or lustfulness, these actions are to be understood figuratively (*Doctr. chr.* 3.12.18). Once the basic ideas communicated in the plainer passages are known, moreover, it is possible to use them as the means for interpreting and understanding figurative portions of Scripture (*Doctr. chr.* 2.9.14).

Augustine's recognition that the figurative language of Scripture presents a difficulty to the interpreter should not be understood as hostility toward figurative language. Interestingly, while Augustine originally finds Scripture's figurative language distasteful, in *De doctrina christiana* he offers a positive perspective on the originality and ambiguity inherent in this figurative language. Augustine admits that he personally finds pleasure in a well-turned metaphor, such as the depiction of the church as a beautiful woman or the holy members of the church as shorn sheep. He suggests that the pleasure found in interpreting these figures encourages the reader to stay engaged in the text (*Doctr. chr.* 2.6.7). Above all, the figurative nature of Scripture encourages the reader actively to search out the meaning of the text and to search out the divine source of the text.[30] Thus, figurative language actually serves an important function in Scripture.

Furthermore, in his discussion of translating Scripture, Augustine suggests that figurative translations of Scripture, those which maintain the figurative language of the original, allow for a range of interpretations. To use a modern expression, figurative language "open ups" the meaning of a text. This can be a positive thing, according to Augustine. For example, he compares the translation of "And do not despise the domestics of thy seed" to the translation "Do not deny the domestics of thy flesh"(*Doctr chr.* 2.12.17). Since the word "seed" is more figurative than "flesh," it allows for a range of possible interpretations. For instance, the use of the word "seed" can be understood as a reference to the Word or Christ. This interpretation allows

[30] Ibid., 81–82.

the verse to describe those "born of the . . . seed," or Christians, as well as the actual descendants of Abraham.

As noted above, Augustine understands that humanity's fallen nature makes it difficult for interpreters to understand Scripture. It is part of humanity's carnal nature to mistake figurative language, which often describes spiritual realities or things, for literal language, as if it described things that are fleshly or physical (*Doctr. chr.* 3.5.9). In the final chapter of *De civitate Dei*, Augustine argues that this mistake is often made by those interpreting the Book of Revelation, which is replete with figurative language. Labeling these interpreters as "chiliasts" or "millenarians," since they interpret Revelation's description of the saints' thousand-year reign literally (Rev 20:1–6), he implies that they are not "spiritual" or "spiritually minded" (*Civ.* 20.7).

In *De doctrina christiana* Augustine offers a view of language, and specifically figurative language, that is shared by many medieval interpreters. In this work Augustine describes language in terms of signs that point to things other than themselves. These signs are conventional or culturally determined. Figurative language, according to Augustine, involves an intentional misuse of language. Defying conventional usage, figurative language uses one sign to point to something other than its proper meaning. Even though figurative language can be pleasing to hear or read, when interpreting Scripture it can be problematic. As figurative language involves a deviation from conventional meaning, it is possible for figurative language to convey multiple meanings. While this can be a positive factor, allowing for layers of meaning in Scripture, it also raises the issue of determining the "correct" interpretations of figurative language. Since fallen humans are naturally inclined to interpret Scripture "carnally," or according to the flesh, it is necessary to have guidelines for interpreting figurative language. Thus, Augustine advocates applying hermeneutical principles culled from Scripture, including the love of God and love of neighbor, to Scripture's figurative language.

Interestingly, one aspect of the conversation about figurative language that Augustine does not include is the association between metaphor and sight. Unlike Aristotle and some of the Roman rhetoricians, who associate the persuasive nature of metaphor with its ability to make ideas "visible" to an audience, in *De doctrina christiana* Augustine does not highlight this aspect of metaphor.

Metaphorical Language and the Fourfold Interpretation of Scripture

Complicating the discussion of ancient and medieval interpretation of Scripture, especially the figurative language of Scripture, is the multileveled rubric—the "threefold" or "fourfold" sense of Scripture—that undergirds, both explicitly and implicitly, much of medieval biblical exegesis. Although interpretive practices differ, the levels of interpretation can be distinguished as the literal or historical, allegorical or spiritual, tropological or moral, and anagogical senses of Scripture. Given that the nomenclature of these categories overlaps with descriptions of different types of language, one must at least raise the question of how this fourfold interpretive approach relates to ancient and medieval discussions about language. Specifically, one must ask how ancient and medieval interpreters understood a text's figurative language in relation to these interpretive categories.

Some ancient and medieval interpreters complicate the issue by implying that the four senses of Scripture include both different methods of Scriptural interpretation and different types of discourse found within Scripture. For example, in *Literal Interpretation of Genesis,* Augustine explains as follows:

> Four ways of expounding the Law are handed down by certain men who treat the Scriptures. Their names can be set forth in Greek, while they are defined and explained in Latin: in accord with history, allegory, analogy, and etiology. It is a matter of history when deeds done—whether by men or by God—are reported. It is a matter of allegory when things spoken in figures are understood. It is a matter of analogy, when the conformity of the Old and New Testaments is shown. It is a matter of etiology when the causes of what is said or done are reported.[31]

Augustine's description of history and etiology suggest that these are types of material that Scripture reports or contains, rather than specific approaches to interpreting Scripture. The same is true for Augustine's description of allegory, which refers to the text's use of figurative language (*figurate dicta*). In contrast, the description of analogy may imply that an interpreter "shows" conformities between the two testaments, although it is possible that NT texts make explicit connections.[32] The imprecision in Augustine's discussion reflects the fact that the distinction between interpretive methods and the type of material within Scripture cannot be clearly demarcated.

---

[31] Augustine, *Literal Interpretation of Genesis,* in *Saint Augustine: On Genesis*, trans. Roland J. Teske (The Fathers of the Church 84; Washington, D.C.: Catholic University of America Press, 1991).

[32] In the introduction to his translation of Augustine's works on Genesis, Roland J. Teske notes that Augustine's language about interpreting Scripture "seems lacking in fixity and precision with different sets of terms that overlap and are remarkably resistant to a systematic presentation." Further, he notes that Augustine's views on interpretation may change over time, further demonstrating the fluidity of these interpretive categories for Augustine.

Henri de Lubac presents the ancient and medieval interpretive method in his two-volume work *Exégèse médiévale*, originally published in 1959.[33] De Lubac systematically addresses the ways in which Christian interpreters in the first twelve centuries of the church understood and practiced the interpretation of the Scriptures. Tracing the history and development of the so-called four senses of Scripture, de Lubac demonstrates the variety and flexibility inherent within ancient and medieval interpretive practices. Not all interpreters, actually few interpreters, systematically employed the four interpretive approaches in Scripture. In fact, the interpretive categories themselves were quite fluid. De Lubac offers a telling quotation from Gregory of Nyssa's commentary on the Song of Songs: "This anagogical contemplation [of Scripture], or this tropology, or this allegory, or whatever other name one wants to call it: we shall not dispute how to speak of it, provided that we can usefully think of it."[34] Clearly, Gregory's understanding of the senses of Scripture, as expressed in this quotation, is fluid and attentive to a passage's function.

De Lubac argues that while ancient and medieval interpreters often delineate a three- or fourfold interpretive paradigm, this paradigm reflects a more fundamental division between the literal/historical sense and the figurative/spiritual sense of Scripture. The quotation from Gregory of Nyssa continues:

> In all these names that designate the spiritual understanding, Scripture fundamentally teaches us just one thing: that it is not absolutely necessary to stop at the letter, . . . but to pass on to immaterial contemplation . . . , in accordance with the dictum: "the letter killeth, but the spirit giveth life."[35]

Drawing on the Pauline distinction between the "letter" and the "spirit," ancient and medieval interpreters tend to approach Scripture as capable of literal interpretation, reading the text from the perspective of the historical author, as well as figurative interpretation. This latter method of interpretation allows the interpreter to "move beyond" the letter of the text. Allegorical, anagogical, and tropological approaches are different versions of the broader category of spiritual or figurative interpretation.

Furthermore, de Lubac notes that figurative interpretation, which describes a variety of different approaches, reflects the understanding of figurative language articulated in the ancient and medieval grammarians.[36]

---

[33] See the recent English translation of Henri de Lubac, *Medieval Exegesis*, trans. E. M. Macierowski; 2 vols. (Grand Rapids, Mich.: William B. Eerdmans, 2000).

[34] Quoted in de Lubac, *Medieval Exegesis*, 2.35.

[35] Quoted in ibid., 2.35.

[36] Ibid., 2.89–90.

This influence is evident in the names given to some of the different categories of figurative or spiritual interpretation: *tropo*logical referring to tropes and *allegor*ical referring to allegory.[37] This is also supported by Venerable Bede, who discusses the different senses of Scripture in the context of his work on figurative language, which we examine below. The idea that words, as signs, can point to things indirectly as well as directly provides a foundation for developing different levels of interpretation. Thus, the traditional understanding of figurative language fosters a great deal of interpretive freedom in medieval biblical interpretation. Naturally, medieval interpreters debated how extensively figurative interpretation should be employed, some suggesting that figurative interpretations are only secondary to literal interpretations.[38]

Rules for Reading: *Figurae* in the Middle Ages

On the one hand, the ancient understanding of figurative language gave rise to the creative and multifaceted interpretation of Scripture; on the other hand, there was a simultaneous impulse toward providing and following guidelines for interpreting figurative language. The latter impulse answered Augustine's concern that interpreters of Scripture familiarize themselves with the tropes in order to understand ambiguities in the Scriptures (Augustine, *Doctr. chr.* 3.29.40). Knowledge of how particular figures are constructed and function provides at least some control on the polysemous nature of figurative language. In this vein, the study and classification of *figurae* flourished in the Middle Ages. Two medieval scholars, one writing in Spain, Isidore of Seville (ca. 560–636), and one writing approximately a century later in England, the Venerable Bede (ca. 673–735), demonstrate the uniformity of this tradition.

The study of grammar involved learning not only guidelines for speaking and writing correctly but also guidelines for the art of interpreting both *scriptura* and the Christian and classical *auctores*. During this period of time, the study of grammar functioned as one of the basic academic disciplines, and it shaped the ways in which individuals within the culture read the foundational texts and, therefore, the ways in which they thought about their world.[39]

One of the predominant ways in which discussions about figures was carried into the Middle Ages is through the encyclopedic works that gath-

---

[37] Ibid., 2.129–30.

[38] Denys Turner, *Eros and Allegory: Medieval Exegesis of the Song of Songs* (Cistercian Studies 156; Kalamazoo, Mich.: Cistercian Publications, 1995), 99.

[39] Irvine persuasively argues that the study of grammar during the medieval period produced a unique textual culture that had far-reaching effects, including social and political effects (*The Making of Textural Culture*, 1–39).

ered together extant information on the various topics of studies. Isidore's *Etymologies*, which devotes twenty books to an elaboration of the seven liberal arts and a summary of world history, proved one of the most popular of these works. Isidore begins this immense work with a book on grammar—the "origin and foundation" of all other subjects of study (*Ety.* 1.5). This book, even apart from the work as a whole, was quite popular in the Middle Ages. As Martin Irvine notes, the influence of *Etymologies* "was enormous: this book, or a set of excerpts from it, was often transmitted independently in the grammatical miscellanies and compilations produced in the early Middle Ages, and its influence endured until the Renaissance."[40]

Isidore's treatment of figurative language comprises a large portion of the book on grammar. In two lengthy chapters, Isidore outlines over twenty figures of speech (*schemata*) and over twenty different tropes (*tropis*) and their subspecies (*Ety.* 1.36–37); Isidore's treatment of figurative language is quite formal or structured. First, Isidore offers a traditional distinction between figures and tropes. Figures, meaning figures of speech, involve using words and sentences in order to embellish (*orno*) a speech or text (*Ety* 1.36.1). Tropes employ a sign (*significatio*) to denote something similar, but in a way that is not proper or traditional (*Ety.* 1.37.1). Second, beginning with figures and then covering tropes, Isidore outlines the various forms following a set pattern: noting the traditional Greek term of a particular figure or trope, offering a Latin translation of the term, offering a terse definition, and then, perhaps, citing an example of the figure or trope. Thus, Isidore's discussion of figurative language generally conveys a sense of classification, much like *Ad Herennium*.[41]

When Isidore discusses metaphor (*translatio*), he breaks the general pattern of his discussion, offering a slightly longer treatment of this particular trope. He explains that metaphor involves the transferring of the meaning of one word to another and outlines different ways in which this transferring of terms occurs: from inanimate to inanimate object, animate to animate object, from inanimate to animate, and from animate to inanimate (*Ety.* 1.37.2–4).[42] He also suggests that metaphor includes the trans-

[40] Ibid., 212. The influence of Isidore's discussion of grammar is seen, for example, in Hugh of St. Victor's suggestion that *Etymologies* be consulted on grammar, along with the works of Donatus, Priscian, and others. He offers this suggestion in *Didascalicon*, written in the late 1120s, which provides an introduction and outline to the subjects studied at the school founded as part of the Abbey of St. Victor (Hugh of St. Victor, *The Didascalicon of Hugh of St. Victor: A Medieval Guide to the Arts*, trans. Jerome Taylor [New York: Columbia University Press, 1961], 2:29).

[41] Irvine argues that Isidore's discussion of figures and tropes reflects a lost, specifically Christian, version of Donatus's grammatical text. This version appears to be partially preserved in other texts (*The Making of Textual Culture*, 226–27).

[42] These categories of different types of metaphor are also outlined by Quintilian, *Inst.* 8.6.9ff.

ferring of a name from one genus to another genus or even from a part to the whole (*Ety.* 1.37.5). This trope is used for the sake of making a speech more elegant (*decoris*). Isidore continues the tradition that defines metaphor as a transferring of names done primarily for decorative effect.

Isidore also describes tropes that involve comparison (*similitudo*) of different terms or things, including parable and simile (*imago*) (*Ety.* 1.37.32–35). As we saw in the discussion of *Ad Herennium*, some interpreters acknowledged a connection between these figures and metaphorical language. The discussion in *Etymologies*, however, is quite brief and does not seem to reflect such a connection.

Another important and influential discussion of figurative language written in the Middle Ages was *De schematibus et tropis* by Venerable Bede. Written at the turn of the eighth century, this short work was written as an instructional text for use in monastic schools.[43] While originally written for an Anglo-Saxon context, this work, as well as other didactic works of Bede, became influential in monastic education through Europe during the time of the Carolingian reform.[44] The influence of this particular work also stemmed from the fact that it was seemingly one of the first texts on *figurae* that uses examples solely from Scripture and Christian authors. This characteristic reflected Bede's assertion that Scripture "surpasses all other writings," not only in terms of antiquity but also in terms of artistic expression. While the Greeks claim to have invented figures and tropes, these stylistic elements were present in Scripture all along. In this way Bede recognizes and extols the figurative language of Scripture.

Bede's use of biblical examples suggests that *De schematibus et tropis* is intended to function as an exegetical guide.[45] He even begins by distinguishing the figurative language of Scripture from the language of "ordinary speech" (*De schematibus* 1.5–20). In order to understand the figurative language of Scripture one must be familiar with the different schemes and figures. In this way, Bede's work provided the guidelines for right understanding.

Although a notable and creative scholar, Bede's discussion of figurative language bore a striking resemblance to those of his predecessors, including Isidore. Not only did Bede follow the pattern of first translating the Greek term into Latin and then offering a definition and example, but he shared Isidore's assumption that figurative language primarily serves a decorative function. Scholars use the language of "form" and "figures" to

---

[43] Ch. W. Jones, "Preface," in *Bedae Venerabilis Opera: Opera Didascalica I* (Corpus Christianorum: Series latina; Turnhout: Brepols, 1975), vii.

[44] Jones, "Preface," vii–viii.

[45] Irvine argues that *De Schematibus et Tropis* is often misclassified as a rhetorical work, when it clearly functions as a guide for the interpretation of Scripture and not as a guide for constructing an original work (*The Making of Textual Culture*, 292).

describe figurative language, "because through it speech is in some way clothed or adorned" (*De schematibus* 1.1). Likewise, Bede's discussion of tropes, including metaphor, echoes that of Isidore and his predecessors. Bede suggests that tropes function either "out of need," to fill a lexical lacuna, or to embellish a speech by transferring a word from its proper meaning to another similar, but not proper, meaning. Metaphor, one of the tropes, occurs when a word or its qualities are transferred to another word.[46] He then notes that this can take a number of forms: inanimate object to inanimate object, inanimate object to animate, and so on.

The medieval tradition of classifying different types of figurative language, as exemplified in the works of Isidore and Bede, can be interpreted in a number of different ways. In one sense, it can be interpreted as parasitic on the classical works of Cicero, Quintilian, and *Ad Herennium*. As such, the medieval scholars appropriated and perpetuated the most pedantic aspects of the classical treatments of figurative language. It is also possible to read the medieval scholars more sympathetically. The simple facts that medieval scholars chose to include discussions of tropes and figures within their works, often devoting a great deal of time to the subject, and that these discussions were widely circulated throughout the Middle Ages point to a general concern for understanding the figurative language in Scripture. Most of all, keeping in mind that the study of grammar serves as an initial step in the process of learning how to interpret Scripture, the rules for reading figures and tropes were only one part of the larger interpretive method employed during the Middle Ages. Understood within a context of the fourfold interpretation of Scripture, which was based on the understanding of figurative language, the seemingly formulaic classification of tropes provides at least one way of preventing innumerable possible interpretations of Scripture.

Another trend in the Middle Ages related to how figurative language was understood is the advent of manuals instructing individuals on writing official letters. As letter writing became an important means of communication within religious and political circles, these texts grew in popularity. In one such text, *Flores rhetorici* (ca. 1087), the Benedictine teacher Alberic of Monte Cassino instructed and warned his audience about the influential nature of metaphorical language.[47]

Metaphor, Alberic suggested, is one of the means by which a writer can embellish or dignify his/her composition. Like the ancient rhetoricians, however, Alberic also claimed that metaphorical language brings an idea to the eyes of the audience. This visual aspect of metaphor contributes to

[46] Bede, *De Schematibus* 2.1.

[47] Alberic of Monte Cassino, *Flores Rhetorici*, in *Readings in Medieval Rhetoric*, ed. Joseph M. Miller et al.; trans. Joseph M. Miller (Bloomington: Indiana University Press, 1973), 131–61.

its persuasive nature. Alberic depicted this persuasive aspect of metaphor in negative terms:

> The metaphor is a trope which frequently appears in writing, and which contributes a certain apparent dignity. For the method of speaking in metaphors has this characteristic: it turns one's attention from the particular qualities of the object [being described]; somehow, by this distraction of attention, it makes the object seem something different; by making it seem different, it clothes it, so to speak, in a fresh new wedding garment; by so clothing it, it sells us on the idea that there is some new nobility bestowed. And what else can I call it but "selling us," when a man takes a story that is petty in its content and heightens it by his treatment so as to convince us that it is all new, all delightful. If a meal were served up in this way, it would disgust us, would nauseate us, would be thrown out.[48]

Using metaphorical language himself, Alberic describes the way in which a metaphor can persuade or even deceive an audience to see something in a new or different manner. The power of metaphorical language makes it potentially dangerous.

For the most part, the medieval scholars who discuss the nature and use of figurative language continued the trend that began in the Latin rhetorical tradition of delineating and classifying different types of tropes. This tradition was based on the assumption that figurative language, including metaphor, involves using a word improperly for the sake of embellishment or ornamentation. Medieval scholars devoted a significant amount of time to delineating and describing the different ways this ornamentation could be accomplished. Within these discussions, metaphor functioned as one of these many different methods. The effect of this was that metaphor, like other figures of speech, was understood primarily as a phenomenon on the surface of the text with little or no relation to the actual meaning of the text. With this view of metaphor, which became the dominant view in the Western literary tradition, it is understandable why subsequent scholars, including biblical scholars, devoted so little time to exploring the ways that metaphor contributes to a text's meaning. It is important to note, however, especially in light of the comments of Alberic, that, even in the medieval context, theory and practice were not always in agreement.

Turning to Modern Theories of Metaphor

In *Death Is the Mother of Beauty: Mind, Metaphor, Criticism*, Mark Turner observes that classical scholars, including Aristotle and Cicero, assumed a relationship between language and thought. Addressing the topic of

[48] Alberic, *Flores,* 146–47.

metaphor within the context of both poetics and rhetoric, classical scholars sought to describe the ways a speaker uses and arranges words to move his or her audience from one way of thinking to another. Metaphor or figurative language in general was assumed to be an effective means of persuading an audience by means of bringing an idea into the audience's sight.[49] It seems, furthermore, that this concern for the relationship between language and cognition was fostered by the fact that the classical scholars were not only rhetorical theorists but also philosophers interested in broad questions about the human capability for thinking and learning.

The classical assumption that figurative language possessed the capability to influence thought has not always been shared by scholars, especially philosophers. In particular, the Western philosophical tradition has historically regarded metaphorical language with disdain. While the roots of this tendency appeared already in late-medieval thought,[50] it flourished within the context of seventeenth-century rationalism and British empiricism.[51]

The philosophical disdain for metaphorical language reflected a broader shift in how scholars understand language to function. Writing on medieval concepts of "denotation," Eco explains that in the writings of Roger Bacon we can see a definite change in the understanding of how words signify or how they communicate meaning. This view eventually became the dominant way scholars described the function of words. While prior to Bacon most scholars maintained the Aristotelian view that words signify both the mental experiences of things and the names of things, as discussed above, Eco writes,

---

[49] Turner, *Death Is the Mother of Beauty*, 3. Another scholar who characterizes conceptual metaphor theory as generally marking a return to classical theories of metaphor is Lynne Cameron in "Operationalising 'Metaphor' for Applied Linguistic Research," in *Researching and Applying Metaphor*, ed. Cameron and Low, 3–28.

[50] One of the most noted and influential scholars of the Middle Ages, Thomas Aquinas, exhibits and perpetuates disapproval of figurative language. Aquinas's dislike of figurative interpretation of the biblical texts is well known. Even though he recognizes that the use of symbolic language in Scripture, in contrast to poetry, is effective and necessary, he emphasizes the importance of the literal reading of Scripture. Beryl Smalley explains that Aquinas's understanding of the literal/historical sense of Scripture includes the intended meaning behind figurative language. That is, the meaning of figurative language is the literal meaning to which it points (*The Study of the Bible in the Middle Ages*, 3rd ed. [Oxford: Basil Blackwell, 1984], 300–302).

[51] Cameron argues that this is actually a twentieth-century phenomenon, as a more cognitive understanding of metaphor is expressed in some seventeenth- and eighteenth-century works. The purpose of the current discussion is not to offer a study on the historical development of theories of metaphor for its own sake. Rather, by sketching out the history in broad strokes we can see the importance of appropriating conceptual theories of metaphor in our interpretation of Revelation. See Cameron, "Operationalising 'Metaphor,'" 9.

> For Roger Bacon signs are not referred to their referent through the mediation of a mental species, but point directly or are posited in order to refer immediately to an object. It does not matter whether this object is an individual (a concrete thing) or a species, a feeling, a passion of the soul. What counts is that between a sign and the object it has been appointed to name, *there is no mental mediation*.[52]

It is assumed that words can and do refer directly to the things they signify, apart from any impression the thing makes on the soul.

Ted Cohen cites works of Thomas Hobbes and John Locke as representative of the tendency to hold figurative language in contempt.[53] Reflecting the view that words signify things, Hobbes, writing in *Leviathan*, describes metaphor as using words "in other senses than that they are ordained for."[54] Figurative language involves deviating from normal word usage, by replacing one word with another. Since words refer directly to things, carrying little or no cognitive content (the impressions things make on the soul), there is no sense that metaphor involves transferring a complex of meanings or impressions from one context to another. Instead, metaphor is simply an indirect and unnecessary way of communicating; instead of referring to one thing, an author refers to another thing. As such, metaphor bears no meaning, apart from the literal sense that lies behind a particular metaphor.

In addition, both Hobbes and Locke asserted that literal language is "more true" than figurative language, as the latter involves replacing words with words that mean other things. By definition, figurative language is deceptive and, therefore, less capable of communicating truth or facts. In and of themselves, metaphors are not verifiable; only the literal claims behind them are verifiable. A claim that is not capable of being empirically verified cannot, within the rationalistic and empirical system of thought, be true. As such, metaphor, in contrast to literal language, is purely ornamental, intended to please an audience.

It is mistaken to assume that this philosophical prejudice against figurative language is limited to these seventeenth-century scholars; rather, the trend continues even into the twentieth century. Cohen explains,

> Although these remarks of Hobbes and Locke may seem remote, their import has prevailed until quite recently. The works of many twentieth-century positivist philosophers and others either state or imply that metaphors are frivolous and inessential, if not dangerous and logically perverse, by denying to

[52] Eco, "Denotation," 59.

[53] Ted Cohen, "Metaphor and the Cultivation of Intimacy," in *On Metaphor*, ed. Sheldon Sacks (Chicago: University of Chicago Press, 1978), 1.

[54] Hobbes, *Leviathan* 1.4, as quoted in Cohen, "Metaphor and the Cultivation of Intimacy," 2.

> them (1) any capacity to contain or transmit knowledge; (2) any direct connection with facts; or (3) any genuine meaning.[55]

In light of these assumptions about metaphorical language, Western philosophers have tended to avoid the exploration of the nature of metaphor, relegating the topic to literary criticism. While literary critics study metaphor, especially particular metaphorical constructions, until recently there has been very little attention given to the relationship between the metaphors as linguistic constructions, including those in literature and in everyday speech, and the mechanics of cognition. Likewise, Max Black, who, as we will see, exercises considerable influence on the discussion of metaphor, notes the ironic fact that while twentieth-century philosophers are fascinated with language and meaning, they generally avoid the topic of metaphor.[56] Turner attributes this, in part, to the academic tendency toward specialization and the resulting separation between academic disciplines. It has been only within the past twenty-five years that the disciplines of literary criticism, linguistics, psychology, philosophy, and anthropology have been drawn together to explore the nature and function of metaphor and metaphorical language.[57]

Max Black: Returning to Metaphor and Thought

In his groundbreaking essay simply entitled "Metaphor" (1954), Black reintroduced the topic of metaphor into philosophical discussion.[58] In this essay, as well as in subsequent works, especially in *Models and Metaphors: Studies in Language and Philosophy*, Black explored the relationship between metaphorical language and cognition, exploring the ways in which metaphorical expressions create new meanings.[59]

Black begins by describing the problems inherent within traditional understandings of metaphor, which he describes as the "substitution theory" and the "comparison theory." The substitution view assumes that metaphor involves replacing one word with another word. Black explains,

> According to a substitution view, the focus of a metaphor, the word or expression having a distinctively metaphorical use within a literal frame, is used to communicate a meaning that might have been expressed literally. The author substitutes M for L; it is the reader's task to invert the substitution, by using

[55] Cohen, "Metaphor and the Cultivation of Intimacy," 3.

[56] Max Black, "Metaphor," in *Proceedings of the Aristotelian Society,* vol. 55 (London: Harrison and Sons, 1955), 273–94.

[57] Turner, *Death Is the Mother of Beauty*, 8–11.

[58] For reference to the influence of this essay on the scholarly discussion about metaphor, see Cohen, "Metaphor and the Cultivation of Intimacy," 3.

[59] Max Black, *Models and Metaphors* (Ithaca, N.Y.: Cornell University Press, 1962).

> the literal meaning of M as a clue to the intended literal meaning of L. Understanding a metaphor is like deciphering a code or unraveling a riddle.[60]

It is assumed that the metaphorical term stands in place of the literal term, and the intended meaning of the statement resides within the literal term. Metaphor functions, according to this view, as a stylistic device. In order to give pleasure to the reader, an author or speaker creatively replaces proper terms with words used in novel and interesting ways.

It is easy to see why the substitution view of metaphor is often attributed to the classical theorists, including Aristotle and Cicero, as Black himself does off-handedly.[61] The classical theorists, especially as they are represented and interpreted within medieval grammars, described metaphor in terms of replacing one word with another and in terms of ornamentation. Unlike the substitution view characterized by Black, however, the classical theorists discussed metaphor within the context of rhetorical theory, which assumes the persuasive power of metaphorical language. Also, even within the medieval tradition there was the assumption that metaphorical language produces multiple meanings, making rules for interpreting metaphors necessary. This assumption is not necessarily shared by the substitution view, which treats metaphor almost like a code that has a singular, literal meaning.[62]

Another view of metaphor that Black addresses is the comparison view. Like the substitution view, this understanding of metaphorical language is also attributed to Aristotle by many modern interpreters. (The fact that different theories of metaphor can be attributed to Aristotle suggests to some extent the complexity of Aristotle's presentation.) As the name suggests, this view assumes that metaphor involves a replacement of terms based on

---

[60] Black, "Metaphor," 280.

[61] Ibid., 281 n. 11.

[62] For an example of the substitution view of metaphor, see John R. Searle, "Metaphor," 83–111. John Searle provides an example of the substitution approach to metaphor, placing it within the context of speech-act theory. In so doing, Searle maintains that metaphor entails a locution (a speech-act) in which the speaker says one thing but means another. As such, metaphor can be described as occurring when an individual says "S is P" but means "S is R." In this way, metaphor is fundamentally a substitution of terms—one predicate is substituted for another.

The metaphorical act of substitution involves a departure from conventional word usage in such a way that the truth conditions of the statement do not correspond to the literal meaning of the statement. This is to say, the metaphorical utterance is an obvious falsehood or semantically nonsensical. Therefore, the utterance is meaningless within the context of the speech act, unless it refers to another set of truth conditions. For example, on one level the utterance "Sally is a block of ice," to use one of Searle's examples, is semantically meaningless. Sally, as a human female, can not possess the qualities of ice—frozen water molecules. This semantically defective utterance suggests to the audience, according to Searle, that the speaker must be referring to a separate set of truth conditions, in which the claim "Sally is a block of ice" is somehow meaningful.

some similarity between the two terms. For example, in the metaphorical statement "Ruth is a lion," there is the assumption that "Ruth" shares some characteristic with a "lion." In this view, metaphor is simply a shortened form of simile; instead of saying "Ruth is *like* a lion," the phrase is abbreviated to "Ruth *is* a lion."

Black's main objection to the comparison view is that it operates with the assumption that words have proper or single meanings. Words can be used in their proper or, in the case of metaphor, improper sense. The description of metaphor as a purposely misapplied word overlooks the fact that the meanings of words are shaped by their context within a sentence or within a larger unit of discourse.[63] In reference to the comparison view, Black comments, with characteristic wit,

> The main objection against a comparison view is that it suffers from a vagueness that borders upon vacuity. We are supposed to be puzzled as to how some expression (M), used metaphorically, can function in place of some literal expression (L) that is held to be an approximate synonym; and the answer offered is that what M stands for (in its literal use) is *similar* to what L stands for. But how informative is this? There is some temptation to think of similarities as "objectively given," so that a question of the form, "Is A like B in respect of P?" has a definite and predetermined answer. If this were so, similes might be governed by rules as strict as those controlling the statements of physics.[64]

Like the substitution view, the comparison view assumes that words refer to single referents. In the comparison view, this assumption allows one to substitute words based on some similarity inherent within their referents. In contrast to this, Black suggests that it might be more helpful to describe metaphors as "creating" similarities between referents.[65]

In contrast to these traditional theories of metaphor, Black describes what he calls the interactionist view of metaphor. Metaphor involves the interaction between two distinct subjects—an interaction created by their placement within a phrase, sentence, or statement. More specifically, metaphor involves placing a particular subject, the "focus," into a new context, the "frame."[66] The frame, which consists of the words or phrases surrounding the focus, brings the focus into relationship with another subject that is either stated or implied. This subject is the primary subject—what the metaphor is primarily *about*. The interaction between the focus and the frame, including the primary subject, creates new meaning for the reader.

---

[63] A similar point is made in Ricoeur, *The Rule of Metaphor*, 18.

[64] Black, "Metaphor," 284

[65] Ibid., 285. This, in my estimation, echoes Aristotle's claim that metaphor requires one to be able to see similarities between different things. See above.

[66] Black, *Models*, 39–40. Black's terminology in *Models and Metaphors* is somewhat vague at points, as it changes midway through the discussion of the interactionist view of metaphor. While he begins using the terms "focus" and "frame" to describe metaphor, he shifts to the language of "primary" and "secondary" subjects.

In moving away from understanding metaphor primarily as a phenomenon involving the substitution of words, Black also argues that a metaphor's subjects, the focus and the primary subject, are actually more like "*system[s] of associated commonplaces.*"[67] The focus and the primary subject, even if they consist of single words, each evoke networks of meanings and associations, including cultural assumptions and fictions. The frame, however, acts as a sort of filter through which particular elements of this network are highlighted and subsequently applied to the principal subject implied in the frame. The sentence that embraces the metaphor highlights and hides different parts of the networks implied in the focus and the primary subject. Using the somewhat simplistic example "Man is a wolf," Black recounts how the system of commonplaces associated with "wolf," the focal word, are filtered through the frame, the sentence as a whole, and applied to the primary subject, "man." He writes,

> A suitable hearer will be led by the wolf-system of implications to construct a corresponding system of implications about the principal subject. But these implications will *not* be those comprised in the commonplaces *normally* implied by literal uses of "man." The new implications must be determined by the pattern of implications associated with literal uses of the word "wolf." Any human traits that can without undue strain be talked about in "wolf-language" will be rendered prominent, and any that cannot will be pushed into the background. The wolf-metaphor suppresses some details, emphasizes others—in short, *organizes* our view of man.[68]

Black's work contributed greatly to the modern fascination with metaphor. By reintroducing the topic of metaphor to philosophical conversation, Black opened up the way for scholars to begin to explore the relationship between metaphor and thought. He made space for the question of how metaphorical language can create meaning. In addition, Black pushed subsequent scholars to move away from regarding metaphor simply as involving a substitution of words; instead, he calls for a more complex understanding of metaphor within the context of a sentence and in relation to the complex networks of meanings conjured up by individual words.

Paul Ricoeur: Metaphor in Terms of Tension

Philosopher Paul Ricoeur built on Black's interactionist theory of metaphor in his works on hermeneutics and the philosophy of language. Like Black, Ricoeur argued that metaphor is a phenomenon of the sentence, rather

---

[67] Ibid., 40.

[68] Ibid., 41.

than a phenomenon occurring at the level of the word.[69] As a sentence, metaphor entails the act of predication in which a speaker attributes the characteristics of one subject to another subject. This act of predication is not simply the substitution of one word and its associations for another; rather, metaphor creates an event of semantic innovation.

In conversation with the work of Black, Ricoeur contends that metaphor does not entail a tension between the two subjects in a sentence as much as it entails tension between two interpretations generated by the sentence. Since metaphor involves the equation of two dissimilar subjects, the interpreter must choose between either preserving the literal and nonsensical meaning of the sentence or accepting the new meaning assigned to the primary subject.[70] This is described in terms of resolving the semantic clash between the "is," the metaphorical act of predication, and the "is not," the literal absurdity of such a predication.[71] This tension creates an extension of meaning in relation to the metaphor's primary subject; for through the tension inherent within a metaphor, the audience or interpreter gains a new insight into the nature of the primary subject being described.

Drawing on the language of Gottlob Frege, Ricouer also describes metaphor in terms of a clash between the *sense* and the *reference* of a sentence. While the sense of the sentence, the surface meaning of the signs within a sentence, defies logic, the reference of the sentence, which refers to the extralinguistic, can be resolved as apt or appropriate.[72] In employing the language of "reference," Ricoeur opposes interpreters who understand the world of the text to be enclosed, not pointing to anything beyond the text. In contrast, he argues that all discourse, including metaphorical or poetic discourse, is about something that is extralinguistic, outside the text. Even though poetic discourse does not necessarily refer to things that are ostensive, things that can be pointed to with a speaker's hand, it does refer to extralinguistic reality. Poetic or literary texts "speak of possible worlds."[73] This contributes to the power of poetic language, for it has not only the ability to change the ways in which one looks at the world, but it

---

[69] This reflects a major theme in Ricoeur's work, that words mean in the context of a sentence and that, subsequently, a sentence is not reducible to the sum of its parts. This claim undergirds Ricoeur's emphasis on the discipline of semantics over and against semiotics. See Ricouer, "Word, Polysemy, Metaphor: Creativity in Language," in *A Ricoeur Reader: Reflection and Imagination*, ed. Mario J. Valdés (Toronto: University of Toronto Press, 1991), 69.

[70] Paul Ricoeur, *Interpretation Theory: Discourse and the Surplus of Meaning* (Fort Worth, Tex: Texas Christian University Press, 1976), 50.

[71] See, for example, Claudia Camp, "Metaphor in Feminist Biblical Interpretation," *Semeia* 61 (1993): 14–15.

[72] Ricoeur, *The Rule of Metaphor*, 74–75. Ricoeur argues that metaphor, as discourse, actually has a dialectical reference that refers both to something beyond the text and to the speaker of the text.

[73] Paul Ricoeur, "Metaphor and the Main Problem of Hermeneutics," in *A Ricoeur Reader*, ed. Valdés, 314.

has the power to change the ways in which one lives and acts in the world.[74] Through metaphor, the process of predicating a subject with characteristics other than its own, it is possible to imagine the world in new and different ways and, subsequently, to change the world.

As metaphor involves the resolution of the tension between a sentence's sense and reference, Ricoeur argues that metaphor does not exist in itself; rather, metaphor exists only through the act of interpretation. It is the event of resolving the tension inherent within metaphor that creates new meaning.[75] Further, within this event, the interpreter decides which connotations of a metaphor are significant within the context of a discourse as a whole. This allows for an abundance of possible meanings:

> It is the reader, in effect, who works out the connotations of the modifier that are likely to be meaningful. A significant trait of living language, in this connection, is the power always to push the frontier of non-sense further back. There are probably no words so incompatible that some poet could not build a bridge between them; the power to create new contextual meanings seems to be truly limitless. Attributions that appear to be "non-sensical" can make sense in some unexpected context. No speaker ever completely exhausts the connotative possibilities of his words.[76]

In this way, metaphor, while logically absurd, can give rise to a multiplicity of interpretations.

Once, however, a metaphor has been read and reread or heard and reheard, once it becomes familiar, the flicker of insight once conveyed in the tension between "is" and "is not" is lost. As Ricoeur explains, once metaphorical associations become part of common parlance, the metaphor is incapable of creating new meaning.[77] Some metaphors are so common, in fact, that they can be called "dead metaphors."

Metaphor as Conceptual Mapping

While Ricoeur highlights the novel aspect of metaphor, others have begun to explore the nature and function of more conventional metaphors that function as important, if often unnoticed, parts of common speech. In so doing, conceptual metaphor theorists, including George Lakoff, Mark

---

[74] Ricoeur, "Word, Polysemy, Metaphor," 85. Ricoeur draws heavily from Aristotle's description of *mimesis* in his explanation of reference. In his essay "Mimesis and Representation," Ricoeur outlines three different aspects of *mimesis* that have a bearing on his understanding of how language relates to extralinguistic reality ("Mimesis and Representation," in *A Ricoeur Reader*, 137–55).

[75] Ricoeur, "Word, Polysemy, Metaphor," 82.

[76] Ricoeur, *The Rule of Metaphor*, 95.

[77] Ricoeur, "Word, Polysemy, Metaphor," 83.

Johnson, and Mark Turner, underscore the connection between thought and metaphorical language, asserting that conventional metaphors reveal the inherently metaphoric nature of human cognition.[78] While conceptual metaphor theory is a relatively recent field of study, its roots are in the classical tradition of Aristotle and Cicero, who assumed a vital connection between thought and language. In fact, Turner expresses a desire to reclaim this aspect of the classical rhetorical tradition.

Turner argues that conceptual metaphor theory, like its classical predecessors, begins with the assumption that "audiences share many things. . . ." In particular, audiences share "conceptual systems, social practices, commonplace knowledge, discourse genres, and every aspect of a common language, including syntax, semantics, morphology, and phonology."[79] Audiences share a wide range of factors that influence the ways in which they interpret a speech, a poem, a letter, or some other form of communication. As we saw above, the ancient theories of rhetoric explore different ways of using an audience's common cognitive system, including the impressions of things on the soul, as Aristotle suggests, to the best effect.

Part of a particular audience's cognitive apparatus, which is shaped by its culture or subculture, includes cognitive models or image schemata. In *The Body in the Mind: The Bodily Basis of Meaning, Imagination, and Reason*, Mark Johnson describes image schemata as "abstract patterns in our experience and understanding that are not propositional in any of the standard senses of that term, and yet they are central to meaning and to the inferences we make."[80] Image schemata are dynamic patterns that develop out of and that help us interpret our experiences.[81] Again Johnson explains, "some of our experiences have a certain recurring structure by virtue of which we can understand them."[82] For instance, in *Death Is the Mother of Beauty*, Turner explores a basic kinship model that is found throughout the Western literary tradition, as well as in the literary productions of many non-Western cultures.[83] The human experience of procreation, which pro-

---

[78] George Lakoff and Mark Johnson, *Metaphors We Live By* (Chicago: University of Chicago Press, 1980).

[79] Turner, *Death Is the Mother of Beauty*, 4.

[80] Mark Johnson, *The Body in the Mind: The Bodily Basis of Meaning, Imagination, and Reason* (Chicago: University of Chicago Press, 1987), 2.

[81] Johnson, *The Body in the Mind*, 102. In contrast, Mieke Bal criticizes conceptual metaphor theory for being too "realist" or too "objectivist." That is, many of the publications associated with conceptual metaphor theory tend to assume that all humans, as embodied creatures, experience life in similar ways. Mieke Bal, "Metaphors He Lives By," *Semeia* 61 (1993): 185–207.

[82] Johnson, *The Body in the Mind*, 102.

[83] Conceptual metaphor theory draws heavily on the observations of cultural anthropology. See, for example, Naomi Quinn's essay, "The Cultural Basis of Metaphor," in *Beyond Metaphor: The Theory of Tropes in Anthropology*, ed. J. Fernandez (Stanford: Stanford University Press, 1991), 56–93.

duces offspring similar to the parents, provides an image schema or basic cognitive model of kinship. There are different elements that make up this model, including the various parties usually associated with kinship (e.g., mother, father, child) and the different relationships between these parties.[84]

Image schemata, such as the kinship model, are idealized models that reflect both bodily experience and cultural assumptions. Not only do the physical human experiences of kinship—including experiences of procreation, gestation, birth, etc.—contribute to the content and shape of the model, but cultural assumptions about kinship also make up parts of the model. Consequently, even though individuals' experiences of kinship may somehow differ from the model, the model still exists as a culturally constructed model.[85]

Image schemata are often used metaphorically to understand or "structure" experiences other than those that they represent. An image schema can be "mapped on to" another experience or a concept as a way of understanding the latter. This metaphorical extension of an image schema resembles Black's suggestion that metaphor involves bringing together two different semantic domains, which include subjects and their networks of associated commonplaces. In contrast to Black, however, conceptual

---

[84] Turner, *Death Is the Mother of Beauty*, 7–8.

[85] A significant challenge to conceptual metaphor theory is offered by cultural anthropologist Naomi Quinn. Investigating the ways in which U.S. Americans describe marriage, Quinn explores the relationship between conceptual metaphors and models and cultural assumptions and predilections. Quinn argues, against conceptual metaphor theorists, that metaphorical mappings are the product of cultural models and not vice versa. While conceptual metaphor theorists seemingly suggest that cultural models of understanding are constrained by metaphorical mappings, metaphorical mappings are actually selected on the basis of preexisting models for understanding particular phenomena. For instance, common marriage metaphors, such as descriptions of marriage as a journey, are employed because they fit with preconceived ideas about marriage, that is, that marriage endures and involves difficulties. Further, Quinn argues that metaphorical mappings do not constrain reasoning about the abstract, even though they may be involved in reasoning about something abstract. If, for example, an individual's reasoning about marriage can no longer be described by a journey metaphor, the individual will often change to another metaphorical description of marriage, such as MARRIAGE IS AN OBJECT. Thus, Quinn concludes that the metaphors are secondary in the reasoning process and do not necessarily shape the ways in which individuals reason about the abstract.

Even though Quinn challenges conceptual metaphor theory, she does not call into question the existence of basic conceptual metaphors or metaphorical mappings. In the most simple terms, the debate between Quinn and conceptual metaphor theory revolves around which comes first, cultural ways of understanding abstract concepts or the metaphorical ways of conceiving abstract concepts. While this is an important question, it has little impact on the claim of this volume, that certain metaphorical mappings lay behind more specific textual metaphors (Quinn, "The Cultural Basis of Metaphor," 56–93; and Claudia Strauss and Naomi Quinn, *A Cognitive Theory of Cultural Meaning* [Cambridge: Cambridge University Press, 1997], 137ff.).

metaphor theory underscores that this merging of domains, called source and target domains, occurs primarily on the conceptual level rather than the linguistic level. Linguistic expressions of a metaphor actually reflect prior conceptual mappings of domains.[86]

A classic example of the way in which an image schema metaphorically structures another domain is the traditional metaphorical connection between the experience of walking down a path or taking a trip (source domain) and a love relationship (target domain). The image schema of walking down a path or road provides a structure for understanding and talking about the more abstract experience of a love relationship. This metaphorical mapping or "basic conceptual metaphor" can be written as LOVE IS A JOURNEY.[87] This basic conceptual metaphor can be expressed in a variety of linguistic forms, including statements such as "Our relationship has reached a dead end" or "We've come to an important turning point in our relationship"; however, the metaphor itself is the conceptual structure *behind* the linguistic expressions.

In a basic conceptual metaphor the source domain's image schema provides the structuring device or pattern that shapes the way in which one conceives of the more abstract referent of the target domain. The network of concepts and relationships inherent in the source domain (e.g., a journey) is said to be "mapped" on to the network of concepts and relationships within the target domain (e.g., a love relationship). In this way the source domain organizes the information within the target domain. A speaker or author selects various aspects of the metaphorical mapping in her expressions. For example, referring to the basic metaphor LOVE IS A JOURNEY, an author's expression of the metaphor can focus on one aspect of the metaphor, such as the destination. This does not mean that the author's audience will not bring other aspects of the basic conceptual metaphor's structure (e.g., twists in the path, junctures, the travelers on the journey, a vehicle for traveling on the journey, etc.) into their reading of the metaphorical expression. Even though an author or speaker may introduce a basic conceptual metaphor into conversation, highlighting and hiding various aspects of the metaphor's structure, an audience is not bound by the author's expression of the metaphor. Rather, the presence of a basic conceptual metaphor, the underlying structure of the expression, seemingly

[86] Conceptual metaphor theory recognizes that metaphors can be expressed in nonlinguistic ways. See, for instance, Alan Cienki, "Metaphoric Gestures and Some of Their Relations to Verbal Metaphoric Expressions," in *Discourse and Cognition: Bridging the Gap*, ed. Jean-Pierre Koenig (Stanford: CSLI, 1998), 189–204.

[87] Within the publications of conceptual metaphor theory, it is standard to describe the mappings of basic conceptual metaphors in all upper-case letters, while individual expressions of the conceptual metaphors are printed in lower-case letters. For the sake of clarity, I will adopt this method of reference throughout this study.

invites audience participation. This necessarily leads to the polyvalence of metaphorical expressions.

While an audience may recognize aspects of a basic conceptual metaphor that an author does not explicitly express (or intend), an author's use of a particular conceptual metaphor in the first place is a means of shaping an audience's thought. A basic conceptual metaphor itself necessarily highlights and hides various aspects of the concept it structures. For instance, drawing again on the above example, using the human experience of a journey to describe a love relationship will highlight various aspects of the love relationship that another basic conceptual metaphor, such as LOVE IS A GAME, will hide and vice versa. As Lakoff and Johnson explain, "the metaphorical structuring involved here is partial, not total. If it were total, one concept would actually be the other, not merely be understood in terms of it."[88] Consequently, an author's use of a particular metaphorical mapping encourages an audience to consider certain aspects of the target domain over other aspects inherent in the domain. This fact explains, at least in part, the rhetorical force of metaphor. By encouraging an audience to conceive of a reality in a specific way and not in another way, an author attempts to shape how an audience thinks about that reality and accordingly speaks and acts in light of that reality.

Understood in terms of cognition, metaphor possesses an amazing rhetorical force. Not only does an author or speaker have the ability to shape the way an audience understands a particular concept through the use of a particular conventional metaphor, but an author or speaker can also use metaphorical mappings to try to challenge conventional ways of envisioning a particular concept. An author or speaker can alter metaphorical mappings to challenge conventional ways of thinking about abstract concepts. This can subsequently change the ways in which individuals act in relation to a particular situation.[89]

---

[88] Lakoff and Johnson, *Metaphors We Live By*, 13.

[89] Donald Schön describes an interesting example of the ability of conceptual metaphors to generate new ways of thinking and acting. Looking at how urban housing has been described in U.S. social policy, Schön observes that the metaphors used to envision urban housing contribute to how problems with urban housing are handled. For instance, conceiving of urban housing as an entity with a sickness in need of healing leads to problem solving that involves an outside authority ("the doctor") analyzing ("diagnosing") the problem and offering a solution ("the cure"). In contrast, envisioning urban housing as a folk community leads to different ways of describing and solving problems associated with housing. This second metaphorical model, according to Schön, involves thinking of ways of "rebuilding" the community and of avoiding the "dislocation" of community members. Schön's analysis demonstrates the power of metaphorical mappings to shape the ways individuals and communities think and speak about *as well as* act in response to abstract concepts ("Generative Metaphor: A Perspective on Problem-Setting in Social Policy," in *Metaphor and Thought*, ed. Ortony, 137–63).

Using Conceptual Metaphor Theory as a Guiding Method

As a reaction against theories of metaphor that focus on metaphor as a linguistic phenomenon, conceptual metaphor theorists downplay the ways metaphor appears in linguistic constructions. Similarly, in an attempt to highlight the pervasive nature of metaphorical thinking, conceptual metaphor theorists (with the notable exception of Turner) focus heavily on metaphor usage in "everyday speech," instead of in literary texts. As a result, Gerard Steen observes, metaphor theory, as articulated by Lakoff, Johnson, and Turner, lacks both a systematic method for analyzing and describing the linguistic expressions of conceptual metaphors in literature and a method for identifying the conceptual metaphors that "stand behind" linguistic metaphors.[90] In response to these lacunae, Steen has begun the process of articulating a method for analyzing and describing metaphor within literary texts. Even though this work remains in its early stages,[91] it provides a guide for our analysis of Revelation.

Ideally, conceptual metaphor theory should provide a method for analyzing a text that allows us to examine the metaphorical language of the text, the "linguistic metaphors," in relation to the conceptual mappings that undergird this language, "the conceptual metaphors." This suggests that our method entails two interrelated tasks: identifying/describing the linguistic metaphors within a given text and identifying/describing the conceptual metaphors that seem to be present within the text. This can be described also in terms of analyzing the "surface" of the text and the metaphorical structures that "undergird" or "lie behind" the text. Steen, furthermore, suggests that careful textual analysis includes articulating *how* one moves from a text's linguistic metaphors to its conceptual metaphors. While the following articulation of a method for analyzing metaphor within literary texts may appear cut and dried, the complexity and fluidity of metaphorical language demands that any analysis of metaphor remain flex-

[90] Gerard Steen, *Understanding Metaphor in Literature: An Empirical Approach* (London: Longman, 1994). See also idem, "From a Linguistic to Conceptual Metaphor in Five Steps," in *Metaphor in Cognitive Linguistics: Selected Papers from the Fifth International Cognitive Linguistics Conference*, ed. Raymond Gibbs and Gerard Steen (Amsterdam: John Benjamins, 1999), 57–77; "Metaphor and Discourse: Towards a Linguistic Checklist for Metaphor Analysis," in *Research and Applying Metaphor*, ed. Lynne Cameron and Graham Low (Cambridge: Cambridge University Press, 1999), 81–104; and "A Rhetoric of Metaphor: Conceptual and Linguistic Metaphor and the Psychology of Literature," in *The Psychology and Sociology of Literature: In Honor of Elrud Ibsch*, ed. Dick Schram and Gerard Steen (Amsterdam: John Benjamins, 2001), 145–63.

[91] Only in early 2002 was a journal published that included a number of articles applying Steen's method to literary texts and articulating the complexities inherent within this method. See *Language and Literature* 11, no. 2 (2002).

ible and heuristic. In this vein, although the following presents the method in terms of linear steps, in numerous instances not all tasks are necessary and many times certain tasks may be performed at the same time or in a different order. Furthermore, it is important to note that this method is not intended to assess or theorize about the ways in which a text's metaphors reproduce meaning in the mind of its author(s) or produce meaning in the mind of its audience.[92] Rather, through employing the tools given to us through conceptual metaphor theory, we intend to examine some of the different ways metaphors are constructed in the text and the ways in which they produce and delimit meaning.

1. Identification of a Metaphorical Expression

The first step that Steen suggests when analyzing metaphor within a literary text or a unit of text entails identifying the components of the metaphorical expression.[93] This involves the interrelated tasks of identifying the focus and frame of the expression.

a. Identifying the Focus. As described in our discussion of Max Black, a metaphor's focus is that which is used to describe or refer to another thing or concept. The focus is the lexical term or phrase that an author uses to describe another concept or term. Even though identifying the focus may sound like a simple task, the matter is complicated by the fact that few metaphorical expressions, especially those in literature, take a propositional form of "a is b."[94] Instead, metaphorical expressions and their foci may be manifest through different grammatical forms. For example, a metaphor's focus may be expressed in a verb, such as "she's *moving* forward in her studies," or a metaphor's focus may be expressed through a noun, "she's on the right *path* now."

b. Identifying the Frame. Identifying the focus of a metaphorical expression involves attention to the expression's frame, which may signal the metaphorical or nonliteral nature of the focus term or terms. The "frame" describes the lexical terms and grammatical structures that surround the focus. For instance, in the above example, "she's . . . forward in her studies" could be understood as the frame, as the verb "moving" could be

---

[92] Peter Crisp, "Metaphorical Propositions: A Rationale," in *Language and Literature* 11, no. 1 (2002): 7–16; Cameron, "Operationalising 'Metaphor,'" 5–6.

[93] Steen, "From a Linguistic to Conceptual Metaphor," 60–61; and "A Rhetoric of Metaphor," 149.

[94] Cameron, "Operationalising 'Metaphor,'" 15. The assumption that metaphor appears in this form stems, in part, from the tendency of conceptual metaphor theorists to use the propositional form of denotation.

understood as the metaphor's focus, which is used to describe making progress or not. Complicating the process of identifying metaphorical expressions, however, is the fact that the distinction between focus and frame is, as Cameron explains, sometimes fuzzy. In this example, it is possible to include "forward" as part of the focus or as part of the frame. The metaphorical expression could be either "progressing is moving forward" or "progressing is moving." In many instances such as this, it is difficult to delineate the focus from the frame because they are grammatically intertwined.

The terms and constructions that comprise the frame often indicate that the focus is not to be taken literally, because doing so would be nonsensical. To draw on the language of Paul Ricoeur, within certain metaphorical expressions the interaction between the focus and the frame result in "semantic impertinence."[95]

The third chapter of Revelation provides an example of this semantic impertinence. In 3:16, John describes the risen Christ using a metaphorical expression as a threat to the people of the church in Laodicea: "I am about to spit you out of my mouth." Putting aside the issue of the personification of a deity, which is itself a metaphorical move, one might assume that the verb "to spit" functions as the focus of the metaphorical expression; for, the notion of spitting out people ("you" or the Laodiceans) is literally absurd. For example, in his comments on Rev 3:16, Aune analyzes the verb in this statement, which he translates as "to vomit." Drawing on OT parallels, he suggests that this verb functions as a "figure of speech" (a metaphor?) to describe the possibility of "utter rejection."[96] Spitting something out of one's mouth or vomiting, however, functions literally as a form of rejection, which suggests that the verb is not the metaphor's focus in this instance. It is only when one reads or applies this verb to people that the expression as a whole functions metaphorically. This suggests that the focus of the metaphorical expression in this verse is "you" and not "to spit out." Instead, "to spit out . . . of my mouth" serves as the frame of our metaphorical expression.

c. Metaphors with a Literal Relationship between the Focus and Frame. As we mentioned above, metaphor resists following logical patterns. In many metaphorical expressions the focus and frame do not create an obvious tension or a semantic impertinence. In certain metaphorical expressions the focus may actually "exhibit a literal relation to the frame."[97] Taken literally, the expression could make sense. For example, shortly after the threat to

[95] E.g., Ricoeur, *The Rule of Metaphor*, 247.

[96] David E. Aune, *Revelation*, 3 vols. (WBC; Dallas, Tex.: Word, 1997–1998), 1:258.

[97] Steen, "From a Linguistic to Conceptual Metaphor," 62.

the Laodiceans mentioned above, the risen Christ tells them, "I counsel you to buy from me gold refined by fire" (3:18). Out of context, this statement makes literal sense: Christ could be, in theory, instructing the Laodiceans to purchase actual pure gold. It is only when read in relation to the expression's context, in which the Laodiceans are chastised for their confidence in wealth (3:17) and told to acquire/put on other metaphorical items (e.g., white robes and eye salve), that the nonliteral or metaphorical nature of the expression becomes evident.

When identifying metaphorical expressions in which the frame coheres logically with the focus, one must infer that a focus refers to something other than itself. Identifying and describing these overlaps with the second task in identifying metaphorical expressions in general—metaphorical idea identification.

2. Identification of the Metaphorical Idea

Identifying the "idea" of the metaphorical expression involves naming and describing that concept or thing to which the focus refers.[98] The idea or referent of the metaphorical expression may be either explicit or implicit.

a. Explicit Referents. A referent may be designated within the metaphorical expression, as in propositional metaphors (A is B). These sorts of metaphorical expressions are explicit. As we well know, however, many literary texts avoid such pedantic metaphorical expressions. Instead, as we will see in Revelation, the referent is either mentioned outside of the metaphorical expression itself or the referent must be inferred by the audience.

b. Co-Textual Implicit Referents. A metaphor's referent may be co-textual, explicit within the text although not within the metaphor clause. The referent can be expressed in a clause adjacent to the metaphorical expression or it can be introduced much earlier within a text. In such an instance, the audience is required to "carry" the referent or target domain, mentioned elsewhere in a text or discourse, to the subject domain.

c. Contextual Implicit Referents. It is also common for a metaphor's referent to be contextual, evident only through inferences made by virtue of some knowledge apart from the text itself. Contextual metaphors require an interpreter to infer the referent by employing "one's knowledge of conventional language use and the world."[99] Although the referent is not

[98] Ibid.

[99] Steen, "Metaphor and Discourse," 91.

named, certain lexical markers (words and phrases) may signal the nature of the referent.

Quite often in Revelation, intertextual allusions, references to various texts and traditions outside of Revelation itself, signal the reader or audience to approach certain terms as metaphorical. These expressions seemingly reflect the assumption that the audience and author share a large body of cultural and religious knowledge, including the Hebrew Bible and early Christian traditions. An example of Revelation's use of contextual metaphors is found in John's description of the heavenly throne room. Witnessing worship around the throne of God, John describes seeing "a lamb standing though it had been slaughtered" (5:6). While John never explicitly states that "Christ is a lamb," various elements of the surrounding text suggest that "Christ" is the referent of the metaphorical expression. Immediately prior to his seeing the lamb, an elder announces the appearance of "the Lion of the Tribe of Judah, the root of David" (5:5). Both titles are Jewish messianic claims.[100] Placing these titles, which are themselves metaphorical, prior to John's reference to the lamb signals that the lamb in 5:6 is to be read in reference to the Messiah, which early Christians believed to be Jesus Christ. This metaphorical expression requires one to infer the referent through common cultural knowledge.

Identifying the referent, whether it is explicit or implicit, yields a metaphorical proposition "a is b."[101] The specific metaphorical proposition that results from our second step is not necessarily a conceptual metaphor.

3. Identifying Conceptual Mappings

Conceptual metaphor theorists argue that linguistic metaphorical expressions reflect prelinguistic metaphorical mappings. Individuals use image schemata, general patterns of concrete things or events, to conceive of more abstract ideas or experiences. As Aristotle suggests, we use one thing to "see" something else. We use the network of ideas and relationships of a particular image schema, the source domain, in order to understand and organize the components of another domain, the target domain. While this happens on a general level, utilizing culturally communicated image schemata or domains, the linguistic expressions of these conceptual metaphors are often more specific.

a. Identifying Conceptual Domains. Since our analysis of metaphor in Revelation requires us to begin with specific metaphorical expressions within

---

[100] Aune, *Revelation*, 1:350.

[101] Following the tradition in conceptual metaphor theory, linguistic metaphorical expressions will be written in lower case letters (a is b) and conceptual metaphors or mappings will be written in capitals (A IS B).

the text, it is necessary to explore whether or not the terms within the specific metaphorical propositions we identify in the text reflect more general domains.[102] In order to do this, we inquire as to whether or not either or both of the components of the metaphorical proposition are specific manifestations of a more general category or domain. This requires not only familiarity with the language of the text but also knowledge of the culture from which the text ensues. What are the categories or domains with which particular things are identified? In some instances the domains appear obvious. Lamps and torches clearly should be understood as specific examples of the more general domain LIGHT SOURCE. Other items and corresponding lexical terms prove more difficult to relate to or place within a general domain. For instance, do stars and the sun function as part of the LIGHT SOURCE domain or as a part of a domain named CELESTIAL BODIES? In cases such as this, it is important to remember that conceptual domains are themselves constructions, having fluid boundaries and overlapping one another.[103] Thus, in the case of stars and the sun we might conclude that giving off light functions as part of Revelation's understanding of the domain CELESTIAL BODIES.

In many cases, knowledge of the text's cultural context is necessary in order to fill out the different components and relationships within a particular domain. Returning to the image of the lamb introduced in Revelation 5, one can ask, first of all, whether LAMB/SHEEP itself qualifies as a domain or whether the conceptual mapping is better understood as ANIMAL. One might even ask whether or not in Revelation's cultural setting, which is urban Asia Minor, lamb might be better understood as part of the domain FOOD. These issues are settled by looking to the cultural context of Revelation, including not only urban Asia Minor but also Jewish textual and religious traditions, on which John draws heavily. In a full analysis of this metaphorical expression, it is likely that we would conclude that the domain ANIMAL is most appropriate, as it can contain the concept of LAMB/SHEEP and relate to the domain FOOD, since in this culture animals are typically food sources. Likewise, we would probably also conclude that ANIMAL is an appropriate domain, since it can also contain the related idea of SACRIFICIAL OBJECT, which is important within Jewish cultic traditions.

b. Reconstructing Metaphorical Mappings. As early as Aristotle, theorists have claimed that metaphor involves seeing and creating similarities

---

[102] Steen, "From a Linguistic to Conceptual Metaphor," 66. Many analyses of metaphor investigate metaphors and metaphorical expressions more from these generalized domains and then identify metaphorical expressions that draw on a particular domain rather than beginning with specific metaphorical expressions within a text and identifying the underlying conceptual mappings and domains.

[103] In fact, the use of the word "domain" is metaphorical: A CONCEPT IS A PIECE OF LAND.

between dissimilar things or ideas. In his method for analyzing metaphor, Steen suggests that it is necessary to reconstruct these conceptual mappings or analogies implicit within metaphorical expressions. This initially involves naming the mapping or conceptual metaphor, such as CHRIST IS AN ANIMAL/LAMB.

Reconstructing the metaphorical mapping also requires us to begin to ask questions about what it means to see one idea or thing in terms of another domain. What aspects of the source domain, which concepts and relationships within this domain, are mapped on to the target? As Black argues, semantic domains are "networks of associated commonplaces"; however, in metaphorical mappings, specific aspects of the source domain may be applied to the target domain. As a result, not only is it necessary to develop some idea of the complexity of different domains, but it is also important to examine how each individual mapping draws on and recasts the domains it encompasses.

When authors cast a conceptual mapping in specific lexical terms and set it within a linguistic frame, they naturally highlight certain aspects of the complex conceptual domains underlying the expression. It is not enough to simply identify the conceptual mappings behind the text. The tendency to stop with identifying conceptual metaphors is one of the major criticisms of conceptual metaphor theory. Thus, for a complete analysis it is necessary to return to the linguistic expression to observe how within this particular expression the metaphorical mapping is being employed.

Returning to the lamb in Revelation 5, by using the lexical term "lamb" as the focus of the metaphorical expression, John highlights particular aspects of the ANIMAL domain: Christ is an animal having characteristics typically associated with lambs. In addition, by placing this focus in a lexical frame that refers to the lamb being slaughtered, John emphasizes a certain aspect of the domain ANIMAL, namely, the possibility that an animal functions as a sacrifice. This is not to suggest that other aspects of the domain ANIMAL and, more specifically, the concept of LAMB do not come into play when John introduces the metaphor; rather, other aspects of the domain naturally do adhere to the metaphorical expression. How these other aspects of the domain are incorporated into the text and into interpretations of the text depends in large part on the interpreter. This is where metaphor becomes particularly unwieldy, because different interpreters draw on different aspects of the mapping implied within a metaphorical expression. Even though an author may try to delimit meaning within a metaphorical expression, by introducing a particular conceptual mapping he or she invites the audience to imagine a variety of different meanings.

4. Conceptual Blends

While metaphorical mappings in their most basic form involve projecting a source domain onto a target domain, mappings can be related in more complex ways. In many literary texts, as well as everyday language, different conceptual domains can be "blended" to create new or different conceptual domains. This happens quite often with personification and animal imagery in fables. For example, in fables an animal character often possesses human characteristics (e.g., the abilities to speak and to reason) in order to communicate something about human behavior. In these instances, the animal is not strictly speaking the source domain for a metaphorical mapping with a human as the target domain; instead, characteristics of both domains, animal and human, are blended to metaphorically depict human behavior.[104]

Throughout Revelation, it is possible to identify possible conceptual blends, including quite complex constructions. In Revelation, as well as other fantastic texts, not only do conceptual blends occur when aspects of source and target domains are blended into one, but also when various domains function as sources in creating a new domain in order to describe a particular target. One of the most prominent blends in the text is the heavenly throne room, initially described in Revelation 4. John's description of this space blends, among other things, aspects of an earthly throne room, including a variety of political symbols (e.g., elders, thrones, crowns), with celestial realities (e.g., thunder and lightning) creating "God's space." In the text, the description of the heavenly throne room does not necessarily function as an end in itself. Rather, the heavenly throne room seemingly describes the character of its chief resident—"the one who sits upon the throne," or God. This reflects a basic conceptual mapping STATES/CHARACTERISTICS ARE OBJECTS. The different objects in the heavenly throne room describe metaphorically the different characteristics of the divine. In this way, John, like many before him, describes a blended space in order to depict the indescribable.

Through this exploration of how metaphorical language has been understood and approached throughout the Western literary and rhetorical traditions, we have seen how metaphor has been described as a tool of persuasion and as a purely ornamental device. The latter characterization, which grows out of the delineation of tropes in the Latin rhetorical tradition, has contributed to the denigration of metaphorical and figurative

---

[104] For a discussion of conceptual blends especially as they are used in fables, see Mark Turner, *The Literary Mind* (New York: Oxford University Press, 1996), 57–84.

language in some strands of Western philosophy. This tendency to scorn metaphor reflects the assumption that words function as signs, pointing directly or, in the case of metaphors, indirectly to what they signify. In this view, metaphors are at best creative ways of signifying concepts and at worst words misused for the sake of style.

Contemporary theories of metaphor generally have sought to emphasize the connection between metaphor and thought, an ancient idea that seems to have been lost in later discussions of metaphor. Conceptual metaphor theorists in particular have worked to underscore how metaphor, including metaphorical expressions in literary texts, bring ideas "before the eyes." Drawing on the insights of conceptual metaphor theory, especially as articulated by Steen, we turn now to an exploration of how Revelation redeploys traditional metaphorical mappings within its own historical context as a means of shaping the ways its audience conceptualizes its identity and its relationship to Christ.

CHAPTER THREE

Envisioning the City as a Woman: A Metaphorical Framework in the Jewish Literary Traditions

As we saw in the last chapter, Aristotle found metaphorical expressions particularly persuasive because of their ability to "set something before the eyes" of an audience. Many subsequent scholars, including conceptual metaphor theorists, have likewise understood the power of metaphor to be contained in its ability to encourage an audience to view one thing in terms of another, especially to make abstract concepts concrete through comparison. These metaphorical comparisons may resonate with human experience, proving to be a useful tool for understanding and communicating a specific idea or set of ideas.[1]

Given this resonance, certain metaphorical comparisons or mappings establish themselves as conventional figures within a given culture or tradition. These conventional metaphorical mappings are often described as "dead metaphors," since they seemingly function as literal truth claims. George Lakoff and Mark Turner note that this designation "assumes that those things in our cognition that are most alive and most active are those that are conscious. On the contrary, those that are most alive and most deeply entrenched, efficient, and powerful are those that are so automatic as to be unconscious and effortless."[2] Conventional metaphors and mappings are not "dead," simply taken for granted.

Such is the case with a key metaphorical mapping used by the prophets of the Hebrew Bible. This mapping envisions a city (target domain) as a

---

[1] These mappings may also conflict with a particular group or subculture's experience of reality. This poses a problem when the metaphorical mapping becomes so entrenched within a cultural context to be understood as "true." Such is the case with metaphorical mappings such as GOD IS A FATHER. While this may resonate with a particular culture's assumptions about the divine, it may also be discordant with the experience of some groups and individuals within that culture. If the metaphorical mapping is equated with literal truth, the mapping risks becoming unhelpful at least and oppressive at worst. For a critical response to conceptual metaphor theory, see Mieke Bal, "Metaphors He Lives By," *Semeia* 61 (1993): 185–207.

[2] George Lakoff and Mark Turner, *More Than Cool Reason: A Field Guide to Poetic Metaphor* (Chicago: University of Chicago Press, 1989), 129.

woman (source domain): A CITY IS A WOMAN. This mapping is important for the study of nuptial imagery in Revelation because (a) the ancient Jewish literary traditions, including the prophets, contribute to Revelation's symbolic world;[3] and (b) prophetic texts provide one of the most extensive uses of nuptial imagery as a metaphorical construction in the Hebrew Bible. Of equal importance, this mapping identifies a conceptual dynamic that informs Revelation's use of nuptial imagery—that a collective (in this case a city) can be mapped as an individual.

While numerous texts in the Hebrew Bible include depictions of brides and weddings, we will be looking specifically at expressions that function metaphorically as a means of informing our later analysis of Revelation's metaphorical language.[4] More specifically, our analysis focuses on texts from Ezekiel and Isaiah that are generally regarded as shaping Revelation's nuptial imagery.[5]

In this chapter we will (1) discuss the tradition of depicting cities as women in the ancient Mediterranean world and (2) explore some of the

---

[3] Gregory K. Beale, *John's Use of the Old Testament in Revelation* (Sheffield: Sheffield Academic Press, 1998). For a discussion of how Revelation exhibits the characteristics of earlier prophetic literature, see David Hill, *New Testament Prophecy* (Atlanta: John Knox Press, 1979), 70–93.

[4] This limits the texts we examine, because certain texts, such as Proverbs and Song of Songs, may include nuptial imagery without using it metaphorically. Revelation's nuptial imagery has been long associated with the depiction of a love relationship in the Song of Songs. This association has been drawn primarily on account of metaphorical or allegorical readings of the Song, which date back to ancient and medieval times and which approach the text as an extended allegory of the relationship between God and Israel. These readings often find the interpretive key for metaphorical readings in the prophetic depictions of the "marriage" between God and Jerusalem or Israel. See E. Ann Matter, *The Voice of My Beloved: The Song of Songs in Western Medieval Christianity* (Philadelphia: University of Pennsylvania Press, 1990); and Denys Turner, *Eros and Allegory: Medieval Exegesis of the Song of Songs* (Kalamazoo, Mich.: Cistercian Publications, 1995).

While a reading of Revelation alongside of the Song might make an interesting project, at least three factors limit the usefulness of such a task for this monograph. First, unlike his use of the prophetic traditions, which explicitly echo the language of the prophetic texts, John does not obviously or explicitly reflect or allude to specific linguistic expressions within the Song. Second, a surface reading of the Song, which weaves together erotic exchanges between two lovers with only a few linguistic references to marriage, suggests little possible connection to the nuptial imagery of Revelation. Third, while the text abounds with poetic and metaphorical expressions, the text does not explicitly suggest that the lovers' relationship be read metaphorically. Nothing in the text creates an explicit analogy between the love relationship depicted in the text and another relationship, namely, a relationship between God and Jerusalem/Israel.

[5] See Jean-Pierre Ruiz, *Ezekiel in the Apocalypse: The Transformation of Prophetic Language in Revelation 16,17–19,10* (Frankfurt am Main: Peter Lang, 1989); Jan Fekkes, *Isaiah and Prophetic Traditions in the Book of Revelation: Visionary Antecedents and Their Development* (JSNTSup 93; Sheffield: JSOT Press, 1994); Jeffrey Vogelsgesang, "The Interpretation of Ezekiel in the Book of Revelation" (Ph.D. diss., Harvard University, 1985).

ways the prophetic texts in the Hebrew Bible employ this tradition in their nuptial and bridal imagery. We will explore how these texts draw on the cultural depiction of cities as women to encourage an audience to "envision" one thing in terms of another. We will explore how in these instances of nuptial imagery certain metaphorical mappings coalesce with the conventional mapping A CITY IS A WOMAN. In so doing, we can gain an understanding of how this mapping can be employed to shape the thought of an audience.

Women and Cities: An Ancient Metaphorical Mapping

The ancient tradition of personifying cities as women, especially in ancient Near Eastern mythic traditions and Greek and Roman art, has long been recognized.[6] It is also acknowledged that the prophetic tradition of using nuptial imagery to describe Jerusalem echoes this conventional metaphorical construct.[7] This tradition began as a way for artists and poets to describe intimate patronage relationships between cities and their deities.[8] The Sumerian poets (ca. 1900 B.C.E.) developed a visual and literary depiction of the "weeping goddess" who mourned cities, including Ur, which had been destroyed.[9] In these "city-laments" a city's patron goddess was identified and even visually depicted as "the lady" or "the queen" of the city or even as the city's "mother."[10] One lament proclaims, "Namrat [a goddess], the beautiful lady was lamenting bitterly, 'Alas, the destroyed city, my destroyed temple!' bitterly she cries" ("Lamentation over the Destruction of Sumer and Ur" 2.125–26 [Michalowski]). In this context, the specific city

[6] A classic article on the topic is Percy Gardner, "Countries and Cities in Ancient Art," *Journal of Hellenic Studies* 9 (1888): 47–81.

[7] Mark E. Biddle, "The Figure of Lady Jerusalem: Identification, Deification and Personification of Cities in the Ancient Near East," in *The Biblical Canon in Comparative Perspective*, ed. K. Lawson Younger, William W. Hallo, Bernard F. Batto (Lewiston, N.Y.: Edwin Mellen, 1991), 173–94; Phyllis A. Bird, "'To Play the Harlot': An Inquiry into an Old Testament Metaphor," in *Missing Persons and Mistaken Identities: Women and Gender in Ancient Israel* (Minneapolis: Fortress Press, 1997), 219–36; repr. from *Gender and Difference in Ancient Israel* (Minneapolis: Fortress Press, 1989), 75–94; Aloysius Fitzgerald, "The Mythological Background for the Presentation of Jerusalem as a Queen and False Worship as Adultery in the OT," *CBQ* 34 (1972): 403–16; and idem, "*BTWLT* and *BT* as Titles for Capital Cities," *CBQ* 37 (1975): 167–83; Tikva Frymer-Kensky, *In the Wake of the Goddesses: Women, Culture and the Biblical Transformation of Pagan Myth* (New York: Fawcett Columbine, 1992); Katheryn Pfisterer Darr, "Ezekiel: Introduction, Commentary, and Reflections," in *The New Interpreter's Bible* (Nashville: Abingdon Press, 2001), 6:1221–25.

[8] Biddle, "The Figure of Lady Jerusalem," 175–79.

[9] Samuel Kramer, "The Weeping Goddess: Sumerian Prototypes of the Mater Dolorosa," *BA* 46 (1983): 69–80. F. W. Dobbs-Allsopp argues for a distinctively Israelite version of the ancient city-laments in *Weep, O Daughter of Zion: A Study of the City-Lament Genre in the Hebrew Bible* (BibOr; Rome: Biblical Institute, 1993).

[10] Biddle, "The Figure of Lady Jerusalem," 175.

being mourned is not necessarily depicted as a woman. The lament, however, depicts the goddess as a woman, attributing to her traits and roles culturally associated with womanhood.[11] This personification maps the conceptual domain WOMAN onto the conceptual domain DEITY or GODDESS; thus, A GODDESS IS A WOMAN.

In West Semitic and Hellenistic contexts, the tradition of associating cities and goddesses grew and changed.[12] Aloysius Fitzgerald notes that in West Semitic mythology cities were often understood and depicted literarily and visually as goddesses and women. Goddesses, pictured as women, came to embody the cities they protected and served. Numerous Phoenician coins, for example, bore legends and images explicitly portraying cities as goddesses. One such coin describes the city Sidon as a goddess.[13] Such depictions employ the mapping A GODDESS IS A WOMAN to describe a city, effectively suggesting A CITY IS A GODDESS IS A WOMAN.

Different aspects of the domain WOMAN could be employed in describing the ancient city. The legend on another Phoenician coin reads, "[coin] of [the city of] the Sidonians, the mother of Cambe, Hippo, Citium [and] Tyre."[14] Here the city of Sidon is described in terms of the traditional feminine role of mother. This legend reflects a more general metaphorical mapping in which a city is envisioned as a woman, since a mother is a role specifically associated with the more general concept WOMAN. This metaphorical mapping can be represented as A CITY IS A WOMAN. Drawing on this mapping, the legend highlights one aspect of the domain WOMAN to illustrate the relationship between Sidon and other cities. The mapping A CITY IS A WOMAN also could be extended by highlighting the social roles of "wife" or "consort." In so doing, some traditions portrayed the city as a woman married to the city's patron deity.[15] We can begin to see how the basic conceptual mappings A CITY IS A WOMAN and A CITY IS A GODDESS can be combined and extended in various ways to communicate different things about the metaphor's referent. The conceptual mapping A CITY IS A WOMAN can be extended into a variety of related

[11] Frymer-Kensky, *In the Wake of the Goddesses*, 36–37.

[12] Biddle, "The Figure of Lady Jerusalem," 179.

[13] Fitzgerald, "The Mythological Background," 406.

[14] Ibid., 406.

[15] Ibid., 405; Biddle, "The Figure of Lady Jerusalem," 179. Even though she notes that ancient Near Eastern cities were personified as women/goddesses, Frymer-Kensky disagrees with Fitzgerald's claim that these goddess-cities were metaphorically "married" to a male deity (*In the Wake of the Goddessess*, 171–72, 269 n. 13). For a similar perspective on Fitzgerald's claims, see Elaine Adler, "The Background for the Metaphor of the Covenant as Marriage in the Hebrew Bible" (Ph.D. diss., University of California, Berkeley, 1990), 144–48. While Adler acknowledges that ancient cities were personified as women, she argues against Fitzgerald's claims that these ancient cities were metaphorically married to deities. Instead, she argues that this metaphorical connection is "at home" within the monotheistic traditions of Israel.

mappings, including A CITY IS A GODDESS, A CITY IS A WIFE, A CITY IS A MOTHER, etc.

Besides attributing different feminine social roles to the goddess-city, it was traditional to envision the city metaphorically in relation to the female body. In her discussions of the ancient Near Eastern antecedents to Ezekiel's marriage metaphor, Julie Galambush describes how the physical concept of a woman could be used to describe the physical structure of a city.[16] Certain parts of a woman's anatomy, such as her uterus, were sometimes mapped onto parts of the city. Thus, the basic conceptual mapping A CITY IS A WOMAN suggests another conceptual mapping, for instance, A TEMPLE IS A WOMB. Characteristics associated with a woman's womb, namely, fertility, were metaphorically extended to a city's temple, making the temple the locus of the deity's fertility.[17] This is yet another way that the conventional mapping A CITY IS A WOMAN could be shaped to meet a particular conceptual or rhetorical need.

The tradition of depicting cities as women proved popular in Hellenistic cities and later in Roman settings as well. Throughout the Mediterranean world, cities were depicted as their patron goddesses and understood as the embodiment of a feminine personification of fortune (*Tyche* in Greek and *Fortuna* in Latin). Percy Gardner explains, "There is a large class of representations in late art of Tyche as the goddess of this or that city, who is in fact the embodiment and representation of the city, and is modified in different places to suit her to the situation, the character, and the inhabitants of each."[18] As a city, Tyche was typically represented as wearing a turreted crown, also known as a mural crown. (Some West Semitic examples also wear the mural crown.) The turreted crown creates a direct visual link between the image of the woman and the city that she embodies. This convention, Mark E. Biddle argues, "makes it clear that the deification of the city represents a fusion of city and goddess and not an abstraction of the principle of protection."[19] The visual image of the goddess wearing a crown of city walls presents a specific expression of the conceptual equation of cities with goddesses and women: A CITY IS A GODDESS and A CITY IS A WOMAN.

One of the most famous of the "Tyches" was, and still is, a statue commissioned for the city of Antioch by Seleucus I at its founding. (A copy of the statue by Eutychides is still extant.) This version depicts the popular image seated on a rock with her feet resting on the river Ornotes (often personified as a man), a central river within the city. Gardner comments on the piece, suggesting that Eutychides "produces on us the impression which

[16] Julie Galambush, *Jerusalem in the Book of Ezekiel: The City as Yahweh's Wife* (SBLDS 130; Atlanta: Scholars Press, 1992), 21–23.

[17] Galambush, *Jerusalem in the Book of Ezekiel*, 22–23.

[18] Gardner, "Countries and Cities," 73.

[19] Biddle, "The Figure of Lady Jerusalem," 181.

the city produced on visitors, a stately city full of wealth, pleasant to dwell in, a queen enthroned giving law to Asia, and yet persuading rather than commanding."[20] The popularity of Tyche of Antioch led to her appearance on various coins, many of which are still extant.

The tradition of using an image of a woman wearing the turreted crown to depict a city extends into the Roman period, pointing to its popularity within the Mediterranean world. While depictions of the city as the goddess Roma are probably the most well known, the custom was even more widespread.[21] Diana E. E. Kleiner observes, for instance, the presence of personified cities on the arch of Trajan at Beneventum.[22] On the arch four women wear their walled crowns, suggesting that the cities of the Roman Empire have gathered around the emperor Trajan. Under the Roman Empire the tradition of depicting women as cities was expanded to include using the female figure to depict nations and groups of people, especially those conquered by the empire. At the Sebasteion in Aphrodisias in Asia Minor, relief images of women represented nations, such as Britain. In this instance, the metaphorical mapping A CITY IS A WOMAN has been extended to A NATION IS A WOMAN.[23]

Throughout the ancient Mediterranean world, the cultural milieu for the authors of the prophetic texts of the Hebrew Bible, this convention of depicting cities through feminine imagery held sway. As we have seen, the conceptual mapping A CITY IS A WOMAN could be extended in various ways, even blended with other mappings (e.g., A GODDESS IS A WOMAN) which results in a variety of different specific expressions. This begins to reveal the way in which simple conceptual mappings can yield a variety of different expressions.

The conceptual mapping A CITY IS A WOMAN, as well as the more specific mapping A CITY IS A WIFE, was readily appropriated and modified by the prophets in the Hebrew Bible (e.g., Hosea 1–3; Ezekiel 16; 23; Isaiah 51–66). This mapping provides the prophets a powerful and persuasive image for describing the relationship between God and God's people, as metonymically represented by the nation of Israel and the city of Jerusalem.[24] In contrast to their neighbors, the prophets did not use femi-

---

[20] Gardner, "Countries and Cities," 75.

[21] For a discussion of the goddess Roma, see Ronald Mellor, "The Goddess Roma," *ANRW* 17.2:950–1030.

[22] Diana E. E. Kleiner, *Roman Sculpture* (New Haven: Yale University Press, 1992), 224–26.

[23] R. R. R. Smith, "*Simulacra Gentium:* The Ethne from the Sebasteion at Aphrodisias," *JRS* 78 (1988): 71.

[24] Metonymy is related to metaphor. As Lakoff and Johnson explain, in metonymy, "we are using one entity to refer to another that is related to it" (*Metaphors We Live By*, 35). This often involves using a part of something to describe the whole. The prophets occasionally use the A CITY IS A WOMAN mapping to describe other cities. For a discussion of Ezekiel's use of

nine imagery to depict the city as a goddess. Instead, they extended the metaphorical mapping A CITY IS A WOMAN.

As we examine how Ezekiel and Isaiah use the mapping A CITY IS A WOMAN within the context of nuptial imagery, our focus is on the contours of this imagery and not on the exegetical details. In particular we are interested in how these texts map the collective as an individual.

"I bound you in fine linen . . . ": The Marriage Metaphor in Ezekiel

Ezekiel's use of the conceptual metaphor A CITY IS A WOMAN, found primarily in chaps. 16 and 23, is the most detailed expression of the A CITY IS A WOMAN mapping in the prophetic texts of the Hebrew Bible. Highlighting specific aspects culturally associated with women and marriage, Ezekiel depicts Jerusalem as the unfaithful or "whoring" wife of Yahweh.[25] As Katheryn Pfisterer Darr explains, Ezekiel weaves these images together to construct "a story of Israel's history that justifies God's impending judgment."[26] This fits into the text's overarching aim of "establishing Judah's sinfulness" as a means for explaining the destruction and chaos during Babylon's occupation of Jerusalem.[27]

Ezekiel 16:1–14

In the following, we will focus on the first major unit of Ezek 16:1–14, since this unit's references to the marriage between Jerusalem and God and to the adornment of the city-woman is one of the most extensive mappings incorporating nuptial imagery and the CITY IS A WOMAN mapping. As

this personification specifically with regard to the oracles against the city of Tyre, see Carol A. Newsom, "A Maker of Metaphors: Ezekiel's Oracles against Tyre," in *Interpreting the Prophets*, ed. James Luther Mays and Paul J. Achtemeier (Philadelphia: Fortress Press, 1987), 188–99.

[25] The terms "whore" and "whoring," which are forms of the Hebrew verb *zānâ*, are problematic English translations. While the verb *zānâ* is linguistically related to the noun typically translated into English as "whore" or "prostitute" (*zônâ*), the verb describes more generally the illicit act of engaging in sexual relations apart from marriage. See Phyllis A. Bird, "'To Play the Harlot': An Inquiry into an Old Testament Metaphor," in *Missing Persons and Mistaken Identities: Women and Gender in Ancient Israel* (Minneapolis: Fortress Press, 1997), 221. Revelation's depiction of the great prostitute in chap. 17 draws heavily on the prophetic images of adultery and promiscuity. While an investigation into Ezekiel's depiction of Jerusalem as an unfaithful wife helps elucidate Revelation's image of the prostitute, it has limited relevance for understanding the text's nuptial imagery.

[26] Katheryn Pfisterer Darr, "Ezekiel's Justifications of God: Teaching Troubling Texts," *JSOT* 55 (1992): 102. See also Pfisterer Darr, "Ezekiel," in *The Women's Bible Commentary*, ed. Carol A. Newsom and Sharon H. Ringe (Louisville, Ky.: Westminster John Knox, 1992), 183–94.

[27] Pfisterer Darr, "Ezekiel's Justifications," 97–98.

such it provides a helpful conversation partner for reading Revelation's nuptial imagery:

> [1]The word of the LORD came to me: [2] Mortal, make known to Jerusalem her abominations, [3]and say, Thus says the Lord God to Jerusalem: Your origin and your birth were in the land of the Canaanites; your father was an Amorite, and your mother a Hittite. [4]As for your birth, on the day you were born your navel cord was not cut, nor were you washed with water to cleanse you, nor rubbed with salt, nor wrapped in cloths. [5]No eye pitied you, to do any of these things for you out of compassion for you; but you were thrown out in the open field, for you were abhorred on the day you were born.
>
> [6]I passed by you, and saw you flailing about in your blood. As you lay in your blood, I said to you, "Live! [7]And grow up like a plant of the field." You grew up and became tall and arrived at full womanhood; your breasts were formed, and your hair had grown; yet you were naked and bare.
>
> [8]I passed by you again and looked on you; you were at the age for love. I spread the edge of my cloak over you, and covered your nakedness: I pledged myself to you and entered into a covenant with you, says the Lord God, and you became mine.
>
> [9]Then I bathed you with water and washed off the blood from you, and anointed you with oil. [10]I clothed you with embroidered cloth and with sandals of fine leather; I bound you in fine linen and covered you with rich fabric. [11] I adorned you with ornaments: I put bracelets on your arms, a chain on your neck, [12]a ring on your nose, earrings in your ears, and a beautiful crown upon your head. [13]You were adorned with gold and silver, while your clothing was of fine linen, rich fabric, and embroidered cloth. You had choice flour and honey and oil for food. You grew exceedingly beautiful, fit to be a queen. [14]Your fame spread among the nations on account of your beauty, for it was perfect because of my splendor that I had bestowed on you, says the Lord God. (Ezek 16:1–14 NRSV)

1. JERUSALEM IS A WOMAN

Ezekiel 16 begins with an explanation of the text's purpose, to "make known to Jerusalem her abominations" (v. 2). In this verse, the subject and audience of the following verses are identified as one and the same—Jerusalem. Instead of describing a city, as one might expect, the text immediately embarks on a description of a human individual, addressed in the second person: "*Your* origin and *your* birth were in the land of the Canaanites . . ." (16:3). As the picture of this person unfolds, it becomes clear that the "you" described in the text is a female. She develops breasts (v. 7); she bleeds, either from menstruation or from her first sexual experience (v. 9);[28] she is adorned in ornaments that can be worn by women (vv. 11–

[28] As Pfisterer Darr observes, the text does not specify whether the blood (the text is plural) with which the woman is covered is birth blood, menstrual blood, or blood resulting from

12; cf. 23:40, 42). Ezekiel sets before the eyes of his audience an image of a young woman. Couched in the second person, the text implies that the young woman being described is actually Jerusalem.[29] Even though Ezekiel 16 does not use the Hebrew word for "woman" (*iššâ*) until v. 30, when it is associated with Jerusalem's adulteries, the chapter employs various elements drawn from the source domain WOMAN to create its image. Characteristics traditionally associated with feminine gender function as a source domain for describing a city, specifically identified as Jerusalem. In this way, Ezekiel draws on and begins to elaborate on the traditional conceptual mapping A CITY IS A WOMAN.

The referent for Ezekiel's metaphorical construction is clearly "Jerusalem," as indicated in God's command that Ezekiel address Jerusalem (16:2).[30] While "Jerusalem" functions as a specific city, a specific version of the more general conceptual domain, it remains to be seen how Ezekiel 16 understands the concept CITY. Does the specification "Jerusalem" function as a description of a locale, a political institution, a social structure, a group of people, or a combination of these options? This question becomes even more complicated when one considers the fact that the Book of Ezekiel was written from within the Babylonian exile, a time when the author and his audience were displaced from the city being described and addressed.[31]

Some scholars argue that the depiction of the young woman in Ezekiel 16 is not simply about the city of Jerusalem. Rather, the capital city functions as a metonym for the nation and its people in general. This reading has a long history beginning with rabbinical interpreters who saw Ezek 16:1–14 "as descriptive of Israel's history from the beginning."[32] The abandoned infant flailing in her blood, they suggest, describes the Israelites' experience in Egypt. Contemporary commentator Moshe Greenberg follows this interpretive tradition. He bases his reading on numerous details in Ezekiel 16, but mainly from the fact that it is with Israel and not

---

intercourse ("Ezekiel," 1228 n. 427). The text seems to favor the last two of these options, given the life history assigned to this character in vv. 4–8. Mary E. Shields suggests that the plural *dāmaîm* intentionally alludes to all these types of blood associated with women ("Multiple Exposures: Body Rhetoric and Gender Characterization in Ezekiel 16," *JFSR* 14 [1998]: 9).

[29] Renita J. Weems, *Battered Love: Marriage, Sex, and Violence in the Hebrew Bible Prophets* (Minneapolis: Fortress Press, 1995), 62.

[30] Because Ezekiel 16 explicitly identifies Jerusalem as the metaphorical referent in v. 2, this text does not require us to identify the metaphorical focus, frame, and referent, as described in chap. 2 and employed elsewhere in this project.

[31] Robert Wilson notes that since Ezekiel often directly addresses "Jerusalem," some scholars posit that the prophet traveled back and forth from Babylon to Jerusalem. As Wilson observes, this scenario fails to recognize that prophets could address an audience without being in its physical presence ("Ezekiel," in *Harper's Bible Commentary*, ed. James L. Mays [San Francisco: HarperCollins, 1988], 655).

[32] Pfisterer Darr, "Ezekiel's Justification," 103.

Jerusalem that God establishes a covenant, which is mentioned in 16:8 (cf. Exod 6:7). This reading corresponds to the concern that the text of Ezekiel as a whole exhibits for the fate of Israel as a nation and not only the city of Jerusalem (e.g., 2:3; 3:1; 7:2).[33]

In contrast to reading Jerusalem as a metonym for Israel, Galambush and Pfisterer Darr assert that the "Jerusalem" of Ezekiel 16 refers to the *city* of Jerusalem and its religious and political components. Galambush, who emphasizes Jerusalem's religious significance, points to Ezekiel's appropriation of the traditional metaphorical equation between cities and women, the metaphorical mapping A CITY IS A WOMAN.[34] She suggests that Ezekiel casts Jerusalem as a woman as part of the conventional metaphorical similarity between cities and women. Galambush implies that Ezekiel 16 employs the feminine imagery *in order to* describe Jerusalem the city and especially its Temple and Temple cult.[35] Pfisterer Darr, likewise, points to the ways in which "Jerusalem" is depicted within the metaphorical construction of chap. 16 as evidence for reading Jerusalem as a reference to the city understood as a complex network of political and religious institutions, practices, and participants. For example, Ezekiel's descriptions of the woman's fine clothing (16:11) seemingly conjure images of the Temple cult.[36] Ezekiel 16 clothes this woman in the garb of Jerusalem and its Temple. Elements from the specific concept "Jerusalem" influence how Ezekiel 16 employs the conceptual domain WOMAN in depicting Jerusalem as a young woman. This demonstrates the permeability of the boundary between source and target domains often found in metaphorical expressions.

Furthermore, even though Ezekiel 16 narrows the target domain of the A CITY IS A WOMAN mapping by characterizing the city as Jerusalem, the structure of the metaphor still allows for different interpretations. These different perspectives on what "Jerusalem" signifies point to the ways in which metaphorical language invites readers to participate in the process of imagining the similarities between Jerusalem and a woman. A text may limit possible interpretations by elaborating on the metaphorical mapping; however, sometimes even an extended elaboration, such as Ezekiel 16, allows for a wide range of interpretive possibilities.

The above readings of "Jerusalem" demonstrate the complexity inherent with the concept CITY. The concept can function as a metonym for the

---

[33] Moshe Greenberg, *Ezekiel 1–20* (AB 22; Garden City, N.Y.: Doubleday, 1983), 301. Joseph Blenkinsopp likewise reads the reference to Jerusalem as a metonym for Israel in general (*Ezekiel* [Louisville, Ky.: John Knox, 1990], 76).

[34] Galambush draws on the work of conceptual metaphor theorists, suggesting, as I maintain, that the depiction of cities as women functioned as a conventional metaphor within Ezekiel's context. See Galambush, *Jerusalem in the Book of Ezekiel*, 7–9.

[35] Ibid., 161.

[36] Pfisterer Darr, "Ezekiel's Justifications," 104.

nation and people, including their history, with which it is related. The conceptual domain CITY includes the institutions and groups, political associations and religious orders, "contained" within the city as well. In whatever manner one understands the conceptual domain CITY and its more specific version "Jerusalem," the depiction of the city as a woman prompts the audience to envision these different elements, associated with Jerusalem, as a personalized entity. The city is an individual with an individual's history, an individual's personality, and an individual's future.

a. JERUSALEM IS AN EMBODIED WOMAN

Feminist scholars highlight Ezekiel's depiction of God's voyeuristic gaze on Jerusalem's body, which Ezekiel 16 describes in detail.[37] This aspect of the text is one of the primary ways in which Ezekiel 16 employs the source domain WOMAN. Among the entailments within the conceptual domain WOMAN, Ezekiel's depiction of Jerusalem highlights the female body. Especially in the first half of chap. 16, the text depicts God recalling Jerusalem's young body, specifically noting her breasts and pubic hair (v. 7). In later verses the text mentions Jerusalem's arms, neck, nose, ears, and head (vv. 11–12). This focus on the "body" of Jerusalem is not necessarily a conceptual mapping separate from JERUSALEM IS A WOMAN; however, given the prominence of this metaphorical extension in this chapter, it is helpful to clarify that Ezekiel 16 employs the more specific mapping JERUSALEM IS AN EMBODIED WOMAN. The focus on Jerusalem's body is arguably one of the most distinctive and disturbing aspects of Ezekiel's personification of the city and his use of the marriage metaphor, especially since the text eventually includes graphic depictions of Jerusalem's sexual use or misuse, according to Ezekiel, of her body (e.g., v. 17) and the subsequent physical "punishment" of Jerusalem through dismembering her body (v. 40).

b. A WOMAN'S BODY PARTS ARE ORNAMENTS; A WOMAN'S BODY IS A PLANT

Ezekiel highlights the embodied nature of Jerusalem in a variety of ways, making full use of the concept of embodiment (BODY). A number of different metaphorical mappings are used to describe the female body, shifting the source domain AN EMBODIED WOMAN to a target domain. Passing by the young Jerusalem, for instance, God comments on her

---

[37] Much work has been done on the misogynistic nature of this text. See, for instance, Linda Day, "Rhetoric and Domestic Violence in Ezek 16," *BibInt* 8 (2000): 230; Peggy L. Day, "The Bitch Had It Coming to Her: Rhetoric and Interpretation in Ezek 16," *BibInt* 8 (2000): 231–54; Fokkelien Van Dijk-Hemmes, "The Metaphorization of Woman in Prophetic Speech: An Analysis of Ezek XXIII," *VT* 43 (1993): 162–70; Shields, "Multiple Exposures," 5–18.

"adornments" (*'adi*), which are specified as her breasts and presumably her pubic hair (v. 7). In this way, Ezekiel equates the external signs of feminine sexuality with ornaments or jewelry, which is how *'adi* functions in 16:11: "I adorned you with ornaments (*'adi*): I put bracelets on your arms, a chain on your neck . . ." (NRSV). This suggests the metaphorical mapping A WOMAN'S BODY PARTS ARE ORNAMENTS. Similarly, Ezekiel describes the maturation of the young Jerusalem's body in terms of plants that sprout in a field (v. 7).[38] In this way, the source domain PLANT is used to describe the target domain A WOMAN'S BODY, suggesting the mapping A WOMAN'S BODY IS A PLANT. In both of these instances, the text overlays one metaphorical mapping over another, constructing a complex web of metaphorical references in its depiction of Jerusalem as a woman.

c. A WOMAN IS AN OBJECT; A CHANGE IN STATUS IS A CHANGE IN CLOTHING

Building on the conceptual mapping JERUSALEM IS AN EMBODIED FEMALE, Ezekiel encourages his audience to envision the adornment of Jerusalem's body. (Ezekiel's adornment imagery is especially pertinent to our investigation into Revelation's nuptial imagery, because Revelation employs similar adornment language.) This event occurs in conjunction with the "marriage" (see below) between God and Jerusalem (v. 8):

> I clothed you with embroidered cloth and with sandals of fine leather; I bound you in fine linen and covered you with rich fabric. I adorned you with ornaments: I put bracelets on your arms, a chain on your neck, a ring on your nose, earrings in your ears, and a beautiful crown upon your head. You were adorned with gold and silver, while your clothing was of fine linen, rich fabric, and embroidered cloth. . . . (16:10–13 NRSV)[39]

The extravagance of Jerusalem's adornments, which resemble the priestly vestments and cultic articles of the Jerusalem Temple (cf. Exod 25:5; 26:14, 36; 27:16), contrasts sharply with her earlier state—absolute nakedness.[40] Prior to the marriage covenant between God and Jerusalem, Ezekiel characterizes Jerusalem's body as dirty and unclothed: "As for your birth, on

---

[38] For a discussion of the translation issues surrounding *rebabah,* which can be rendered in terms of sprouting, see Greenberg, *Ezekiel,* 276; also Pfisterer Darr, "Ezekiel," 1227.

[39] The question of whether this process of adornment entails specifically the bridal outfit remains undecided by commentators; however, given their textual proximity and the lack of an explicit transition, the process of adornment is associated with the wedding. Greenberg notes that most modern commentaries hold that this adornment refers to the bridal outfit, although he disagrees with this characterization (*Ezekiel,* 279).

[40] Galambush, *Jerusalem in the Book of Ezekiel,* 95; Pfisterer Darr, "Ezekiel's Justifications," 102.

the day you were born your navel cord was not cut, nor were you washed with water to cleanse you, nor rubbed with salt, nor wrapped in cloths" (16:4 NRSV). Even as she reaches puberty, according to the text, Jerusalem is "naked and bare," her breasts and pubic hair visible to all (v. 7).[41] It is only when God enters into a covenant or marriage relationship with Jerusalem that God covers Jerusalem's nakedness (16:11). God covers Jerusalem's naked body with a cloak and thereby separates Jerusalem's body from the glances of others.

The image of Jerusalem's adornment suggests a number of conceptual mappings. First, throughout the description of Jerusalem's adornment God is the sole actor: God covers, adorns, clothes, binds, and bedecks Jerusalem. Mary Shields writes, "The actions are all God's; she is a mannequin, an object to be acted upon. The marks of ownership—the best and richest of clothing, the jewelry, and the 'glorious crown'—indicate her husband's status. . . ."[42] The description of Jerusalem being acted on in these verses indicates that the woman described in the passage (referred to only with second-person pronouns) is understood primarily as an object. Rather than depicting a woman who actively chooses, embraces, or accepts God's adornment, the text metaphorically equates this woman with an object: A WOMAN IS AN OBJECT.

Second, another metaphorical mapping assumed in the adornment language of 16:1–14 relates to the status of Jerusalem before and after her adornment. As we noted above, prior to Jerusalem's covenant relationship with God she is characterized as naked and dirty. Since the referent of these descriptions is the city Jerusalem, which cannot actually be naked, nakedness or physical appearance must function metaphorically. At the most basic level, the text suggests that Jerusalem's original state of nakedness relates to her alienation from God. It is only after Jerusalem's covenant with God, described in 16:8, that she is covered and then clothed. The text actually describes this in terms of God's granting his splendor to Jerusalem: "You grew exceedingly beautiful, fit to be a queen. Your fame [name] spread among the nations on account of your beauty, for it was perfect because of my splendor that I had bestowed on you, says the Lord God" (vv. 13–14 NRSV).[43]

These lines emphasize Jerusalem's transition from one status to another. Through the event of being clothed, Jerusalem moves from foundling (vv. 4–6, 8) to one suited for royalty (v. 14). These two social

---

[41] Jerusalem's original nakedness is highlighted again later in the chapter: "you did not remember the days of your youth, when you were *naked and bare*, flailing about in your blood" (16:22 NRSV).

[42] Shields, "Multiple Exposures," 10.

[43] The two references to beauty in vv. 13–14 are related terms, *yapa* and *yopi*, which are used elsewhere in Ezekiel. Notably, *yopi* is used in the following verse, which describes Jerusalem using her beauty to commit adultery (v. 15).

states are opposite extremes of a spectrum—from an unwanted outsider to one possessing status, authority, and power. Jerusalem moves from being forgotten and abandoned to being known by all. Changing external appearances functions as a transition from one status to another, reflecting the conceptual mapping A CHANGE IN STATUS IS A CHANGE IN CLOTHING.[44] These verses also suggest the related mapping, STATUS IS A GARMENT.

The metaphorical mappings of Ezekiel 16 shape the rhetoric of this text. An important aspect of this involves having the audience view itself moving from one state of existence to another. The audience is given no option but to look at itself flailing about naked, but then also to see that only "marriage" to God can move them out of this state. This transition is depicted through the detailed account of God's adorning the body of Jerusalem (A CHANGE IN STATUS IS A CHANGE OF CLOTHING). God grants Jerusalem a new status by adorning her (STATUS IS A GARMENT). This depiction, however, assumes that the woman Jerusalem is a passive object (A WOMAN IS AN OBJECT) which must rely on God for this change in existence.

2. A CITY'S HISTORY IS A WOMAN'S LIFE.

Ezekiel 16 unfolds as a narrative that begins with a reference to the conception and birth (v. 3) of this metaphorical woman. The text continues with a description of the young woman's puberty (vv. 6–7) and her marriage (vv. 8–14). Eventually she even bears children (vv. 20–21).[45] Birth, puberty, marriage, and childbearing function as the key events of feminine gender in the ancient Mediterranean world and, more specifically, within the ancient Israelite world.[46] The text draws on the traditional events within

[44] Several scholars have read the language of clothing in relation to the concepts of honor and shame. Lyn Bechtel notes, for instance, that the Hebrew word *'erwa*, which is typically translated as "nakedness," also connotes a sense of "shameful exposure." Thus, the act of clothing involves a transition from a state of shame to a state of honor. The concepts of honor and shame are notoriously complex, because shame involves both positive and negative elements. This can be seen in Ezekiel 16, when God punishes Jerusalem's shamelessness, indicated by her nakedness, by shaming "her" through stripping (16:36–37) (Lyn M. Bechtel, "Shame as a Sanction of Social Control in Biblical Israel: Judicial, Political, and Social Shaming," *JSOT* 49 [1991]: 67). For a discussion of shame in Ezekiel with special reference to chap. 16, see Jacqueline E. Lapsley, "Shame and Self-Knowledge: The Positive Role of Shame in Ezekiel's View of the Moral Self," in *The Book of Ezekiel: Theological and Anthropological Perspectives*, ed. Margaret S. Odell and John T. Strong (Atlanta: Society of Biblical Literature, 2000), 143–73.

[45] Following rabbinical interpretive tradition, some modern scholars make explicit connections between the events described in chap. 16 and actual events from Israel's history. For a critique of this approach, see Pfisterer Darr, "Ezekiel's Justifications," 103–4.

[46] For a succinct discussion of the social roles of women in ancient Israel and as depicted in the Hebrew Bible, see Phyllis Bird, "Women (Old Testament)," *ABD* 6:951–57; repr. in *Missing Persons and Mistaken Identities: Women and Gender in Ancient Israel* (Minneapolis: Fortress Press, 1997), 52–66.

a woman's life to present "the life cycle" of Jerusalem.[47] These events are used to describe stages and transitions in the history and development of Jerusalem, suggesting the conceptual mapping A CITY'S HISTORY IS A WOMAN'S LIFE. As we will see, one of the most significant events described in the text is the "marriage," which functions as a turning point in Jerusalem's life.

3. A WEDDING IS A POLITICAL COVENANT IS A WEDDING; THE RELATIONSHIP BETWEEN GOD AND JERUSALEM IS A MARRIAGE

As noted above, the woman Jerusalem's life takes a marked turn for the better when God initiates a covenantal relationship with her. This event is described in 16:8, when God recalls, "I spread the edge of my cloak over you, and covered your nakedness: I pledged myself to you and entered into a covenant [*bĕrît*] with you . . . and you became mine" (NRSV). Set within a context of a woman's life cycle (see above), this description suggests for many interpreters the marriage between God and Jerusalem.[48] Ezekiel's use of the source domain WOMAN, which includes the concept of a woman's life cycle, encourages the audience to think of this event as a wedding or marriage. Additionally, the text's suggestion that God spreads his cloak over the young woman alludes to a marriage rite (Ruth 3:9), and encourages the audience to read this "covenant" as a wedding.[49]

Besides covering Jerusalem, God also swears an oath to Jerusalem and, likewise, enters into a covenant (*bĕrît*) with Jerusalem (see Ezek 16:59–63). In Ezekiel, the term used for swearing an oath occurs only one other time within a decidedly political context, referring to the relationship between the people of Jerusalem and the king of Babylon (21:23). Likewise, in Ezekiel the term *bĕrît* suggests a political relationship. In chap. 17, for instance, "covenant" refers to agreements made between political figures (e.g., 17:13–14, 18). The language of covenant is especially laden with meaning since it is the term used to describe the agreements made between God and the people of Israel, including the covenants between God and Noah, God and Abraham, and the covenant made on Mount Sinai.[50] Given the

---

[47] Weems, *Battered Love*, 59; Moshe Greenberg, *Ezechiel 1–20* (Herders Theologischer Kommentar zum Alten Testament; Freiburg im Breisgau: Herder, 2001), 322.

[48] E.g., Galambush, *Jerusalem in the Book of Ezekiel*, 94; Pfisterer Darr, "Ezekiel," 1228.

[49] In the case of Ruth, she is the one who instructs Boaz to spread his cloak over her (Greenberg, *Ezekiel*, 277). See Galambush for a brief discussion of some of the problems in using Ruth 3:9 as evidence for interpreting this practice as a marriage rite (*Jerusalem in the Book of Ezekiel*, 94 n.15).

[50] Blenkisopp warns about making exact connections between the covenant mentioned in this verse and the various covenants in Israel's history. He does suggest, however, that the reference is probably best understood in relation to the covenant between God and Abraham (Genesis 17) (*Ezekiel*, 78). Corrine Patton notes that the uses of covenant language in Ezekiel

significance of covenants in Israel's history, Greenberg suggests that the language in Ezek 16:8 be understood "as a fusion of the divine oath to the patriarchs to give their descendants the land of Canaan (e.g., Gen 26:3; Deut 1:8, etc.) and the solemn declaration of mutual obligation connected with the Exodus and covenant with the people (in the priestly writings and Deuteronomy)."[51] In all of these instances the language of covenant functions to describe political or religio-political relationships.

Placed within the context of Ezekiel's vision of Jerusalem as a woman (A CITY IS A WOMAN), the audience is prompted to understand 16:8 as a wedding reference. The text, however, blurs the boundaries between the source and target domains of this mapping as it employs covenant language in a supposed wedding scenario. In some sense, v. 8 suggests that A WEDDING IS A POLITICAL COVENANT, while the passage in general, which uses feminine imagery to describe Jerusalem, suggests that the mapping is A POLITICAL COVENANT IS A WEDDING. In light of this blending of the interpersonal and the political, which is not without precedent in the Hebrew Bible,[52] we can represent the mapping in v. 8 as A WEDDING IS A POLITICAL COVENANT IS A WEDDING.

Furthermore, Ezekiel's use of wedding imagery to characterize the relationship between God and Jerusalem encourages the audience to begin imagining the relationship between the two as a marriage: THE RELATIONSHIP BETWEEN GOD AND JERUSALEM IS A MARRIAGE. This conceptual mapping anticipates 16:15–48. In these verses the marriage mapping provides a framework for describing Jerusalem as the unfaithful wife of God.

4. GOD IS A HUSBAND

By casting Jerusalem as the "wife" in this scenario, Ezekiel implies that God exhibits some of the characteristics and roles of the "husband": GOD IS A HUSBAND. Some modern interpreters seemingly assume that one of the

---

are highly ambiguous. Although chap. 20 offers a retelling of the story of Israel, she argues that the only reference to covenant in this chapter is in conjunction with a future restoration of Israel and is not specifically the Sinaitic covenant ("'I Myself Gave Them Laws That Were Not Good': Ezek 20 and the Exodus Traditions," *JSOT* 69 [1996]: 75 n. 10).

[51] Greenberg, *Ezekiel*, 278.

[52] This metaphorical association appears throughout the Hebrew Bible (e.g., Deut 6:5; 10:12; 1 Kgs 10:9; Hosea 2). In a recent article, Susan Ackerman explores connections between the ways in which the Hebrew Bible uses love language to describe interpersonal relationships and the ways in which love language describes covenant or political relationships. She concludes that in both realms the language functions similarly, being very one-sided and hierarchical. The hierarchically superior individual "loves," whether emotionally or covenantally, the supposed inferior. She suggests that this is why it is so easy for some authors, including Ezekiel, to slip between the language of interpersonal love and the language of covenant ("The Personal Is Political: Covenantal and Affectionate Love (*'ĀHĀB, 'AHĀBÂ*) in the Hebrew Bible," *VT* 52 [2002]: 447–48).

roles of the husband is to care for or love his wife; thus, God's actions within this text are often interpreted in terms of compassion and love, even if the text is not so explicit. In fact, the text never uses the language of love to describe the relationship between Jerusalem and God, even though this language describes marriage relationships in the Hebrew Bible (e.g., Gen 29:18, 30). This demonstrates the complexity inherent within metaphorical language, as audiences are able to bring to their interpretations aspects of the subject domain that may or may not be intended in the text.[53]

Our discussion of Ezekiel's depiction of Jerusalem helps us to see the contours of the metaphorical mapping A CITY IS A WOMAN. It also helps us to see how this mapping can be employed within the context of nuptial imagery. This investigation also brings to light some of the possible metaphorical mappings used in constructing a nuptial image. Now we turn to Isaiah, again with an eye to how the mapping A CITY IS A WOMAN is constructed and figures into the text's nuptial imagery.

"And like a bride you shall bind them on . . .": Visions of Zion in the Isaian Corpus

One of the unifying threads in Isaiah is the text's focus on the fate of the city of Jerusalem, or Zion.[54] This city takes on special significance in the final third of the book (chaps. 40–66).[55] In these chapters, the prophet seeks to comfort a nation that has experienced exile and a not-so-glorious homecoming.[56] Within this context, Isaiah often depicts the city as a woman (e.g., 40:2; 51:17–20; 52:2; 66:7–11),[57] drawing on the conventional metaphori-

---

[53] Day, "Rhetoric and Domestic Violence," 208; Shields, "Multiple Exposures," 8.

[54] Barry G. Webb, "Zion in Transformation: A Literary Approach to Isaiah," in *The Bible in Three Dimensions: Essays in Celebration of Forty Years of Biblical Studies at the University of Sheffield*, ed. David J. A. Clines et al. (Sheffield: JSOT, 1990), 69–71.

[55] Christopher R. Seitz, "The Book of Isaiah 40–66: Introduction, Commentary, and Reflections," in *New Interpreter's Bible* (Nashville: Abingdon Press, 2001), 6:431. Isaiah is generally understood to be a composite work with either two or three parts. The text's Zion imagery falls, for the most part, in the sections considered to be Second (chaps. 40–55) and Third (chaps. 56–66) Isaiah. Recently, there has been a push toward reading the text as a unified whole. See, for example, the commentary by Brevard S. Childs, *Isaiah* (OTL; Louisville: Westminster John Knox, 2001). For a discussion of the issues involved in reading the text as a unity, see, especially, David M. Carr, "Reaching for Unity in Isaiah," *JSOT* 57 (1993): 61–80. See also John N. Oswalt, *The Book of Isaiah: Chapters 40–66* (NICOT; Grand Rapids, Mich.: William B. Eerdmans, 1998), 3–16; John D. W. Watts, *Isaiah 1–33* (WBC; Waco, Tex.; Word, 1985), xliv-lvii.

[56] Susan Ackerman, "Isaiah," in *The Women's Bible Commentary*, ed. Newsom and Ringe, 165–66. The issue of Isaiah's rhetorical situation is bound closely to the question of whether or not the book is a composite work and whether, as a composite, it is by two or three different authors.

[57] The image of "daughter Zion" appears throughout the entire text (see 1:8, 21; 10:30–32; 37:22), although it is in the final third that this character, sometimes unnamed, is most

cal association between women and cities. In the following discussion we will focus on four depictions of Zion in Isaiah that draw on this association (49:14–21; 61:10; 62:1–5; 65:7–11). As above, we will identify some of the central metaphorical mappings in these texts as a means of understanding how the conventional metaphorical mapping A CITY IS A WOMAN can be constructed and employed within the context of nuptial imagery.

Isaiah 49:14–21

One of the first explicit uses of wedding imagery in Isaiah occurs in chap. 49, when Isaiah describes a conversation between a forlorn Zion and God, which begins with Zion's complaint:

> 14But Zion said, "The LORD has forsaken me, my Lord has forgotten me." 15Can
> a woman forget her nursing child, or show no compassion for the child of her
> womb? Even these may forget, yet I will not forget you. 16See, I have inscribed
> you on the palms of my hands; your walls are continually before me. 17Your
> builders[58] outdo your destroyers, and those who laid you waste go away from
> you. 18Lift up your eyes all around and see; they all gather, they come to you.
> As I live, says the LORD, you shall put all of them on like an ornament, and like
> a bride you shall bind them on.
>
> 19Surely your waste and your desolate places and your devastated land—
> surely now you will be too crowded for your inhabitants, and those who swal-
> lowed you up will be far away. 20The children born in the time of your
> bereavement will yet say in your hearing, "The place is too crowded for me;
> make room for me to settle." 21Then you will say in your heart, "Who has borne
> me these? I was bereaved and barren, exiled and put away—so who has reared
> these? I was left alone—where then have these come from?"

1. A CITY IS A WIFE; GOD IS A HUSBAND

The prophet begins these verses with an explicit personification of the city Zion,[59] as he describes her speaking a lament (v. 14). The phrase "But Zion

---

fully developed. The development of this character, John F. A. Sawyer argues, serves as a parallel to the "servant songs" in chaps. 40ff. ("Daughter of Zion and Servant of the Lord in Isaiah: A Comparison," *JSOT* 44 [1989]: 91). See also Kathleen M. O'Connor, "'Speak Tenderly to Jerusalem': Second Isaiah's Reception and Use of Daughter Zion," *PSB* 20, no. 3 (1999): 281–94.

58 The Hebrew is unclear as the MT reads *bānayik* or "sons." This is difficult to reconcile with the text, which describes Zion as a building with walls. The Hebrew for "builders" consists of the same consonants as sons, which leads some commentators to believe that the text should be rendered as referring to builders. See John N. Oswalt, *The Book of Isaiah: Chapters 40–66* (New International Commentary on the Old Testament; Grand Rapids, Mich.: William B. Eerdmans, 1998), 307.

59 Zion is a clearly a city in the text, although the concept of city can be complex, as described above. Such is the case with Isaiah's depiction of Zion. Carol Newsom notes that in

said . . ." functions as a metaphorical frame, since a city does not literally speak. By attributing to Zion a human activity, speaking, the text signals that the audience should interpret the following conversation as a metaphorical construction. We might suggest that the mapping here is A CITY IS A HUMAN; however, Isaiah's earlier use of the image of "daughter Zion" (e.g., 1:8) suggests the more specific mapping A CITY IS A WOMAN. (This is a *co-textual* referent according to the language articulated in the previous chapter.)

The words that Zion "speaks" draw on this personification. Zion wonders why God, whom she describes as her "lord" or "husband," has forgotten her.[60] This verse effectively casts Zion as a wife, the feminine counterpart to her husband. Placed in the "mouth" of a city, these words confirm that Isaiah draws on the metaphorical mapping A CITY IS A WOMAN in his depiction of Zion. The juxtaposition of God and lord or husband also functions as part of a metaphorical expression. When one hears the reference to the husband, after the parallel reference to God, it becomes clear that the term "husband" is not to be taken literally. To return to the language of chap. 2, this term serves as a metaphorical focus. It is a term used to describe something other than its literal referent. In this case, the metaphorical frame includes the focus's referent—God. In this way the text encourages the audience to envision Zion as a wife (A CITY IS A WIFE) and God as a husband (A DEITY IS A HUSBAND).

After Zion's lament in which she expresses her grief over seemingly being forgotten by God, the text depicts God responding by comparing his relationship to Zion to that of a mother and child. God assures Zion that he cannot forget her, just as a mother will not forget her nursing child or the child from her womb.[61] This comparison casts God in the role of mother, suggesting GOD IS A MOTHER.[62] This mapping points to the fact that the use of nuptial imagery does not always follow a strict pattern of

---

Isaiah's depiction, "Zion's geographical location is stressed. She is the destination of Yahweh and of those whom Yahweh brings" ("Response to Norman K. Gottwald, 'Social Class and Ideology in Isaiah 40–55,'" *Semeia* 59 [1992]: 76). Likewise, O'Connor notes the complexity of Zion, "[Zion] is the future; her new life is already imagined. Capital city, monarchical center, and divine dwelling place, her revivification and restoration lures the exiled people homeward" ("'Speak Tenderly to Jerusalem,'" 294).

[60] See Amos 4:1. The use of *'ădonay* could be understood as a nonmetaphorical reference to God, because it is a common replacement for the divine name. One ancient scribe from Qumran makes clear that the term should be read as a reference to God and not, apparently, another "lord" or "husband," because he writes in the divine name above *'ădonay* (1QIs[a]) (Oswalt, *The Book of Isaiah*, 301). In rendering *'ădonay* as a reference to God as husband, I am following the reading of this passage suggested by Sawyer, "Daughter of Zion," 92ff.

[61] Ackerman, "Isaiah," 167.

[62] John J. Schmitt, "The Motherhood of God and Zion as Mother," *RB* 92 (1985): 557–69.

depicting God as the "husband" of Jerusalem.[63] The quick shift in mappings in these verses is important: (1) it shows the weakness of understandings of metaphor that use a substitution view and (2) it anticipates the quick shifts between mappings in Revelation.

As these verses progress, Isaiah blends together elements from both the source domain WOMAN and the target domain CITY in his description of Zion. After the prophet encourages the audience to imagine Zion as a wife, he addresses the wife in the second person singular, but as a "you" that has walls and builders (vv. 16–17), drawing on the concept CITY. The text then depicts Zion as having eyes with which to see (v. 18), drawing on the concept WOMAN. In this way, Isaiah creates for his audience a conceptually blended image of Zion. Arguably, this blended image can be represented as A CITY IS A WOMAN IS A CITY.

2. ZION IS A BRIDE; PEOPLE ARE ORNAMENTS

God addresses Zion's lament by encouraging "her" to look up and see the returning exiles (v. 18). By attributing actions to Zion, Isaiah continues to draw on the mapping A CITY IS A WOMAN. Describing Zion's reception of the exiles, Isaiah draws on the fact that women have bodies that can be clothed and adorned (ZION IS AN EMBODIED WOMAN). Thus he writes, "you shall put them on like an ornament and you shall bind them on like a bride" (v. 18). These two similes function as metaphorical expressions as well. By saying that one thing is *like* another, Isaiah creates a metaphorical comparison between two dissimilar things. In the first half of the sentence, Isaiah implies PEOPLE (specifically returning exiles) ARE ORNAMENTS. In the second half of the sentence, Isaiah assumes the metaphorical mapping ZION (indicated by the "you") IS A BRIDE.

A bridal ornament suggests an element of finery (e.g., Isa 61:10; Jer 2:32). The metaphorical equation between the exiles and a bridal ornament implies that those who have suffered as exiles should be understood as valuable and precious. For Zion, to "bind them on" suggests that they become attached to her. In addition, the metaphorical description of Zion binding on or adorning herself with these "ornaments" connotes her active participation in incorporating the exiles into or onto herself. By describing the exiles as ornaments, the text implies that they are objects that can be put on or left off, accepted or rejected. Thus, by depicting Zion adorning herself with the exiles, the text envisions Zion readily accepting those who have been exiled. Unlike the adorned bride of Ezekiel 16, who is passively adorned by God, Zion is an active participant in her adornment. Here the city-bride is a subject and not an object: A CITY IS A SUBJECT.

---

[63] See also 42:14, in which God is compared to a woman in labor (Ackerman, "Isaiah," 167).

3. A CITY IS A MOTHER; A CITY'S INHABITANTS ARE ITS CHILDREN

Elaborating on the conceptual mapping A CITY IS A WOMAN, the text moves from the bridal imagery of 49:18 into imagery that depicts Zion as mother. Zion becomes so crowded after the return of the exiles that she asks, "Who has borne me these?" (v. 21). This birth language implies that Zion is now a mother with children (v. 20). This reflects the more specific conceptual mappings A CITY IS A MOTHER and A CITY'S INHABITANTS ARE ITS CHILDREN. The exiles, who are initially described as Zion's bridal ornaments, become the bride's children. This provides a marked contrast with the beginning of the pericope, which describes Zion's lament over being forsaken: The one who was once abandoned is now overcrowded.

Isaiah 61:10

In Isaiah 61–62 the prophet proclaims the good news of God's salvation to the city of Zion, the city which earlier appeared forlorn (49:14). In 61:10 Zion responds to this hopeful proclamation:[64] "I will greatly rejoice in the LORD, my whole being shall exult in my God; for he has clothed me with the garments of salvation; he has covered me with the robe of righteousness, as a bridegroom decks himself with a garland, and as a bride adorns herself with her jewels" (61:10 NRSV).

1. A CITY IS A WOMAN; A CITY IS AN EMBODIED WOMAN

Again we see Isaiah employing the conventional mapping A CITY IS A WOMAN, as the city of Zion proclaims that her entire "being" will exult in the Lord. The audience is encouraged to imagine a city as an individual possessing a being or soul. The collective, Zion, bears the hallmark of the human person.

Isaiah 61:10 also encourages the audience to envision the city as a woman with a body. Zion praises God, because God has "clothed" and "covered" her. The language of being clothed implies that Zion has a body that is capable of being clothed. In this way, Isaiah specifies that not only is Zion

---

[64] The text does not specifically identify Zion as the speaker of this verse. While many scholars believe this to be the case (e.g., Oswalt, *The Book of Isaiah*, 574), these verses can also be read as a part of the "servant's song" in vv. 1–7. Childs points out that the Targum introduces vv. 10–11 with the phrase "Jerusalem has said," which indicates that the speaker should be understood as the city. Childs, however, opts for reading the verses as coming from the servant of the previous verses (*Isaiah*, 506). Since Revelation scholars often point to this verse as informing John's depiction of Jerusalem's adornment, we will proceed with the assumption that Zion is the speaker. Beale offers an extended discussion of Isa 61:10 in his analysis of Revelation's nuptial imagery. See Beale, *The Book of Revelation*, 939–41.

a woman, but Zion is an embodied woman (A CITY IS AN EMBODIED WOMAN).

2. QUALITIES OF BEING ARE GARMENTS;
   A CHANGE IN BEING IS A CHANGE OF CLOTHING

The verse continues as Zion praises God for the types of garments he has given to her: "he has clothed me with the garments of salvation, he has covered me with the robe of righteousness." By describing these garments in terms of salvation and righteousness, the text clearly establishes that we are dealing with metaphorical clothing. The abstract concepts of salvation and righteousness, which may be described as qualities of being, are depicted as pieces of clothing that can be put on and worn, and suggest the conceptual mapping QUALITIES OF BEING ARE GARMENTS.

There is a metaphorical connection between the inner character or nature of an entity and its outward appearance (e.g., Isa 3:18–4:1). The presence of the "garments" of salvation and righteousness on Zion metaphorically suggests the presence of these characteristics within the city (see Isa 52:1). Thus changing a garment marks a change in being or character (e.g., 61:3): CHANGING BEING IS CHANGING GARMENTS.

Isaiah 61:10 compares the change Zion undergoes through being clothed by God to being adorned for a wedding: "as a bridegroom decks himself with a garland, and as a bride adorns herself with her jewels." While this text clearly personifies Zion, encouraging the audience to imagine her as human with a body, this comparison does not explicitly describe Zion as a bride. God's act of clothing Zion, of granting her "garments" of salvation and righteousness, is compared to a bridegroom and bride's preparation for their wedding. It appears, therefore, that this nuptial reference functions as part of the mapping CHANGING BEING IS CHANGING GARMENTS.

The use of nuptial imagery in 61:10 makes clear that different conceptual mappings can be employed through seemingly similar metaphorical expressions. Whereas the nuptial imagery in Isa 49:18 alludes to a conceptual mapping equating Zion with a bride, the nuptial imagery in 61:10 makes no such explicit connection.

Isaiah 62:4–5

In chap. 62, Isaiah again employs nuptial imagery as it weaves together images of Zion the city and Zion the woman:

> 4You shall no more be termed Forsaken, and your land shall no more be termed Desolate; but you shall be called My Delight Is in Her, and your land Married; for the LORD delights in you, and your land shall be married. 5For as a young

man marries a young woman, so shall your builder marry you and as the bridegroom rejoices over the bride, so shall your God rejoice over you. (62:4–5 NRSV)

1. STATUS IS A NAME; A CHANGE IN STATUS IS A CHANGE IN NAME

Isaiah 62:4 begins with the prophet's announcement that Zion's name will be changed. Addressing the city in the second person, the prophet informs Zion that she will no longer be called "Forsaken" and "Desolate," but "My Delight Is in Her" (Hephzibah) and "Married" (Beulah). The names that Zion currently bears, "Forsaken" and "Desolate," echo Zion's lament in 49:14: "The LORD has forsaken me. . . ." The one who is forsaken is named Forsaken (cf. 62:12). The names of Zion reflect her state of being. This suggests a conceptual mapping such as STATUS IS A NAME.

Now, according to the prophet, Zion will be assigned new names that indicate a radical change in status. The one who was forgotten will be married and cherished. Baruch Halpern explains, "Nomenclature establishes the place of the named, its right relationship to all about it. Naming . . . therefore signifies an abrupt change in status. The namer's power is the power to direct the (re-) creation toward its proper function."[65] Zion's name change implies, therefore, a change in her status: A CHANGE IN STATUS IS A CHANGE IN NAME.

2. GOD IS A BRIDEGROOM; ZION IS A BRIDE; THE RELATIONSHIP BETWEEN GOD AND ZION IS A MARRIAGE

Isaiah 62:5 attributes Zion's change in status, from one that is forsaken to one that is cherished (e.g., "My Delight Is in Her"), to God's intention to marry the city. The speaker, presumably God, draws an explicit analogy between his relationship with Zion and the relationship between a bridegroom and a bride.[66] In so doing the verse reflects three interrelated conceptual mappings: GOD IS A BRIDEGROOM, ZION IS A BRIDE, and, finally, THE RELATIONSHIP BETWEEN GOD AND ZION IS A MARRIAGE. The fact that Zion is not a woman and that this is not a literal marriage is made clear as the text describes God as Zion's builder. The target domain CITY comes into view, reminding the audience that the text's description of a woman who marries God is really a description of a city. Again we see the permeable boundaries between conceptual domains.

Even though a metaphorical mapping may be conventional, such as the A CITY IS A WOMAN mapping, it can still be the foundation for creative

---

[65] Baruch Halpern, "The New Names of Isaiah 62:4: Jeremiah's Reception in the Restoration and the Politics of 'Third Isaiah,'" *JBL* 117 (1998): 627.

[66] Ackerman, "Isaiah," 167.

thought. As we have seen, Ezekiel and Isaiah both employ this mapping in various ways in conjunction with images of weddings and brides. We have seen some of the many ways this mapping can be employed and some of the mappings that each author uses in specifically creating nuptial imagery. Most generally we see the elasticity of the A CITY IS A WOMAN mapping. This elasticity is related to the different ways in which authors highlight and expand on different aspects of the mapping as they depict the city's "wedding" or "marriage." Whether an author highlights the woman's social role or her embodied nature determines the overall use and function of the metaphor. Similarly, the ways in which a particular presentation links this central mapping to other conceptual mappings shape the meaning of the metaphor and the ways in which it functions.

Arguments about whether or not John actually had these prophetic traditions in mind when he composed Revelation and its nuptial images are problematic, especially since there are few direct linguistic similarities between Revelation's nuptial imagery and the prophetic depictions of Jerusalem as the wife of God. Instead, as we will see in chap. 5, it is the creative use of the conventional that makes Ezekiel and Isaiah precursors to John, the author of Revelation.

CHAPTER FOUR

Unveiling the Bride: Nuptial Traditions and Roman Social Discourse

While the Book of Revelation's nuptial imagery reflects the metaphorical framework employed in Jewish literary traditions that depict a community as a woman, this nuptial imagery also refers to cultural and social realities (i.e., marriage, brides, weddings, etc.) existing within the text's assumed cultural context. Written within and addressed to communities living in first-century Asia Minor,[1] a Roman province, Revelation's nuptial imagery reflects and responds to its surrounding cultural context. Since Revelation addresses the ways Christian communities relate themselves to the broader non-Christian culture, the text reflects aspects of this culture.[2] As we turn

[1] Revelation clearly identifies itself with Asia Minor (1:4), but the dating of the text is difficult. While traditionally assigned to sometime during the end of Domitian's reign (ca. 96–97 C.E.), the evidence for this dating is far from certain. Steven J. Friesen provides an instructive method for dating the text of Revelation and reading it in relation to its context. The text of Revelation itself is not specific on dating, and internal evidence suggests only a late-first-century, post–70 C.E., date. In light of this, Friesen proposes that scholars read Revelation against the broad backdrop of late-first-century Asia Minor instead of trying to force the text to fit a more specific period of time. In so doing, Friesen implies that Revelation scholars need to resist the temptation to align details in the text with specific historical personages and events. Like other texts, Revelation should be read in relation to other social discourses within the empire. Thus, Friesen reads the text in relation to Roman social discourses of the late first century (*Imperial Cults and the Apocalypse of John: Reading Revelation in the Ruins* [Oxford: Oxford University Press, 2001]). For details regarding the dating of Revelation, especially in relation to the question of whether the text functions as a response to actual or perceived persecution, see Adela Yarbro Collins, *Crisis and Catharsis: The Power of the Apocalypse* (Philadelphia: Westminster Press, 1984), 54–83; and Leonard L. Thompson, *The Book of Revelation: Apocalypse and Empire* (New York: Oxford University Press, 1990).

[2] In his examination of how wealth functions in Revelation, Robert M. Royalty similarly addresses the way Revelation draws on Jewish narrative or literary conventions while interacting with the Greco-Roman social world. He writes, "In this chapter, we turn to the ways in which the imagery and motifs of wealth and trade in Revelation would have been heard in the cities of Asia Minor around 95–100 C.E. . . . As we have seen, the language and characters of the Apocalypse originate in the narrative worlds of Jewish prophetic and apocalyptic literature. So what do demonic beasts and angelic guides have to do with philosophical treatises and polished speeches? The anti-Roman stance of the Apocalypse deepens this sense of dissonance between the narrative world of Revelation, with its prophetic and apocalyptic Jewish sources, and the social world of Greco-Roman culture. But Greek culture and Roman authority are major moral issues in the Apocalypse because this text came to life in a Greco-Roman

to our analysis of Revelation's nuptial imagery, we must initially address some of the ways brides and marriages were depicted in the social discourse of the first-century Roman milieu. This gives us some sense of the richness of the source domains pertaining to marriage (e.g., WEDDING, BRIDE) as we examine how John employs nuptial imagery metaphorically. This material also may contain a clue to the function of the nuptial imagery in Revelation.

Family and marriage played an important role in Roman social discourse. One aspect of this discourse involved depicting the imperial family as the ideal family, which was worthy of emulation. In light of this, one question we need to ask at the conclusion of our analysis is whether Revelation's use of nuptial imagery is a response or criticism of Roman social discourse.

Unveiling the Context of Revelation

The complexity of Revelation's social and cultural environment proves difficult to untangle, for during this time Greek-speaking and previously Hellenized Asia Minor was a province of the Roman Empire.[3] The Roman Empire is famous for its appropriation and glamorization of the ideals and traditions of the Greek East. Horace articulates this irony: "Captive Greece captured the victor and brought the arts to rustic Latium" (*Epodes* 2.1.156 [Zanker]).[4] It also appears, however, that the leaders of the Roman Empire actively sought to further Roman social and political influence throughout the Greek world, including the province of Asia Minor.[5] Leonard Thomp-

context." In fact, Royalty states, "Few of the Christians who heard the Apocalypse would have had the knowledge of the Hebrew scriptures that John had, whereas all would be conversant in the public aspects of Greco-Roman culture that organized social life in the cities of Asia Minor" (*The Streets of Heaven: The Ideology of Wealth in the Apocalypse of John* [Macon, Ga.: Mercer University Press, 1998], 81).

[3] For a classic discussion on the relationship between the Roman Empire and the Greek East, including Asia Minor, see G. W. Bowersock, *Augustus and the Greek World* (Oxford: Clarendon Press, 1965). Bowersock ends his monograph with the claim that Augustus encouraged "a union of Rome and the East which had begun under the Republic. The result was an extraordinary continuity from the second century B.C. to the third century A.D., and the first Princeps deserves no small share of the credit. That continuity underlies the Greek renaissance of the second century and helps to explain the growth and consolidation of the empire . . ." (*Augustus*, 149). While the Romans had a variety of connections (political, economic, and cultural) with Asia Minor as early as the second century B.C.E., Andrew Lintott notes that the empire began to formally establish control of the region in 133 B.C.E., when the last king of Pergamum died (*Imperium Romanum: Politics and Administration* [London: Routledge, 1993], 10).

[4] As quoted in Paul Zanker, *The Power of Images in the Age of Augustus*, trans. Alan Shapiro (Ann Arbor, Mich.: University of Michigan Press, 1988), 1.

[5] Riet Van Bremen characterizes Asia Minor as the functional "centre of the Greek world" during the Hellenistic and Roman periods, *The Limits of Participation: Women and Civic Life in the Hellenistic and Roman Periods* (Amsterdam: J. C. Gieben, 1996), 6. See also Mary T.

son notes, for instance, that while the Roman Empire did not seek to change the democratic structure of the Greek cities in Asia, the governing of the cities nonetheless was overseen by Roman officials.[6] Since there were definite benefits to being part of the empire, the cities of Asia Minor themselves embraced much that the empire had to offer. Not only did the empire offer the cities of Asia Minor financial aid after natural disasters, such as the earthquakes that hit Laodicea and Thyatira (Suetonius, *Tiberius* 8), for example, but inclusion in the empire brought about general economic recovery as well (Strabo, *Geography* 641, 578).[7]

In response to the empire's patronage, the cities in Asia Minor and many individuals in the upper classes sought to honor the empire and its rulers. This took many forms. For instance, reflecting a popular trend of dedicating public art work to Roman patrons, Plancia Magna, a noble woman and priestess in the imperial cult at Pergamum, dedicated an elaborate gate to the imperial family during the time of Hadrian (117–138 C.E.).[8] In addition, the cities of Asia Minor adopted the Roman imperial cult as a means of demonstrating their gratitude toward the empire.[9] Even though there existed no tradition of dedicating temples to living imperial figures in Rome itself, a number of such temples were erected throughout Asia, including the cities to which Revelation is addressed. Dio Cassius writes,

> At that time [ca. 29 B.C.E.] Caesar [Octavian] was attending to general matters, and he permitted the establishment of precincts to Rome and to (his) father Caesar—calling him the hero Julius—in Ephesos and in Nicea, for these were then the most distinguished cities in Asia and in Bithynia respectively. He ordered the Romans who had settled among them to honor these two. But he allowed the foreigners—whom he called Hellenes—to consecrate precincts to him, the Asians in Pergamon and the Bithynians in Nicomedia. Beginning there, this (practice) continued under other emperors, not only among the Hellenic nationalities but also among the others, in so far as they are subject to the Romans. For in the city (of Rome) and in the rest of Italy there is no one who dared to do such a thing, however worthy of renown. (*Roman History* 51.20.6–9 [Friesen, *Imperial*, 25–26])[10]

Boatwright, "The City Gate of Plancia Magna in Perge," in *Roman Art in Context: An Anthology*, ed. Eve D'Ambra (Upper Saddle River, N.J.: Prentice Hall, 1993), 189–207.

[6] Thompson, *The Book of Revelation,* 149.

[7] Bowersock, *Augustus*, 99.

[8] Van Bremen, *The Limits of Participation*, 104ff. The gate of Plancia Magna is particularly fascinating since it includes a number of statues representing members of the imperial family, especially its female members.

[9] Bowersock, *Augustus*, 112–21; Steven J. Friesen, *Twice Neokoros: Ephesus, Asia and the Cult of the Flavian Imperial Family* (Leiden: E. J. Brill, 1993); S. R. F. Price, *Rituals and Power: The Roman Imperial Cult in Asia Minor* (Cambridge: Cambridge University Press, 1984).

[10] Tacitus notes the presence of a temple dedicated to Roma in Smyrna, one of the cities mentioned in Revelation, as early as 195 B.C.E. (*Annals* 4.56).

Even though the cities, as cities, and the urban upper classes demonstrated their loyalty to the empire through public tributes and adopting the imperial cult, not all people in Asia Minor eagerly embraced Roman rule. In particular, it is quite possible that lower-class attitudes toward the empire in Asia Minor ranged from ambivalence to anger, in light of upper-class Roman elitism.[11] Thus, given the complexity of the Greco-Roman milieu of Asia Minor in which Revelation is situated and to which it responds, it is essential to gain some sense of the social discourse in which the text and its imagery participate.

The Social Discourse of Roman "Family Values"

Every social movement or group, including empires and even relatively small religious movements, operates with a discourse that embodies the rules, modes of being, and relationships of the movement or group and that defines the group.[12] Drawing on the insights of Edward Said's exploration of the relationship between narrative discourse and imperialism, Steven Friesen argues that like subsequent empires, the Roman Empire maintained and legitimated its exercise of power through an imperial discourse.[13] This discourse seeks to legitimate the power of the empire and communicates the ideals of the empire and its founding myths. The empire actually used a variety of means of presenting its discourse. In his noted work *The Power of Images in the Age of Augustus*, Paul Zanker demonstrates that Augustus initiated an unprecedented program of communicating the ideals of the empire and his program of social and religious renewal through imagistic means. This program included "not only 'works of art,' buildings, and poetic imagery, but also religious ritual, clothing, state ceremony, the emperor's conduct and forms of social intercourse. . . ."[14] In this way, the ideals of the Augustan reform were disseminated throughout the empire and to every strata of society. At the center of Rome's imperial discourse was its depiction of the beginnings of the Roman Empire, specifically the reign of Augustus, as the founding of a "new world order."[15] Part of Augustus's new world was a program of social renewal that highlighted the importance of the *domus* (the household) in maintaining Roman peace and power.[16] Not only was the imperial household understood as crucial to

---

[11] Bowersock, *Augustus*, 101.

[12] Edward W. Said, *Culture and Imperialism* (New York: Vintage Books, 1993).

[13] Friesen, *Imperial Cults*, 19.

[14] Zanker, *The Power of Images*, 3.

[15] Friesen, *Imperial Cults*, 123.

[16] The definitions of what constituted a *domus* and a *familia* are debated among scholars. The question of how these concepts were understood by Romans remains unanswered, which reflects the ambiguity inherent in the ancient sources. Some scholars, notably Richard P. Saller

Roman peace (e.g., Ovid, *Fasti* 1.709–22), but the importance of individual families in maintaining civil order and peace was emphasized. In *De officiis* (ca. 46–43 B.C.E.) Cicero describes the family, including parents and children, as the "nursery" of the state (*Off.* 1.54). Likewise, writing in the early third century C.E., Dio Cassius depicts Augustus praising married citizens with children as "helping to replenish the fatherland" so that "the Romans of later days will become a mighty multitude" (*Roman History* 56.2 [Cary, LCL]).

Legislation served as one of the ways that the empire sought to promote marriage, including the traditional gender roles associated with marriage, and to discourage adultery, as well as to encourage childbearing (e.g., Dio Cassius, *Roman History* 56.1–10; Plutarch, *Caesar* 15).[17] One character in Plutarch's *Amatorius* comments, "since [marriage is] necessary for producing children, there's no harm in legislators talking it up and singing its praises to the masses" (*Amat.* 750 [Minar, LCL]). The movement was couched in terms of returning the empire, which was described as being in decline, to the pristine state of the earlier republic. In the *Res Gestae Divi Augusti* (ca. 14 C.E.), an inscription inscribed on a temple in Ankara, Asia Minor, but found in other locations as well, Augustus is depicted as proclaiming, "By the new laws, carried with me as [sponsor,] many model traditions of our ancestors that were falling out of use in our [generation] *I restored* and [handed on] as *models* of many things to be imitated by posterity."[18] The "new laws" described in the inscription include the *Lex Julia de*

---

and Brent D. Shaw, suggest that the Roman conception of the family was similar to the contemporary notion of the "nuclear family" (mother-father-children); other scholars note that the Romans did not even possess a term describing such an idea. Addressing the problem of "constructing" the ancient family, Dale B. Martin points out that while *domus* describes those living in a physical house, including kin and slaves and possibly others, *familia* could also describe both kin and slaves ("The Construction of the Ancient Family: Methodological Considerations," *JRS* 86 [1996]: 40–60). See also Richard P. Saller and Brent D. Shaw, "Tombstones and Roman Family Relations in the Principate: Civilians, Soldiers, and Slaves," *JRS* 74 (1984): 124–56; and Beryl Rawson, "The Roman Family," in *The Family in Ancient Rome: New Perspectives*, ed. Beryl Rawson (Ithaca, N.Y.: Cornell University Press, 1986), 14.

[17] Suzanne Dixon, *The Roman Family* (Baltimore: Johns Hopkins University Press, 1992), 61–97; Judith Evans Grubbs, *Law and Family in Late Antiquity: The Emperor Constantine's Marriage Legislation* (Oxford: Oxford University Press, 1995), 103–12; Susan Treggiari, *Roman Marriage: Iusti Coniuges from the Time of Cicero to the Time of Ulpian* (Oxford: Clarendon Press, 1991), 60–80.

[18] *The "Res Gestae" of Augustus*, in *The Roman Empire: Augustus to Hadrian*, ed. and trans. Robert K. Sherk (Cambridge: Cambridge University Press, 1988), 8.5. This inscription recounting the works of Augustus is purported to be authored by Augustus himself, who wrote it prior to his death to be hung in his mausoleum. While the original inscription may have been on his tomb in Rome, fragments of the text have been discovered throughout the Mediterranean world, including an inscription in Ankara, which is the most complete. See also Suetonius, *Divus Augustus* 34; and Tacitus, *Annales* 3.25.

maritandis ordinibus (18 B.C.E.) and the *Lex Papia Poppaea* (9 C.E.).[19] Among other things, these laws made public crimes of adultery and love affairs between married people with different partners.[20] This is particularly interesting, since marriage and divorce were not legislated; rather, consent (*affectus maritalis*) between the parties involved created marriage and divorce.[21]

The Augustan discourse about the importance of marriage and the family was perpetuated not only through legislation aimed at citizens but, as suggested above, through forms of social discourse that reached most, if not all, sectors of the Roman Empire. The ideals of the Roman *domus* were communicated through monumental art, such as the *Ara Pacis* and the frieze at the *Forum Transitorium* (which was commissioned by Domitian)[22] in Rome and the relief, located in Libya, of Septimus Severus and his family (ca. 206 C.E.).[23] Likewise, coinage served as a means of communicating imperial views about the family and gender. Even though the Augustan legislation applied only to Roman citizens, all classes of people were exposed to the Roman social discourse about the ideal *domus*. As Beryl Rawson observes, the imagistic social propaganda of the Roman Empire was so pervasive that "people could not have been oblivious to it, and it must have influenced their perceptions."[24] The general acceptance of the empire's social discourse can be seen, in part, through funerary art and family monuments of the time, which clearly mimic imperial themes and assumptions.

It would be mistaken to assume that the social reform advocated by Augustus ended with his reign or that of the Julio Claudians; rather, sub-

[19] Full copies of these pieces of legislation are no longer extant. Treggiari notes that the differences between these two sets of legislation are not even completely clear. In fact, after 9 C.E. these two pieces of legislation are often referred to in tandem as the "Julian and Papian Law" (*Roman Marriage*, 60–80).

[20] Leo Ferrero Radista, "Augustus' Legislation Concerning Marriage, Procreation, Love Affairs and Adultery," *Aufstieg und Niedergang der römischen Welt* II.13 (Berlin: Walter de Gruyter, 1980), 307ff.

[21] Ulpian notes that it is similarly consent and not sexual relations that create a marriage: "*non enim coitus matrimonium facit, sed maritalis affectio* . . ." (*Digest* 24.1.32.13).

[22] Eve D'Ambra argues that the main frieze of the Forum Transitorium, which depicts the myth of Arachne, should be understood within the context of Domitian's policy of cultural renewal and moral reform. In part, the frieze functions to reify traditional ideals of feminine gender through images of spinning and weaving. In contrast to Arachne, who challenges the goddess Minerva, one section of the frieze depicts ideal women rushing to Minerva to learn the arts representing feminine virtue, spinning and weaving. Other extant sections of the frieze also depict and commend the traditional role of the Roman matron through the depictions of personified virtues and women weaving, which suggest that fulfillment of this role functions as "the cornerstone of society" (*Private Lives, Imperial Virtues: The Frieze of the Forum Transitorium in Rome* [Princeton: Princeton University Press, 1993]).

[23] An image of this relief can be found in Elaine Fantham et al., *Women in the Classical World: Image and Text* (New York: Oxford University Press, 1994), 359.

[24] Beryl Rawson, "From 'Daily Life' to 'Demography,'" in *Women in Antiquity: New Assessments*, ed. Richard Hawley and Barbara Levick (London: Routledge, 1995), 16.

sequent emperors, including the Flavians, embraced the tradition. Domitian, who reigned during the time in which Revelation is assumed to have been written, seems to have been particularly fervent in his acceptance of Augustan social ideals. Despite some polemical traditions that portray Domitian as a sex-crazed tyrant, evidence suggests that he embraced (at least politically) and promoted Augustan moral codes.[25] Martial comments in one of his infamous epigrams,

> It used to be a game to betray the sacred marriage torch and a game to castrate innocent males. You forbid both, Caesar, and come to the aid of future generations; for by your order their birth is made safe. Under your rule no man shall be either eunuch or adulterer. Formerly (alas for our morals!) even a eunuch was an adulterer. (6.2 [Ker, LCL])

Domitian's devotion to the goddess Minerva, who embodies marital characteristics and protects the domestic domain (even teaching young women the arts of spinning and weaving) similarly reflects his commitment to maintaining the traditional values of the *domus*.[26]

Another aspect of the Augustan reform that was perpetuated by subsequent rulers involved presenting the imperial family as *the* ideal family. This served a number of purposes, including establishing lines of succession, as well as perpetuating imperial ideals about the *domus*.[27] For instance, Suetonius recounts that the emperor Augustus bragged that he only wore cloth spun by the women of his family, rather than cloth that was purchased (Suetonius, *Divus Augustus* 73). Among other things, as we will discuss below, this suggested both the chastity and economy of the Augustan women. Ironically, propaganda concerning the imperial family often contradicted reality, as was the case with Augustus's own family. While Augustan imagery sought to depict the women of the *domus Augusti* as possessing piety and chastity,[28] Augustus's daughter Julia, the mother of his adopted sons, was eventually banished for her adultery (Dio Cassius, *Roman History* 55.10, 15–16; Suetonius, *Aug.* 65).[29]

---

[25] Much scholarly attention has been given to the portrayal of Domitian, primarily found in Suetonius's biography, as a philanderer and adulterer, as well as one who engaged in incest with his niece Julia. Interestingly, Suetonius does acknowledge that Domitian sought to correct "public morals" and enforced laws on adultery, in spite of committing adultery himself, (*Domitianus* 8). Drawing together the various sources, Brian Jones suggests that the depiction of Domitian's sexual misbehavior is likely standard vituperation. Jones's work is considered one of the standard scholarly works on the controversial emperor (*The Emperor Domitian* [London: Routledge, 1992], 39).

[26] D'Ambra, *Private Lives*, 11.

[27] Mark D. Fullerton, "The *Domus Augusti* in Imperial Iconography of 13–12 B.C.," *AJA* 89 (1985): 473–83.

[28] Fantham, *Women in the Classical World*, 295–96; Fullerton, "The *Domus Augusti*," 480ff.

[29] Radista, "Augustus's Legislation," 290–95. See also Susan Fischler, "Social Stereotypes

During the time of the Flavians, the trend of idealizing the imperial family and presenting them as a model for behavior continued. During the reign of Domitian, images of the emperor and his wife, Domitia Longina, emphasized their similarity and marital harmony (although Domitia was exiled for a short time for supposedly committing adultery).[30] In coinage from Asia Minor, Domitia is depicted as Venus, which suggests that she bears the same characteristics as the goddess, while elsewhere, including other coins, she was associated with Juno, who was hailed for her chastity.[31] Further, Domitia's role as mother, specifically as the mother of the divinized son of Domitian (the son died before Domitian became emperor), was emphasized on coins emblazoned with the legend MATER DIVI CAESARIS.[32] In imperial propaganda, Domitia embodied all of the essential characteristics of the ideal woman: concord with her mate, sexual attractiveness, chastity, and a maternal nature.

Wives, Brides, Marriages, and Weddings in the Greco-Roman Milieu[33]

The characteristics attributed to Domitia Longina reflect some of the ideals expected of women and wives during the time of the Roman Empire. In his *Roman History*, Dio depicts Augustus describing the attributes of an ideal wife, "For is there anything better than a wife who is chaste, domestic, a good house-keeper, a rearer of children; one to gladden you in health, to tend you in sickness: to be your partner in good fortune, to console you in misfortune; to restrain the mad passion of youth and to temper the unseasonable harshness of old age?" (*Roman History* 56.3.3 [Cary, LCL]). While Dio's accuracy in reporting Augustus's speech is questionable, since he wrote in the early third century C.E., he does capture the view of feminine gender that was communicated within Augustan reform and within subsequent reigns.

The initial characteristic mentioned in the speech attributed to Augustus is chastity, or sexual self-control (σωφροσύνη in Greek and *pudicitia* in

---

and Historical Analysis: The Case of the Imperial Women at Rome," in *Women in Ancient Societies: An Illusion of the Night*, ed. Léonie J. Archer, Susan Fischler, and Maria Wyke (Basingstoke: Macmillan, 1994), 115–33.

[30] Eric R. Varner, "Domitia Longina and the Politics of Portraiture," *AJA* 99 (1995): 192.

[31] Ibid., 200–202.

[32] Ibid., 188.

[33] The primary sources from this period, including texts and material culture, vary in their depictions of women and marriage; however, certain characterizations appear again and again. The works of feminist classicists develop a sense of how feminine gender was understood and constructed in the Greek and Roman contexts. See Gillian Clark, "Roman Women," *Greece and Rome* 28 (1981): 193; and Sarah B. Pomeroy, "The Study of Women in Antiquity: Past, Present, and Future," *AJP* 112 (1991): 263–68.

Latin), one of the most common virtues ascribed to women in the ancient world.[34] Writing about the same time as the author of Revelation (90–100 C.E.), Plutarch notes the importance of this characteristic in marriage, "Herodotus was wrong to say that a woman doffs her modesty when she doffs her clothes. The opposite is true: a good woman wears modesty in place of clothes, and the sign of great love is modesty towards each other" (*Advice* 139.10 [Russell]). According to Plutarch's estimation, modesty or chastity does not exclude the sexual aspect of marriage, but consists of an attitude of respect between husband and wife, such that the wife keeps her body only for her husband and the husband is careful to avoid coming home smelling of a lover (*Advice* 142.31, 143.44)!

The importance of a woman's chastity was underscored in Roman myth, as well as in law and other forms of discourse.[35] David Cohen observes that "The ideological significance of chastity in Roman consciousness is manifest in the patterns of crucial events in their invented early history."[36] Among other mythic traditions, Livy (first century C.E.) tells the story of Lucretia, whose chastity is tested by her husband, one of the first consuls of the Roman Republic, and his friends. Lucretia is proven chaste, as she was found working her wool late at night rather than engaging in illicit affairs. In spite of this or, perhaps, on account of this, one of her husband's companions, the king's son, eventually rapes her. Informing her husband and father about the rape, Lucretia laments the loss of her chastity: "what can be well with a woman when she has lost her honor [*pudicitia*]?" (Livy 1.58.7 [Foster, LCL]). She has lost her defining characteristic. Although Lucretia's husband and father reassure her that she is not guilty of any crime, they do suggest that she is the "author" (*auctorem*) of the crime. In other words, Lucretia bears some responsibility in the loss of her honor. Consequently, Lucretia takes her own life so that she might not set a negative example for future women (Livy 1.58.7–8). Furthermore, Livy suggests that outrage over Lucretia's death led to the expulsion of the ruling dynasty which in turn made way for the free Roman Republic. With this myth the story of Rome's foundation is closely linked to the preservation of female chastity.[37]

---

[34] Sarah B. Pomeroy, "Reflections on Plutarch, *Advice to the Bride and Groom*: Something Old, Something New, Something Borrowed," in *Plutarch's Advice to the Bride and Groom and A Consolation to His Wife: English Translations, Commentary, Interpretive Essays, and Bibliography*, ed. Sarah B. Pomeroy (New York: Oxford University Press, 1999), 48.

[35] David Cohen, "The Augustan Law on Adultery: The Social and Cultural Context," in *The Family in Italy from Antiquity to the Present*, ed. David I. Kertzer and Richard P. Saller (New Haven: Yale University Press, 1991), 109–27; and Hans-Friedrich Mueller, "*Vita, Pudicitia, Libertus*: Juno, Gender, and Religious Politics in Valerius Maximus," *Transactions of the American Philological Association* 128 (1998): 221–63.

[36] Cohen, "The Augustan Law on Adultery," 114.

[37] Mueller, "*Vita, Pudicitia, Libertus*," 228. The story of Lucretia is also recounted by Ovid, *Fasti* 2.6.

Conversely, a major component of Roman social discourse entailed lamenting female licentiousness as a sign of the decline of the empire.[38] Juvenal's notorious sixth satire provides an extreme example of this tendency, depicting modern Roman women as sex-starved and corrupt, lacking *pudicitia*.[39] Commonly labeled "The Ways of Women," the sixth satire begins by describing, perhaps ironically, an idyllic past in which wives were faithful to their husbands and they "gave suck to lusty babes." Juvenal soon moves on to describe how "Chastity" has fled to heaven and women have taken to adultery. In one particularly graphic passage, Juvenal describes two women, Maura and Tullia, urinating upon the ancient altar of Chastity or Pudicitia and then "riding" one another (6.305–27). Likewise, Horace, a proponent of the Augustan reforms, comments in a poem written ca. 32 B.C.E., "Teeming with sin, our times have sullied first the marriage bed, our offspring, and our homes [*domos*]. . . . Our parents' age, worse than our grandsires', has brought forth us less worthy and destined soon to yield an offspring still more wicked" (Horace, *Carmina* 3.6 [Bennet, LCL]). In both Juvenal and Horace unrestrained feminine sexuality or lack of sexual self-control serves as a metonym for the overall decline of the empire. It is important to remember, however, that this topic functions within moral argumentation and is not likely an accurate description of ancient reality.

In the same ode quoted above, Horace asserts that "The maiden (*virgo*) . . . trains herself in coquetry e'en now and plans unholy amours, with passion unrestrained" (Horace, *Carm.* 3.6 [Bennet, LCL]). Even before marriage, Horace suggests, the virgin trains in sexual promiscuity and infidelity. Horace's concern, justified by reality or not, reflects the Greco-Roman concern with a bride's virginity upon marriage.[40] It seems that this concern with a bride's virginity compelled the Romans in particular to marry girls off at around fourteen years of age (even though the legal age for Roman marriage was twelve).[41] A bride's chastity, as well as that of a wife, can be described in the metaphorical terms of moral purity or cleanliness. In this vein, Plutarch suggests that the presence of fire and water at the Roman marriage ceremony likely symbolizes that a "married woman must remain pure [καθαράν] and clean [ἁγνήν]" (Plutarch, *Quaestiones romanae et graecae* 1).

Chastity and modesty, as well as virginity before marriage, prove to be some of the most prevalent themes in Greco-Roman discussions of feminine gender.[42] These characteristics were understood to be valuable at the

[38] Suzanne Dixon, *Reading Roman Women: Sources, Genres and Real Life* (London: Duckworth, 2001), 56–65.

[39] Susanna H. Braund, "Juvenal–Misogynist or Misogamist?" *JRS* 82 (1992): 71–86.

[40] E.g., Catullus 62.20–26; see also Treggiari, *Roman Marriage*, 105–7.

[41] Clark, "Roman Women," 200.

[42] The Latin term *pudicitia* refers to sexual control in general, including a bride's virginity and a woman's chastity within marriage (Braund, "Juvenal," 74).

level of the individual family or household and as important civic ideals. In *The Limits of Participation: Women and Civic Life in the Greek East in the Hellenistic and Roman Periods*, Riet Van Bremen maintains that the seemingly domestic quality of "feminine modesty" (σωφροσύνη) was understood to have civic value. Upper-class women were especially expected to possess this value not only in relation to their families but also in relation to their cities.[43] Prominent women would be lauded publicly for possessing feminine ideals, such as chastity or modesty. Van Bremen notes that Apollonis, from the city of Kyzikos in Asia Minor, was honored with numerous statues throughout the city. One such statue was placed in the civic office where couples registered their marriages. Its inscription read, "The people, and the Romans who trade in the city, [honour] Apollonis, daughter of Prokles, because of the *aret* (virtue) of her husband and parents, and because of her own *sophrosyn* (feminine modesty)."[44] Similar inscriptions were on other statutes, but the location of this particular statue explicitly suggests that Apollonis served as a model for other women. Like imperial women, prominent women throughout the empire served as models of feminine virtues, including modesty.

As noted above, σώφρων can be translated as "self-control" or "moderation." Ancient authors did not understand this only in terms of sexual self-control when describing the feminine gender; rather, the value of moderation should be evident in all aspects of a woman's life. Moderation serves as an important characteristic in women, partly because of the feminine role as keeper of the *domus*, which demands economic moderation.[45] As Dio describes, a good wife is "domestic, a good house-keeper" (Dio Cassius 56.3.3). In the Greco-Roman context, wool working or spinning (*lanificium*) was the paradigmatic domestic responsibility of women. Clark notes, "By the first century B.C. there were ready-made fabrics for those who could afford them . . . but *lanificium* was part of traditional devotion to the home and was still, for most women, an essential part of household economy."[46] Wool working metonymically represented all of a woman's domestic skill and devotion. For example, a certain Claudia is said to have "kept house, made wool," and a certain Amymone was "very good and very beautiful, a wool-maker, pious, righteous, thrifty, chaste, staying at home."[47] Likewise,

[43] Van Bremen describes this in terms of "the domestication of public life." As the Roman period progressed, not only were members of the ruling elite understood as *the* moral exemplars of a city, but they also functioned in a paternalistic relationship to fellow citizens, serving as the "mothers" and "fathers" of the city (*The Limits of Participation*, 165–66).

[44] As quoted in Van Bremen, *The Limits of Participation*, 3.

[45] In the first-century C.E. essays "That Women Too Should Study Philosophy" and "Should Daughters Receive the Same Education as Sons?" Musonius Rufus pinpoints household management as the most important job of a wife (Cora E. Lutz, trans., "Musonius Rufus: the Roman Socrates," *Yale Classical Studies* 10 [1947]: 3–147).

[46] Clark, "Roman Women," 198; see Columella, *De re rustica* 12.preface.

[47] Translated from the *CIL* by Treggiari, *Roman Marriage*, 243.

many funerary monuments depict women with wool-working implements, such as a ball of yarn or with baskets for wool.[48] Wool working and cloth production, including spinning and weaving, were significant markers of idealized feminine gender.[49] A "good wife" produced the clothing for those within her home, including her own garments. This ideal functioned as part of the imperial ideological discourse about the family. As mentioned above, the emperor Augustus reportedly bragged that he only wore clothing spun by the women of his family (Suetonius, *Aug.* 73). Again, the imperial family served as a model of the ideal family to be emulated by other Romans.

Demonstrating the polyvalence of metaphorical language, spinning and weaving also served as a metaphor for a woman's moral behavior.[50] Returning to the story of Lucretia, we see that the text asserts her chastity by depicting her at home spinning. A woman who works wool remains within the *domus* or home and is not out and about looking for sexual adventures. A funeral monument from Smyrna visually represents the connection between wool working and staying within the home. The monument depicts an interior, through columns and window, which suggests the enclosed home. Inside the home, a seated woman receives a spindle from a servant.[51]

Besides possessing self-control and domestic skills, the ideal wife, according to Dio's *Augustus,* rears children. In fact, the Augustan legislation on marriage mentioned above rewarded women for fulfilling this ideal[52] (although these efforts were not necessarily successful in encouraging marriage and childbearing) (Tacitus, *Annals* 3.25). A variety of sources assert that procreation is one of the primary reasons for marriage. For instance, a second-century dowry document located in Egypt, describes the marriage between two Roman citizens as complying "with the Julian law concerning marriage which was passed for the purpose of procreating children."[53] Like other ideal characteristics, the fecundity of the imperial women was asserted.

---

[48] E.g., Dixon, *Reading Roman Women,* plate 15; Eve D'Ambra, "The Cult of Virtues and the Funerary Relief of Ulpia Epigone," *Roman Art in Context: An Anthology*, ed. Eve D'Ambra (Upper Saddle River, N.J.: Prentice Hall, 1993), 109.

[49] For instance, on a tombstone located in Phrygia, symbols of feminine gender, including wool-working tools, as well as a mirror and shoes, are grouped together–in contrast to symbols of masculine gender. See Fantham, *Women in the Classical World*, 371.

[50] D'Ambra, "Cult of Virtues," 109–10.

[51] An image of this monument is included in Fantham, *Women in the Classical World*, 158.

[52] In Roman law, women required guardianship by a male. Free-born women could escape guardianship by bearing three children, while freed women could receive the same privilege by bearing four children. Bearing children also provided women with privileges when it came to inheriting from their husbands (Treggiari, *Roman Marriage*, 69–73).

[53] Reprinted by Jane Rowlandson, ed., *Women and Society in Greek and Roman Egypt: A Sourcebook* (Cambridge: Cambridge University Press, 1998), 182. See also *Digest* 24.3.1 and Catullus 61.205.

Reminding us that literary depictions of gender do not always represent the complexities of reality is the eulogy for Turia, written on her tombstone sometime between 12 and 8 B.C.E. In her eulogy, Turia's husband describes how they longed for a child, although they never had one. Reflecting the societal assumption that a male should have a male heir, Turia offered to divorce her husband so that he could bear a child with another woman: "Disconsolate to see me without children you wished to put an end to my chagrin by proposing to me a divorce, offering to yield the place to another spouse more fertile. . . ."[54]

The final characteristics that Dio's *Augustus* ascribes to an ideal wife reflect the Greco-Roman belief that marriage functioned as partnership, albeit unequal, characterized by harmony and concord. A wife, Dio writes, is "to gladden you in health, to tend you in sickness; to be your partner in good fortune, to console you in misfortune; to restrain the mad passion of youth and to temper the unseasonable harshness of old age. . . ." The assumption that marriage is a partnership between eligible parties[55] underlies Roman legal definitions of marriage. In the *Digest*, Modestinus asserts that "Marriage is the *coniunctio*, the joining together of a man and woman and the sharing of their entire life, the joint participation in rights human and divine."[56] The fact that Roman marriages were predicated on the mutual assent of the parties involved, which was described as *affectio maritalis* (a marital attitude), and not upon a legal contract, likewise reflected the assumption that marriage was a partnership.[57] A marriage ended only when this mutual consent dissolves.

The underlying conviction that marriage was ideally a partnership seems to have been widely assumed. Epitaphs throughout the empire from a wide range of social classes laud the values of partnership and marital harmony.[58] One tomb reads, "we lived harmonious and with equal character,"[59] while another describes the ideal of harmony indirectly by praising

[54] As quoted in Eva Cantarella, "Marriage and Sexuality in Republican Rome: A Roman Conjugal Love Story," in *The Sleep of Reason: Erotic Experience and Sexual Ethics in Ancient Greece and Rome*, ed. Martha C. Nussbaum and Julia Sihvola (Chicago: University of Chicago Press, 2002), 277.

[55] As Treggiari points out, Roman marriage could occur legally only between eligible parties. Basically the rule was, as described in *Tituli Ulpiani* 5.3–5, "Roman citizens have *conubium* [the capacity to marry] with Roman citizens, but with Latins and foreigners only if the privilege was granted. There is no *conubium* with slaves" (as quoted in Treggiari, *Roman Marriage*, 43).

[56] *Digest* 23.2.1, as quoted in Jane Gardner, *Women in Roman Law and Society* (London: Croom Helm, 1986), 47.

[57] Along these lines, in *Digest* 24.1.32.13 Ulpian notes that it is the *affectio maritalis* and not sexual relations that constitute a marriage: "*non enim coitus matrimonium facit, sed maritalis affectio*. . . ." See also Quintillian, *Institutio* 5.11.32; and Treggiari *Roman Marriage*, 54–57.

[58] Treggiari, *Roman Marriage*, 249–53; Suzanne Dixon, "The Sentimental Ideal of the Roman Family," in *Marriage, Divorce, and Children in Ancient Rome*, ed. Beryl Rawson (Oxford: Clarendon Press, 1991), 101–9.

[59] Translated from the *CIL* by Treggiari, *Roman Marriage*, 245.

a wife who was married to her husband thirty years without a quarrel![60] The assumption that husbands and wives were partners in creating and maintaining the *domus* could be implied in an epitaph, such as this husband's words: "Everything we have won by your hard work."[61] In addition, whether reflecting reality or not, many epitaphs suggest that mutual love and affection accompanied the marriage partnership. Thus, a silversmith from Citra claims, "Laughter and luxury I always delighted in, in the company of my dear friends, but such a life after the death of my chaste lady Valeria I did not find; while I could I had an enjoyable life with my holy wife."[62]

The almost ubiquitous image of a couple grasping hands (*dextrarum iunctio*), depicted on funerary monuments throughout the empire, points to the popularity of the concept of marital harmony. While the handshake motif has a long history in Greco-Roman art and conveys a number of concepts, it generally communicates agreement and harmony between those involved. The motif appears in political contexts, depicting the harmony between two figures, such as Domitian and his son Titus.[63] In the context of funerary monuments established by nonimperial families, the handclasp seemingly indicates the harmonious relationship between a wife and husband. While some scholars suggest that the gesture signifies an actual marriage ceremony, which was thought to include a handclasp between the bride and groom, others argue that it could "be seen as a representation of the moment of parting on the death of one partner, and an allusion to the continued fidelity of the couple to one another after death."[64] Whether the handclasp alludes to the actual marriage ceremony or not, this gesture visually and metonymically communicates the Greco-Roman values of partnership (*societas*/κοινωνία) and harmony/agreement (*concordia*/ὁμονοία). In certain instances, specifically on coinage representing imperial couples, the

[60] Translated from the *CIL* by Natalie Kampen in Fantham, *Women in the Classical World*, 369–70.

[61] *CIL* 6.9693, as translated by Treggiari, *Roman Marriage*, 244.

[62] *CIL* 8.7156, as translated by Treggiari, *Roman Marriage*, 246.

[63] The handshake motif appears in the context of political relationships, as well as personal relationships. Louis Reekmans notes, for instance, that a coin from 80 or 81 C.E. depicts Domitian and Titus clasping hands as an indication of their concord ("La 'dextrarum iunctio' dans l'iconographie romaine et paléochrétienne," *Bulletin de l'Institut historique Belge à Rome* 31 [1958]: 33). See also Glenys Davies, "The Significance of the Handshake Motif in Classical Funerary Art," *AJA* 89 (1985): 627–40

[64] Davies, "The Significance of the Handshake Motif," 632. Interestingly, the handshake motif occurs between some same-sex couples, who are not necessarily political figures. While Davies argues that this means the handclasp is not indicative of a marriage-type of relationship, given the assumption that marriage is only between male and female individuals, a few scholars interpret this to mean that some ancient same-sex couples lived as family units. See Bernadette J. Brooten, *Love Between Women: Early Christian Responses to Female Homoeroticism* (Chicago: University of Chicago Press, 1996), 59–60.

handclasp between a couple is accompanied by a legend or personification referring to *concordia*.[65]

Ideally, the partnership bonds created through marriage survived even death, as suggested in one particular funerary altar relief depicting a couple grasping hands, while the husband lay on his funeral deathbed. Even though Roman law encouraged remarriage after the death of a partner, the popular view of marriage was that the relationship between husband and wife lasted *in perpetuum* (in eternity).[66] Thus, Plutarch describes marriage as a "life-long partnership" (ἐπι βίου κοινωνίᾳ). As such, Plutarch argues, a marriage should actually be like a living organism, which is composed of parts that actually *live* together (*Advice* 34). In a marriage, people work together for a common purpose, which during this time includes maintenance of the *domus*.

Moreover, harmony in marriage involved the woman's appropriation of her husband's social status and rank. Diogenes Laertius, writing in the third century C.E., illustrates this ideal in his description of the female philosopher Hipparchia, who fell in love with and married the notorious Cynic philosopher Crates. Despite the pleas of her parents and the warnings issued by Crates himself, Hipparchia adopts the unconventional lifestyle of her mate, including his itinerant ways and his style of clothing (Diogenes Laertius, *Lives of the Philosophers* 6.2–3). Plutarch offers a telling metaphor, suggesting that a wife is quite like a mirror that reflects the true likeness of her husband, even his character (*Advice* 14).

Weddings in the Greco-Roman Milieu

Weddings within Revelation's Greco-Roman surroundings reflected and reinforced the values and characteristics associated with marriage and feminine gender roles within marriage discussed above. Even though there apparently could be and were variations in how individuals conducted wedding ceremonies, depictions of weddings from the Greco-Roman milieu reveal some traditional assumptions about wedding procedures.[67]

The numerous depictions of weddings in funerary and other monumental art point to the cultural importance of this event within this context.[68] Natalie Boymel Kampen suggests that the tradition of depicting weddings, including the *dextrarum iunctio*, on tombs functions as a way of

---

[65] Davies, "The Significance of the Handshake Motif," 638.

[66] Diana E. E. Kleiner, *Roman Imperial Funerary Altars with Portraits* (Rome: Bretschneider, 1987), 53; Treggiari, *Roman Marriage*, 260.

[67] Treggiari, *Roman Marriage*, 161.

[68] Dixon, *Reading Roman Women*, 65; and Susan Wood, "Alcestis on Roman Sarcophagi," *AJA* 82 (1978): 504.

indicating metonymically the deceased's possession of *concordia*.[69] By depicting the wedding of the deceased on a tomb, a family asserted the deceased's possession of important social virtues.

As an event, the wedding was a significant event, if not *the* significant event, in marking feminine identity and role As we will see, in the Greco-Roman milieu the role of "bride" (*nova nupta*, νύμφη) functioned as a transitional role, marking a female's shift in social identity from virgin to matron.[70] As such, the wedding incorporated a number of elements that represented the girl's readiness to take on the role of a wife in maintaining the *domus*.

The female's transition from virgin to matron was suggested by the main element of the wedding—the procession. The procession was literally "door to door," beginning at the home of the bride, her father's home, and ending at her new home, that of the bridegroom (Catullus 61.30). As Plutarch indicates in his *Roman Questions,* the wedding procession involves the bride *leaving* her home and *entering*, by being carried over the threshold, into a new home (*Quaestiones romanae et graecae* 29–30). Assuming the same direction of the wedding procession (bride's home toward the bridegroom's home), Catullus describes the bride's grief as she leaves her mother's home, "her mother's bosom," and "weeps that she must go" (Catullus 61.60, 80 [Cornish, LCL]).[71] Notably, it is the bride who made the procession to a new home, whether by wagon or by foot, and not the bridegroom, which implies that the wedding marked the woman's transition from one place to another. As her entrance into a new home demanded that the bride take on a new social role, the wedding procession can be understood as visually representing her transition into this new social identity. The wedding procession is typically described as *ducere uxorem* (lit., "to lead a wife"), which seems to suggest the groom's active role in leading his bride through this transition. In spite of this, Pomponius indicates that this event can take place even without the physical presence of the bridegroom:

> A woman can, it is agreed, marry a man who is absent either by means of a letter from him or by means of a messenger, *if she is led to his house*. But a woman who is absent cannot be married by a husband either through a letter or by a messenger from her. For *deductio* is necessary to the house of the husband, not

[69] Natalie Boymel Kampen, "Biographical Narration and Roman Funerary Art," *AJA* 85 (1981): 52.

[70] The importance of this event in the social understanding of feminine gender is evident when Pliny, writing around 100 C.E., offers a heartfelt lament at the death of a young girl who died before her wedding. (Pliny, *Letters* 5.16.6).

[71] See also Catullus 62.20–6.

the wife, for the former is the domicile of the marriage. (Pomponius, as cited in Ulpian, *Dig.* 23.2.5 [Treggiari 167])

The wedding clearly signals the woman's transition, not the groom's, although *ducere* ("to lead") implies that the bride is a passive participant in this event.

During the wedding procession, the bride or her attendants carried tools associated with wool working and weaving, such as spindles and distaffs. Popular for centuries, images of this tradition adorn classical Greek vases depicting weddings. The bride and her representative carried the symbols of a good wife, again suggesting that the wedding involves the female's adoption of the identity of a loyal and industrious matron. As Plutarch notes, the spindle was a token of a woman's "industry" (*Quaest. rom.* 30). Thus, in making the transition from one role to another, the bride adopted the symbols of her *new* role.

Another tradition frequently evident in ancient descriptions of weddings, including literary and artistic depictions, was the presence of torches carried by attendants. Plutarch wonders about this in his *Roman Questions,* asking whether the presence of torches reflects the symbolic connection between light and birth (*Quaest. rom.* 2).[72] Further, in Roman weddings there was typically fire and water present, possibly suggesting essential elements in the home, although Plutarch suggests they represent the bride's purity (*Quaest. rom.* 1).[73] Finally, another prominent theme, especially in the poems of Catullus, is that of the bridal bed, located in the home of the bridegroom. For Catullus, the physical consummation of the marriage appears to be the culmination of the wedding: "See how your husband within, reclining on a purple couch, is all eagerness for you . . . ," and "Now you may come, bridegroom; your wife is in the bride-chamber, shining with flowery face, like a white daisy or yellow poppy."[74]

Banquets appear to have been an important element of the wedding event, although it is not completely clear whether they took place before or after the wedding procession.[75] A number of wedding invitations found at Oxyrhynchos reflect a stylized form that closely links dining and the wedding. One third-century C.E. invitation reads, "Thermouthis invites you to dine at the marriage of her daughter in her home tomorrow, which is the

[72] See also Catullus 61.80.

[73] See also Ovid, *Fasti* 4.791–92; Treggiari, *Roman Marriage*, 168.

[74] Catullus 61.165, 185. See also Augustine, *Civ. Dei* 6.9.3, 7.24.2; Plutarch, *Quaestiones romanae et graecae* 65; Tacitus, *Annals* 15.37.9.

[75] Catullus 62.1–6 describes a banquet before the wedding procession. See, however, Treggiari, who notes that a dinner took place the day after the wedding (*Roman Marriage*, 169).

18th. . . ."[76] While these celebratory dinners naturally varied in extravagance according to the economic standing of those hosting, usually the bride's family, they were clearly much more special than typical meals.[77] Accepting invitations to the wedding, including the banquet, was apparently understood to be a duty (*officium*), indicating the social importance of this event (e.g., Suetonius, *Divus Claudius* 26.3; *Nero* 28.1).[78]

Adornment and the Bride

Adornment proves a popular topos in Greco-Roman depictions of feminine gender. Maria Wyke emphasizes the ambivalent nature of these depictions in her investigation of the rhetoric of adornment.[79] On one hand, a woman's external appearance can contribute positively to the public status of her husband.[80] By wearing the *stola* (a full-length garment worn over a tunic) or *palla* (a mantle with which one could cover the head), for instance, a first-century married woman (*matrona*) communicated her modesty, which reflected positively on her husband and family.[81] On the other hand, Wyke notes, the assumption that women were preoccupied with their outward appearances proved for many Greco-Roman writers that women were generally petty and inferior to men.[82] In this vein, Seneca praises his mother, while implying the ostentatious tendency of modern women:

> Unchastity, the greatest evil of our time, has never classed you with the great majority of women; jewels have not moved you, nor pearls; to your eyes the glitter of riches has not seemed the greatest boon of the human race; you, who were soundly trained in an old-fashioned and strict household, have not been perverted by the imitation of worse women that leads even the virtuous into pitfalls . . . never have you, in the manner of other women whose only recommendation lies in their beauty, tried to conceal your pregnancy as if an

---

[76] *P.Oxy.* XII 1579, as quoted in Jane Rowlandson, ed., *Women and Society in Greek and Roman Egypt: A Sourcebook* (Cambridge: Cambridge University Press, 1998), 320.

[77] Catullus, for instance, describes the "rich tables" of the wedding banquet (62.1–5); see Treggiari, *Roman Marriage*,162.

[78] Treggiari, *Roman Marriage,* 162.

[79] Maria Wyke, "Woman in the Mirror: The Rhetoric of Adornment in the Roman World," in *Women in Ancient Societies*, ed. Archer et al., 134–51.

[80] Wyke, "Woman in the Mirror,"142.

[81] A. T. Croom, *Roman Clothing and Fashion* (Charleston, S.C.: Tempus, 2000), 73–88; Judith Lynn Sebesta, "Symbolism in the Costume of the Roman Woman," in *The World of Roman Costume*, ed. Judith Lynn Sebesta and Larissa Bonfante (Madison, Wis.: University of Wisconsin, 1994), 48–49; and "Women's Costume and Feminine Civic Morality in Augustan Rome," in *Gender and Body in the Ancient Mediterranean*, ed. Maria Wyke (Malden, Mass.: Blackwell, 1998), 113.

[82] Wyke, "Woman in the Mirror," 139.

> unseemly burden, nor have you ever crushed the hope of children that were being nurtured in your body; you have not defiled your face with paints and cosmetics; never have you fancied the kind of dress that exposed no greater nakedness by being removed. (Seneca, *Consolation to his Mother* [Gummere])

Alongside unchastity and abortion for the sake of vanity, Seneca condemns concern with adornment. Not simply the topic of moralists like Seneca, in Roman comedy women's concern over appearance "helps define the female gender as time-wasting, frivolous, unconcerned with true civic life, and as an inherently sexual being, since female self-construction is read as part of a precise seductive strategy to appeal to men."[83] The belief that women were absorbed with their outward appearance, rather than their inward nature, was often visually depicted through images of a woman gazing into a mirror. An example of this is on a grave stele located in Trier's *Landesmuseum*, which depicts a seated woman gazing into a mirror while she is attended by servants ready to assist her beauty regimen.

The image of a woman's adornment played an important role in Greco-Roman representations of weddings. The "Projecta Casket," now in the British Museum, provides one example. Dated to the fourth century C.E., the small silver casket bears on its top an image of a couple and an inscription with the couple's name (Secundus and Projecta), which suggests that it was a wedding gift.[84] Two sides of the small box bear illustrations of the bride's wedding preparations: On one side the bride is led to a public bath house by attendants, while on the other side she sits as she pins her hair while looking into a mirror held by an attendant. This second scene mimics another illustration of the casket in which the goddess Venus, semi-naked, pins her hair as she holds a mirror. Wyke argues that the "mirror" images of the bride and Venus imply the bride's erotic possibilities. Most of all, the depiction of the bride's adornment, as well as other depictions of women's adornment, points to the crafted or constructed nature of female appearance in antiquity.[85] The fact that the woman's appearance was constructed primarily for the benefit of the men around her is made clear in book 3 of Ovid's *Ars Amatoria*, which is addressed to women. In this work, Ovid instructs women on how to alter their appearance to please their male love interests.[86]

---

[83] Ibid., 136.

[84] Electronic images of the "Projecta Casket" and a full description of its details can be found online at www.thebritishmuseum.ac.uk. A print image of this casket can be found accompanying Wyke's article, "Woman in the Mirror," plate 3.

[85] Wyke, "Woman in the Mirror," 144.

[86] Molly Myerowitz, "The Domestication of Desire: Ovid's *Parva Tabella* and the Theater of Love," in *Pornography and Representation in Greece and Rome*, ed. Amy Richlin (New York: Oxford University Press, 1992), 135–36.

The meaning-laden nature of feminine dress and adornment is seen particularly in the bride's costume, which includes a number of pieces that bear symbolic meaning. The bride's costume exemplifies her transitional nature, since in the Greco-Roman milieu outward appearance indicates social role and identity.[87] The bride's appearance was arranged prior to the procession with the assistance of other women in her family. Just prior to her wedding, the bride changed from a child's tunic, worn by both girls and boys, to the tunic worn exclusively by matrons.[88] The bride changed out of the androgynous garment of the child into a garment specifically associated with feminine gender, which suggests that feminine gender was something appropriated or adopted during the wedding. Moreover, the bride-to-be wove her garment, the *tunica recta*, herself, indicating her preparedness for adopting her new role, which included *lanificium* (Xenophon, *Oeconomicus* 5–6).

The bridal garment included a number of pieces that suggest the ideal characteristics of the bride's new role as wife. The bride's tunic was tied with a belt made of pure wool (*cingulum*), suggesting both her matronly duties of spinning and weaving as well as her sexual purity. In addition, the belt was knotted with a Herculean knot, known for its difficulty to undo, indicating that the bride's sexuality was accessible only to her husband. This reflects a metaphorical connection between social role and garments, because part of a matron's role was to remain sexually faithful to her husband as a way of producing legitimate heirs.

The bridal costume further communicated the new wife's role as sexual partner and future mother through the veil or *flammeum* (Catullus 61.10).[89] That a wedding could be described simply as *mulier nubit,* which refers literally to the veiling of a woman, reflects the importance of this piece of the bride's costume.[90] In fact, the veil symbolically suggests a number of things about the bride and feminine gender. Covering the hair, which was also bound in a hairnet created by the bride, communicates that the bride is chaste or modest. Bound and covered hair reflects a sense of control over one's sexuality, in contrast to the unkempt hair of one who is supposedly promiscuous.[91] The lifting of this veil (ἀνακαλύπτω) served as the culmination of the wedding procession, when the bride arrived at her hus-

---

[87] Sebesta, "Women's Costume," 105–17.

[88] Treggiari, *Roman Marriage*, 163.

[89] Laetitia La Follette, "The Costume of the Roman Bride," *The World of Roman Costume*, ed. Sebesta and Bonfante, 54ff.

[90] Wood, "Alcestis on Roman Sarcophagi," 506.

[91] Sebesta,"Women's Costume," 110–11; see also La Follette, "The Costume of the Roman Bride," 56. For an association between unkempt hair and unchastity, see the description of Messalina in Tacitus, *Annals* 11.31.4, in Sandra R. Joshel, "Female Desire and the Discourse of Empire: Tacitus's Messalina," in *Roman Sexualities*, ed. Judith P. Hallett and Marilyn B. Skinner (Princeton: Princeton University Press, 1997), 243.

band's home. The bride's sexuality or her chastity is "revealed" to her husband, suggesting that a woman's sexuality is an object intended only for her husband.[92]

Discourse about the family and home played an important role within the social world of the Book of Revelation. A dominant voice was that of the state, which sought to further Augustan social ideals throughout the empire. Through a variety of means, including legislation and state-sponsored imagery, the state emphasized the importance of marriage and procreation, encouraging people to support the empire through their domestic lives. Marrying and raising a family was part of one's civic duty. In making these claims, imperial discourse asserted the ideal nature of the imperial family, setting the imperial family up to be emulated.

Within this milieu, weddings played an important social role. The wedding event functioned as a tool for constructing feminine gender to meet the social ideals set out by the empire. The wedding itself contains a number of elements that reinforce assumptions about the ideal feminine role and the importance of bearing children. In particular, the wedding served as the defining event in constructing ideal feminine gender. It is at the wedding that a girl made the important transition into being a woman and a wife. Descriptions of weddings within the Greco-Roman context suggested that it was as a bride that the female, donning the *tunica recta* and the *flammeum*, appropriated the roles and attributes of the Greco-Roman ideal woman.

As we turn to Revelation's nuptial imagery in the next chapter, we must inquire as to how this understanding of marriage and the wedding event might relate to John's depiction of the bride of the Lamb. What significance does Revelation's depiction of the Lamb's wedding have in a context where depictions of marriage and weddings are almost ubiquitous? What sort of function does Revelation's bridal imagery have in a context where being a bride marks an important social transition?

---

[92] Giulia Sissa, *Greek Virginity*, trans. Arthur Goldhammer (Cambridge, Mass.: Harvard University Press, 1990); Treggiari, *Roman Marriage* 168–69.

CHAPTER FIVE

"Alleluia . . . the wedding of the Lamb has come": Reading Revelation's Nuptial Imagery

Following our discussion of the depiction of brides and marriage in Roman social discourse, we turn to the text of Revelation itself. In our analysis we explore the specific ways in which Revelation's nuptial imagery is constructed. Following the procedure articulated in chap. 2, we will examine particular linguistic expressions that employ nuptial language and images and then outline conceptual mappings that undergird these expressions. The conceptual mappings outlined in chap. 3 will help us see some of the ways in which Revelation's nuptial imagery functions in conjunction with conceptual mappings undergirding the text, especially the conventional A CITY IS A WOMAN mapping. In addition, our earlier analysis of weddings and marriage in Revelation's Greco-Roman milieu will assist us as we identify some of the particular ways that Revelation elaborates on conventional mappings.

Throughout Revelation, John addresses the issue of the nascent Christian communities' identity, especially in relation to the larger world and, more importantly, in relation to God. As Paul Minear points out, John's vision depicts the eschatological community of the church as a present reality in which individual churches, namely, the churches of Asia Minor, can and should participate.[1] To this end, Revelation is addressed not to individual believers but to church communities, specifically, "the seven churches in Asia" (1:4); the number seven suggests the wholeness of the Christian

[1] Paul S. Minear, "Ontology and Ecclesiology in the Apocalypse," *NTS* 13 (1967): 92–93. Dieter Georgi suggests that Revelation's concern for ecclesial identity or understanding culminates at the conclusion of the work in the visions of the heavenly Jerusalem in 21:1–8 and 21:9–22:5. The use of a "prophetic perfect tense" in these pericopes challenges the communities who comprise Revelation's audience to live as the new Jerusalem in the present. In so doing, Revelation describes the heavenly Jerusalem as a version of the ideal Hellenistic city, but where God permeates the city and its residents, rather than being limited to a sacred space in the city center (Georgi, "Die Visionen vom Himmlischen Jerusalem in Apk 21 und 22," in *Kirche: Festschrift für Günther Bornkamm zum 75. Geburtstag*, ed. Lührmann and Strecker [Tübingen: J. C. B. Mohr, 1980] 351–32). See also Edouard Cothenet, "L'Église, Épouse du Christ (Éph 5; Apoc 19 et 21)," in *L'Église dans la Liturgie*, ed. Achille M. Triacca and A. Pistoia (Rome: Edizioni Liturgiche, 1980), 97.

community.[2] Revelation's concern for communities is underscored by the fact that the vision begins with the risen Christ dictating seven "letters" to these communities, describing their current situations. John offers his audience a variety of images through which to envision its identity: as a kingdom of priests (1:6), as the reconstituted twelve tribes of Israel (Rev 7:4–8),[3] as a virginal multitude standing on Mount Zion (Revelation 14),[4] and as the children of a woman fleeing a dragon (Rev 12:17).[5] One of the culminating community images is that of a woman, specifically a bride, who marries the Lamb, John's metaphorical description of the crucified and risen Christ (Rev 19:6–9).[6] Echoing Hebrew Bible prophetic traditions, John blends this nuptial imagery with that of a heavenly city, a new Jerusalem (Rev 21:1–10).

As suggested in the first chapter, few modern scholars have explored the use and function of nuptial imagery in Revelation. Instead, scholars generally focus on the city image represented by the new Jerusalem.[7] In contrast, in the following analysis we will explore the ways John sets the image of the bride before the eyes of his audience (to return to Aristotle's description of metaphorical language). We have previously examined conceptual metaphors underlying nuptial imagery in Hebrew Bible traditions, inquiring into the ways these metaphors have been constructed to shape an audience's self-understanding. Now we will address the ways in which John's

---

[2] See Alfred Loisy, *L'Apocalypse de Jean* (Paris: Emile Nourry, 1923), 23; Jacques Ellul, *Apocalypse: The Book of Revelation*, trans. George W. Schreiner (New York: Seabury Press, 1977), 36–51; Ugo Vanni, "Liturgical Dialogue as a Literary Form in the Book of Revelation," *NTS* 37 (1991): 355.

[3] Otto Böcher, "Israel und die Kirche in der Johannesapokalypse," in *Kirche in Zeit und Endzeit: Aufsätze zur Offenbarung des Johannes* (Neukirchen: Neukirchener Verlag, 1983), 35–36.

[4] Mathias Rissi, *The Future of the World: An Exegetical Study of Revelation 19.11–22.15* (Studies in Biblical Theology 23; Naperville, Ill.: Alec R. Allenson, 1972), 14. *Contra* Yarbro Collins, who suggests that the 144,000 describes a "special group within the body of the saints and not Christians in general." In making this claim, Yarbro Collins distinguishes between the 144,000, described both in Revelation 7 and 14, and the innumerable multitude described in 7:9 (*Crisis and Catharsis: The Power of the Apocalypse* [Philadelphia: Westminster Press, 1984], 127).

[5] G. B. Caird, *The Revelation of St. John* (Black's New Testament Commentaries 19; Peabody, Mass.: Hendrickson, 1966), 159. Traditionally, the woman clothed in the sun (Revelation 12) has been understood as a community image, especially as a depiction of the Christian church. Some of the earliest scholarly commentators on Revelation, including Victorinus of Pettau (d. 304), have made this connection (Pierre Prigent, *Apocalypse 12: Histoire de l'exégèse* [Tübingen: Mohr Siebeck, 1959] 8). This continues to be a popular reading of the text. See, for instance, Cothenet, "L'Eglise," 98; and Prigent, *L'Apocalypse de Saint Jean*, 2nd ed. (Commentaire du Nouveau Testament; Geneva: Labor et Fides, 1988), 176, 184.

[6] Not all scholars interpret the bride of the Lamb or the new Jerusalem as a community image. This issue will be addressed below.

[7] J. A. Du Rand offers a discussion of the history of interpretation surrounding the image of the new Jerusalem, which suggests that the city aspect of the new Jerusalem has predominated modern scholarship. See J. A. Du Rand, "The Imagery of the Heavenly Jerusalem (Revelation 21:9–22:5)," *Neot* 22 (1988): 65–86.

nuptial imagery draws on these traditions and conceptual mappings. In conjunction with this, we will inquire into the ways Revelation's nuptial imagery might reflect Greco-Roman conventions about weddings, marriages, and brides. Overall, we will explore the function of Revelation's nuptial imagery by examining the conceptual mappings that it entails.

Locating Revelation's Nuptial Imagery

Locating Revelation's nuptial imagery within the complex structure of the text is not a clear-cut task, as Ruben Zimmermann's *Geschlechtermetaphorik und Gottesverhältnis* indicates. Zimmermann argues that a number of images in Revelation's narrative that are not traditionally read as nuptial imagery can be understood in these terms. For instance, he posits that the crown or wreath (στέφανος) of life promised to those who remain faithful (2:10) in the letter to the church in Smyrna alludes to the bridal crown worn in Greco-Roman weddings.[8] As a network of culturally held ideas, images, and relationships associated with a particular abstract concept, conceptual domains can be alluded to by a variety of different images. Since crowns were used as part of the Greco-Roman wedding ceremony it is possible that the reference in 2:10 can be understood as an allusion to the metaphorical marriage described later in Revelation. However, just because an image *can* refer to a particular conceptual domain does not mean that it *necessarily* points to that domain. Given the mutivalence of words, a single referent, such as "crown," can signal any number of conceptual domains. While στέφανος can function as part of the nuptial domain, according to Gregory M. Stevenson's analysis, it typically refers to conceptual domains related to athletic and musical competitions and to benefaction.[9] Stevenson also suggests that since competitions were often part of religious festivals, the στέφανος conveys a sense that the wearer is worthy of a deity's honor.[10] While this does not exclude the connection between the crown and weddings, it does suggest that the likely connection is to a domain other than the nuptial domain.

---

[8] Ruben Zimmermann, *Geschlechtermetaphorik und Gottesverhältnis: Traditionsgeschichte und Theologie eines Bildfelds in Urchristentum un antiker Umwelt* (Tübingen: Mohr Siebeck, 2001), 447–49. Likewise, Zimmermann suggests that the image of 144,000 redeemed on Mount Zion, with its explicit reference to chastity (14:4), can be understood as part of Revelation's nuptial imagery (*Geschlechtermetaphorik*, 456–59). See also idem, "Die Virginitäts-Metapher in Apk 14:4–5 im Horizont von Befleckung, Loskauf und Erstlingsfrucht," *NovT* 45 (2003): 45–71.

[9] Gregory M. Stevenson, "Conceptual Background to Golden Crown Imagery in the Apocalypse of John (4:4, 10; 14:14)," *JBL* 114 (1995): 257–72. For a discussion of crown imagery in relation to Revelation's ideology of wealth, see Robert M. Royalty, Jr., *The Streets of Heaven: The Ideology of Wealth in the Apocalypse of John* (Macon, Ga.: Mercer University Press, 1998), 99–101.

[10] Stevenson, "Conceptual Background," 259.

In light of the complexity of identifying Revelation's nuptial imagery, we will focus our attention on linguistic markers that specifically pertain to the domain of marriage and weddings. Explicit linguistic markers may include any words that are generally used in reference to the wedding event or the act of marrying, as well as words referring to the participants in a wedding. These referents include, although are not limited to, "wedding" (γάμος), "to marry" (γαμέω),[11] "to give in marriage" (γαμίζω or γαμίσκω), "bride" (νύμφη), and "bridegroom" (νυμφίος).[12]

Using linguistic markers as our tools for identifying Revelation's nuptial imagery, we see that the text includes only a few explicit nuptial references: (1) 18:23 includes references to a bride (νύμφη) and bridegroom (νυμφίος); (2) in 19:7 the word γάμος is used in a hymn celebrating the wedding of the Lamb; (3) immediately following the hymn an angel offers a beatitude (19:9) that refers to a wedding banquet (τὸ δεῖπνον τοῦ γάμου); (4) 21:3 compares the new Jerusalem to a bride (νύμφη); (5) 21:9 again describes the new Jerusalem as a bride (νύμφη); and (6) in the liturgylike closing of the text the bride speaks in unison with the spirit (22:17). We will reserve our analysis of the first explicit use of nuptial language (18:23) for an appendix, since this language does not technically function as a metaphorical expression. Thus, we now turn our attention to the wedding of the Lamb described in Revelation 19.

A Wedding Celebration: Revelation 19:6–8

The first major use of explicit nuptial imagery occurs in Rev 19:7, which heralds the "wedding (γάμος) of the Lamb."[13] This reference is set within a carefully constructed hymnic unit[14] that serves as a bridge between the

[11] Interestingly, the verbal forms referring to marriage do not show up in the text of Revelation. For a full list of the Greek words related to the semantic domain of "marriage," see Johannes P. Louw and Eugene A. Nida, *Greek-English Lexicon of the New Testament Based on Semantic Domains*, 2 vols.; 2nd ed. (New York: United Bible Societies, 1988), 1:456–57.

[12] Below we will discuss the problems with translating γυνή, which can be rendered as "woman" or "wife," and ἀνήρ, which can be rendered as "man" or "husband." Both of these terms are used in Revelation within the context of nuptial imagery. We will discuss them as we analyze the texts in which they are found.

[13] I choose to capitalize "Lamb" since the term functions as a character's name throughout the narrative.

[14] Not simply "interruptions" within the narrative progression, Revelation's hymns unite varied imagery and provide a context for all of Revelation's eschatological action. John's view of "the things which must happen" occurs only after and on account of his spiritual ascent through the door of heaven and into the heavenly throne room (Rev 4:1–2). Throughout the text this throne room is characterized primarily as a place of worship (Rev 4–5; 11:15–19; 12:10–12; 15:1–4). Only from this place of worship, which offers a heavenly perspective, does John have the ability to view the unfolding of events (past, present, future) on the earth. Moreover, since the worship activity takes place continually in heaven, it interprets and colors

depiction of Babylon's judgment (17:1–18:24) and the depiction of Christ's victory over the beast (19:11–21).[15] In the final stanza of this hymn the celebration of God's triumph over Babylon gradually gives way to another type of celebration:

> [6]And I heard something like the voice of a multitude and like the sound of many waters and like the sound of great thunderings, saying: "Alleluia, for the Lord our God, the Almighty, has begun to reign. [7]Let us praise and exult and give glory to Him; for the wedding of the Lamb has come and his wife has prepared herself. [8]And it has been given to her that she be clothed in linen, shining [and] clean; for the linen is the righteous deeds of the saints." (19:6–8)

Proclaimed by the throngs of heaven, along with the announcement of God's reign, this wedding is a momentous event within John's depiction of "the things that must happen soon" (1:1). This image invites the audience to imagine a royal wedding and the Christian community as Christ's bride, putting on a new identity marked by purity and faithfulness.

1. GOD IS A KING; GOD IS AN EMPEROR

Revelation 19:6–8 is shaped by the imagery of God's reign (ἐβασίλευσεν κύριος ὁ θεός), a reality announced by the heavenly chorus in v. 7.[16] The

the events witnessed by John (e.g., Rev 12:10–12). The narrative structure reflects this interpretive function, as the hymns and narrative action alternate throughout the text. See Leonard L. Thompson, *The Book of Revelation: Apocalypse and Empire* (Oxford: Oxford University Press, 1990), 53–63; and idem, "Cult and Eschatology in the Apocalypse of John," *JR* 49 (1969): 330–50.

[15] Given that the text unites the image of the prostitute with that of the wife of the Lamb, scholars are divided on whether 19:1–10 should be read with the preceding chapters or the following chapters, which describe the coming of Christ's reign and the descent of the new Jerusalem. Those who choose to read the text with the preceding material seem to be in the majority, reading 19:1–10 primarily as the heavenly worship that ensues as a result of God's judgment of the Prostitute. See, for example, Lucien Cerfaux and Jules Cambier, *L'Apocalypse de Saint Jean lue aux Chrétiens* (LD 17; Paris: Les Éditions du Cerf, 1964), 160ff.; and Elisabeth Schüssler Fiorenza, *Revelation: Vision of a Just World* (Minneapolis: Fortress Press, 1991), 101. In contrast, some scholars read this passage as a prelude to the Lamb's victory over evil and his future reign, events that are depicted in 19:11–22:6. Boring is the primary contemporary proponent of this reading, although he likewise acknowledges a sense of continuity between 19:1–10 and chaps. 17 and 18 (Eugene Boring, *Revelation* [IBC; Louisville: John Knox Press, 1989], 191f.). Exemplifying this scholarly ambivalence, Caird divides this passage between verses 4 and 5, reading the first half of the scene with the end of chap. 18 and the second half as the introduction to the following material concerning "the reign of God" (232f.). It seems, however, that the uncertainty about where to place 19:1–10 points to the fact that this unit does not "belong" properly to either the preceding material or the following material. Jean-Pierre Ruiz points out that the passage includes both a *recapitulation* of the preceding chaps. 17 and 18, and an *anticipation* of the following material (*Ezekiel in the Apocalypse: The Transformation of Prophetic Language in Revelation 16,17–19,10* [Frankfurt am Main: Peter Lang, 1989], 482ff.).

[16] Revelation's use of the aorist verbs βασίλευσεν (v. 6) and ἦλθεν (v. 7) to describe these

image of God's reign metaphorically depicts God as a human king and, even more specifically, an imperial emperor. As we will see below, this functions as part of Revelation's critique of Roman institutions of power.[17] The image of God's reign is important to our analysis of Revelation's nuptial imagery, since the announcement of the beginning of God's reign in v. 6 prompts the audience to interpret the following events, including the preparation of the Lamb's bride, in light of this reign.

a. GOD IS A HUMAN

The imagery of God's reign builds on the basic conceptual mapping GOD IS A HUMAN. Some interpreters are reticent to acknowledge that Revelation engages in this type of anthropomorphizing. Bauckham, for example, downplays this by arguing that John does not "dwell on the visible form of the One who sits on the throne."[18] The text, however, need not include an extended discussion of the visible form of God to conjure the visual image of God as a human. This stems from the power of metaphorical language in which one or two simple references, such as the mention of God's "hand" (5:1), can tap into a rich conceptual domain, in this case the domain HUMAN PERSON. The mention of the hand of God or the suggestion that God "sits" implies that the source domain HUMAN PERSON is being used to image the target domain GOD. In these specific instances, moreover, the source domain draws on physical human attributes, and suggests that GOD IS AN EMBODIED HUMAN.[19]

---

respective events creates some translation difficulties. The aorist in koine Greek has been typically understood as verbal *tense* referring to past actions in their totality. Following this line of translation, Rev 19:6–7 would be rendered into English as "God reigned" and the wedding of the Lamb "came." Contemporary linguists and translators suggest this understanding of the aorist is too simplistic, arguing that aorist is more properly a verbal *aspect* (referring to the way an author represents action) and not a *tense* (which describes the temporal quality of the action). In this vein, K. L. McKay characterizes the aorist aspect as quite flexible, capable of describing a whole series of actions in their totality or to a simple singular event. He suggests that when used with a stative verb, such "to reign" or even "to come," it can be translated as referring to a process of action that has begun. Similarly, many critical commentators on Revelation treat βασίλευσεν as an inceptive aorist, describing action that has begun. See David E. Aune, *Revelation*, 3 vols. (WBC; Dallas: Word, 1997–1998), 3:1016; Gregory K. Beale, *The Book of Revelation: A Commentary on the Greek Text* (NIGTC; Grand Rapids: Eerdmans, 1999), 932. For a discussion of verbal aspect, see Buist M. Fanning, *Verbal Aspect in New Testament Greek* (Oxford: Clarendon Press, 1990); and K. L. McKay, *A New Syntax of the Verb in New Testament Greek: An Aspectual Approach* (Studies in Biblical Greek 5; New York: Peter Lang, 1994).

[17] Steven J. Friesen, *Imperial Cults and the Apocalypse of John: Reading Revelation in the Ruins* (Oxford: Oxford University Press, 2001), 201–9.

[18] Richard Bauckham, *The Theology of the Book of Revelation* (New Testament Theology; Cambridge: Cambridge University Press, 1993), 32.

[19] *Contra* Bauckham who asserts that the Book of Revelation resists anthropomorphism in its descriptions of God (*The Theology of the Book of Revelation*, 44–45). Stephen Moore also

b. GOD IS A KING; GOD IS AN EMPEROR

The text narrows the mapping GOD IS A HUMAN by highlighting a particular social role within the source domain HUMAN PERSON. The language of God's reign in 19:7 depicts God performing a particular human social role, specifically the role of king. This is not to suggest that the text of Revelation asserts that God simply fulfills human roles and functions; rather, remembering that metaphorical mappings involve equating two *unlike* things, the text envisions God as a human king in order to bring aspects of the target domain (GOD) into view. This does not mean the text ascribes to God all human characteristics; instead, the textual mapping is selective, highlighting a physical and a social aspect of the complex domain A HUMAN PERSON.[20] In this way, John narrows the very basic mapping GOD IS A HUMAN to make a more specific conceptual mapping GOD IS A KING.

The conceptual mapping GOD IS A KING appears throughout the entire text of Revelation. Especially within the reoccurring scenes of heavenly worship, John employs imagery of kingship, royalty, and political power to depict God (e.g., 4:2–11).[21] For instance, Revelation's circumlocution for describing the deity is "the one who sits upon the throne" (e.g., 4:2, 9; 5:1, 13; 7:10).[22] The throne functions as a metonym for the king, who in this case is God. John's use of this mapping draws on a long-held tradition of depicting God as king in the Hebrew Bible. The ubiquitous nature of this within Revelation and its literary forebears may lead one to believe that it is not a metaphor or that it is a "dead metaphor." That is, one might assume, erroneously I believe, that John uses the metaphorical mapping as simple ornamentation apart from any specific meaning. However, given the lengths to which John develops the imagery of God's reign, even describing in detail the throne room of God, it seems to be much more than meaningless ornamentation.

Revelation's depiction of God as king and lord over all can be understood as part of Revelation's response to Roman imperial discourse.[23] Throughout the text, John ascribes to God titles that were commonly used in reference to rulers within the Roman milieu, such as "master" (δεσπότης, 6:10) and "lord" (κύριος, e.g., 4:8) and "the all-powerful one" (ὁ παντοκράτωρ,

---

disagrees with Bauckham's assessment, "The Beatific Vision as a Posing Exhibition: Revelation's Hypermasculine Deity," *JSNT* 60 (1995): 30.

[20] The scope of this project makes it impossible to fully examine what aspects of kingship John highlights in his depiction of God, although this might prove to be a fascinating future project.

[21] Thompson, *The Book of Revelation*, 65.

[22] Bauckham, *The Theology of the Book of Revelation*, 31–32.

[23] Eugene Boring, "The Theology of Revelation: 'The Lord Our God the Almighty Reigns,'" *Int* 40 (1986): 257–69; Schüssler Fiorenza, *Revelation*, 58–59.

1:8; 4:8; 19:6)[24] and ascribes to God a "kingdom" or "empire" (βασιλεία) (11:15; 12:10).[25] This suggests that one of the ways that the conceptual mapping GOD IS A KING might be interpreted within John's rhetorical situation is more specifically as GOD IS AN EMPEROR.

The traditional conceptual imaging of God as a king is expanded in Revelation's context to the image of God as an emperor. This expansion occurs through John's application of titles and characteristics to God that were appropriate to a Roman Emperor and through John's assertion that the Lamb, or Christ, who exists in a closely interconnected relationship with the "one who sits upon the throne" (5:6, 13; 7:17), is the one who rules over the nations of the earth (1:5). The fact that God and Christ are more than mere kings, that they exercise an imperial type of authority over the world's kings, is made explicit later in chap. 19: "And he [Christ] has his name written upon his garment and upon his thigh, 'King of kings' and 'Lord of lords'" (19:16). Clearly, Revelation's depiction of God and Christ functions to challenge imperial claims to ultimate authority through the conceptual mapping GOD IS AN EMPEROR.

In chap. 3 we saw how the prophetic texts depict God as a husband. In Revelation 19, however, John narrows the GOD IS A HUMAN mapping to describe God as a king and *not* as a husband. While these social roles are not mutually exclusive (a king can be a husband), it seems striking that the text of Revelation, so influenced by the Hebrew prophets, resists depicting God as a husband or bridegroom. One wonders if the depiction of God at the pinnacle of human sociopolitical order figures so importantly in Revelation's purview that depicting God in the role of bridegroom might somehow diminish that claim.

2. WEDDING as a Metadomain

We have focused on the use of conceptual domains in metaphorical mappings; however, it is also possible to think of domains more generally. Conceptual domains also function as metadomains through which the audience understands and organizes various aspects of a text.[26]

---

[24] Aune, *Revelation*, 1:310; Schüssler Fiorenza, *Revelation*, 59. Greek titles for Roman emperors included titles and attributes often, but not always, associated with divinity. This causes problems for modern interpreters whose understanding of divinity is typically shaped by the Christian tradition, which understands divinity in a way different from that of the ancient Greeks. See S. R. F. Price, "God and Emperors: The Greek Language of the Roman Imperial Cult," *The Journal of Hellenic Studies* 104 (1984): 79–95.

[25] Wes Howard-Brook and Anthony Gwyther, *Unveiling Empire: Reading Revelation Then and Now* (Maryknoll, N.Y.: Orbis Books, 1999), 224–25.

[26] Gilles Fauconnier and Mark Turner describe these as conceptual frames. Since this language overlaps with the language of a metaphorical frame, as described in chap. 2, I have chosen to describe these as "metadomains." For a description of "conceptual frames," see

After announcing God's kingship, the hymn immediately proclaims the advent of the Lamb's wedding. By making reference to a wedding event (γάμος) Rev 19:7 introduces a conceptual domain or metadomain, WEDDING, which influences the way one understands the surrounding signifiers, such as "woman," "Lamb," "garment," etc. The conceptual domain WEDDING conjures for the audience a number of culturally communicated entailments, including a number of different roles or participants (e.g., bridegroom, bride, other family members) and related concepts (*manus*, fidelity, etc.). In addition, introduction of the conceptual domain WEDDING can signal the audience to imagine specific social, religious, economic, and familial meanings.

By placing the image of the Lamb's wedding in the same hymnic stanza as the announcement of God's reign, Rev 19:7 clearly associates the wedding of the Lamb with God's kingly reign. On account of this wedding, all the inhabitants of heaven give glory to *God* and not specifically to the Lamb. Although Revelation generally resists depicting the relationship between God and Christ in familial terms,[27] the placement of the Lamb's wedding in relation to God's kingly reign might suggest to some a familial relationship, perhaps a father-son relationship, between God and the Lamb. Within Roman imperial discourse, marriage and familial imagery function to cement the social and political authority of the imperial family. Wedding and family imagery could also be used to reinforce dynastic connections between members of the imperial family.[28] The "Marriage Cameo" (ca. 50 C.E.), for instance, depicts Claudius and his wife, Agrippina the Younger, facing Tiberius and his mother, Livia (the wife of Augustus).[29] While this gem was likely for private use, it reflects the ways in which family groupings can be used to establish dynastic and familial links. In this case, Claudius and his wife, Agrippina, are linked back to Augustus through his father and his grandmother. Visual representations of royal family groups, including images of weddings and married couples, establish and reinforce the relationships between members of the family, including the patriarch

Fauconnier and Turner, *The Way We Think: Conceptual Blending and the Mind's Hidden Complexities* (New York: Basic Books, 2002), 120–22, 251–55.

[27] The only exception to this occurs in the introduction to the letter to the church at Thyatira, where the risen Christ refers to himself as the "son of God" (2:18).

[28] Susan Fischler notes the role of imperial women visually depicting dynastic connections ("Social Stereotypes and Historical Analysis: The Case of the Imperial Women at Rome," in *Women in Ancient Societies: An Illusion of the Night*, ed. Léonie J. Archer, Susan Fischler, and Maria Wyke [Basingstoke: Macmillan, 1994], 129). For a discussion of deification of Roman imperial women as a part of the empire's political ideology, see Marleen B. Flory, "The Deification of Roman Women," *Ancient History Bulletin* 9.3–4 (1995): 127–34.

[29] Kleiner, D. E. E, *Roman Sculpture* (New Haven: Yale University Press, 1992), 151–52, fig. 127. This cameo, also known as the Gemma Claudia, is viewable at the Kunsthistorisches Museum (Vienna) website, although the figures are identified differently than in Kleiner's account. See http://khm.at/.

and his successor. The presentation of the Lamb's wedding within a context celebrating the reign of God recalls such dynastic imagery. This does not necessarily imply that Revelation 19 mimics these traditions. Rather, the nuptial imagery of this chapter, combining the conceptual domain WEDDING with the image of God as an emperor, functions similarly to the imperial traditions of using marital images to emphasize imperial dynastic ties.

As we described in the previous chapter, in the Roman milieu the imperial family served to represent the ideal *domus*. Iconography promoting this view permeated the empire. In light of this, it is conceivable that Revelation responds to this by offering its own wedding tableau. Instead of an image of an imperial couple, such as the image from the Sebasteion in Aphrodisas, Asia Minor, depicting Claudius and his wife, Agrippina the Younger, clasping hands as in a wedding (*dextrarum iunctio*),[30] Revelation presents an image of the Lamb's wedding to his bride, which accompanies God's reign. In contrast to the imagery of the Roman imperial *domus divina*,[31] Revelation presents a counterimage of a royal wedding. Steven J. Friesen similarly notes how Revelation's nuptial imagery appropriates the traditional Roman gender conventions, that of the bride and groom, in order to pursue its own "subversive religious goals."[32]

2. AN EVENT IS AN OBJECT; TIME IS A PATH

Reflecting some very abstract metaphorical mappings, Rev 19:7 casts the wedding (γάμος) as the subject of a verb of movement, ἦλθεν: "the wedding of the Lamb *has come*."[33] In Revelation, the verb ἔρχομαι and its conjugations often describe the movement of animate objects, such as the Lamb (5:7) or angels (8:3; 17:1). Revelation also uses these verbs metaphorically to describe "the coming" of times, such as "the hour of crisis" (14:7), and events, such as "the great day of God's wrath" (6:17). This use of ἔρχομαι, which depicts events and times as objects that move is conventional, yet nonetheless metaphorical. In the case of v. 7, the Lamb's wedding, an event,

---

[30] A coin minted in Ephesus ca. 50–51 C.E. also depicts the imperial couple Claudius and Agrippina. This suggests that images of emperors and their wives could be circulated as an image of the ideal married couple or the ideal bridegroom and bride. An image of this coin can be viewed online. See "Boston 60.522," coin, *Perseus Project Database*, Tufts University, 5 Mar. 2004; www.perseus.tufts.edu.

[31] Flory, "The Deification of Roman Women," 134. See also Fullerton, "The *Domus Augusti* in Imperial Iconography of 13–12 B.C.," *AJA* 89 (1985): 473–83.

[32] Friesen, *Imperial Cults*, 178.

[33] Although John uses the aorist tense (ἦλθεν), as in v. 6, this does not suggest that the marriage is an event that has come and is now over, which would be translated as "the wedding of the Lamb came." Instead, I translate ἦλθεν as "has come" in order to convey that in some sense the wedding has already happened (hence the use of the aorist), but that its results still effect the present (Smyth §1923, §1940).

is metaphorically described as a moving object that can come or arrive: AN EVENT IS AN OBJECT.

The AN EVENT IS AN OBJECT mapping can be combined with the conventional mapping TIME IS A PATH to describe the progression of time and the occurrence of events within time.[34] In such a scenario the progression of time can either be envisioned in terms of humans moving along a path toward and away from events, metaphorically understood as objects on the path, or the path and its events/objects can be understood as moving toward and away from stationary humans. An analysis of Revelation's view of time is beyond the scope of this project, since the concept of time permeates the narrative, which is described as revealing "the things which must happen soon" (1:1). However, even a cursory glance over the text reveals that Revelation often envisions time as a path on which objects/events move. As noted above, John describes specific hours, such as the hour of God's judgment (14:7), and days, such as the day of Babylon's judgment (17:8), as "coming." These specific expressions reflect an assumption that events are objects (EVENTS ARE OBJECTS) that move along the path of time (TIME IS A PATH). Likewise, in 19:7 the wedding of the Lamb "arrives," like an object moving along a path.

Revelation's metaphorical depiction of events "coming" and "going" assumes a relatively passive human audience. The events come and go regardless of the audience's actions. As Lakoff and Turner explain, "we are stationary and moments of time move by us, approaching us from the future and going away from us into the past."[35] The hymn of Revelation 19 announces that God's imperial reign has begun and the Lamb's wedding has come, apart from any action by humanity.

3. THE UNION BETWEEN CHRIST AND THE COMMUNITY IS A MARRIAGE

The proclamation that "the wedding of the Lamb has come" invites the audience to envision a metaphorical wedding. Even though WEDDING can be understood as metadomain through which the surrounding verses should be understood, WEDDING also functions as a domain within a metaphorical construction. As described in chap. 2, identifying the component parts of a metaphorical expression can be complicated, since the distinction between a metaphorical focus and frame is often unclear. In a

---

[34] George Lakoff and Mark Johnson, *Metaphors We Live By* (Chicago: University of Chicago Press, 1980), 41–45; George Lakoff and Mark Turner, *More Than Cool Reason: A Field Guide to Poetic Metaphor* (Chicago: University of Chicago Press, 1989), 44–46.

[35] Here Lakoff and Turner describe the metaphor that they call TIME MOVES, which is best understood as a blend of metaphorical mappings, such as TIME IS A PATH and EVENTS ARE OBJECTS or, even, EVENTS ARE ACTIONS (*More Than Cool Reason*, 44).

simple metaphorical expression, the frame helps identify the focus, the lexical term that serves as the metaphorical source domain. The frame indicates that the focus is not to be taken literally, by placing the focal term into a context in which it cannot be taken literally. The use of the term "Lamb" in the phrase "the wedding of the Lamb" compels the audience to interpret "wedding" metaphorically, since neither lambs, nor the deities that they may metaphorically represent (see below), *actually* wed. By qualifying this wedding as "the Lamb's," John signals that this wedding functions metaphorically. The expression's immediate textual context, however, offers little in the way of determining the target domain to which "wedding" refers. In his discussion of metaphor, Gerard Steen notes that a metaphor's referent is often *contextual*, evident only through inferences to a text's cultural context.[36] Such is the case with the wedding metaphor at play in Rev 19:7.

Within Revelation's cultural milieu, a divine figure could be understood as *metaphorically* married to a city or a community. In chap. 3, we saw that this imagery plays a role in the prophetic texts of the Hebrew Bible, including those which John explicitly echoes. John presumes that his audience possesses some familiarity with the Jewish literary traditions and apparently builds some metaphorical mappings around this assumption.[37] These texts often employ the metaphorical mappings A CITY IS A WOMAN and THE RELATIONSHIP BETWEEN GOD AND JERUSALEM IS A MARRIAGE, highlighting different aspects of this mapping for different rhetorical purposes. As we saw with Ezekiel 16, for example, it is possible to highlight different points in time in a marriage relationship, such as the betrothal and the wedding, to describe particular aspects of the relationship between God and Israel.

There likewise exists a precedent of employing marriage and, more specifically, wedding language to describe the union between the Christian community and Christ. In 2 Corinthians, Paul metaphorically describes the Corinthian community as a bride that he presents to Christ for marriage: "I betrothed (ἁρμόζομαι) you (the Corinthians) to one husband . . . Christ" (11:2 NRSV). Since the plural you (ὑμᾶς) cannot refer to an actual entity that has been betrothed to *one* husband, one recognizes that this betrothal cannot be understood in literal or actual terms. The verb ἁρμόζομαι, "to promise in marriage," therefore, functions as a metaphorical focus. Looking at the expression's immediate surrounding, Paul clearly uses the term

---

[36] Gerard Steen, "Metaphor and Discourse: Towards a Linguistic Checklist for Metaphor Analysis," in *Research and Applying Metaphor*, ed. Lynne Cameron and Graham Low (Cambridge: Cambridge University Press, 1999), 91.

[37] For example, John's vision of the four living creatures in the heavenly throne room echoes the vision in Ezekiel 1. John's vision draws on the images from the earlier texts, but reformulates them subsequently creating a unique vision.

to describe one aspect of the relationship between Christ and the Corinthians—the time when Paul initiated the relationship between the two parties. In this vein we can argue that the metaphorical expression in 2 Cor 11:2 could be written as, "the beginning of the relationship between Christ and the Corinthians is a betrothal." Especially since Paul is particularly interested in the continuing relationship between Christ and the Corinthians, the expression reflects a more general equation between this relationship and marriage. The conceptual mapping undergirding this text is, therefore, THE UNION BETWEEN CHRIST AND THE COMMUNITY IS A MARRIAGE. Additionally, like the prophets of the Hebrew Bible, Paul compels the audience to envision the collective, the Corinthian community, as an individual, specifically a woman and bride.

The author of Ephesians, a letter to one of the churches supposedly addressed in Revelation as well, also draws a metaphorical connection between the relationship of "the church" and Christ and a human marriage relationship: "Wives, be subject to your husbands as you are to the Lord; for the husband is the head of the wife just as Christ is the head of the church . . ." (Eph 5:22–23). As E. Elizabeth Johnson observes, in this instance the author of Ephesians reverses the traditional marriage metaphor of the Hebrew Bible prophets:

> The prophetic metaphor uses human marriage to illustrate or explain God's faithful relationship to Israel despite Israel's faithlessness. The writer of Ephesians, however, reverses the direction of the comparison by using Christ's relationship to the church to illustrate how men ought to relate to their wives and women to their husbands.[38]

To put this in the terms of conceptual metaphor theory, the author of Ephesians uses the relationship between Christ and the church as a *source domain* to describe and subsequently regulate the nature of relationships within a human marriage, which functions as *target domain*. Thus, Ephesians employs the general mapping A MARRIAGE IS THE UNION BETWEEN CHRIST AND THE COMMUNITY. The reversal of this metaphorical motif implies the ubiquitous nature of the mapping within the first-century Christian environment: That the "marriage" between Christ and the church functions as a source domain for describing a human relationship suggests that the former, THE UNION BETWEEN A DEITY (or CHRIST) AND THE COMMUNITY IS A MARRIAGE, is a conventional metaphorical mapping within the milieu.

The significant cultural precedents for employing marriage imagery to describe a union between a deity, including Christ, and a community force

---

[38] E. Elizabeth Johnson, "Ephesians," in *The Women's Bible Commentary*, ed. Carol A. Newsom and Sharon H. Ringe (Louisville, Ky.: Westminster John Knox Press, 1992), 340.

us to consider the possibility that Revelation's reference to the wedding of the Lamb reflects a similar metaphorical equation. As we proceed in our analysis of Revelation's nuptial imagery we will see that the text does, in fact, employ the general metaphorical mapping THE UNION BETWEEN CHRIST AND THE COMMUNITY IS A MARRIAGE.

The assertion that Revelation's nuptial imagery employs a common cultural mapping does not imply that John slavishly borrows a tradition whole cloth. Rather, like Ezekiel and Isaiah before him, John shapes the conventional to fit his own rhetorical purposes. Simply by casting the traditional marriage metaphor as a wedding (γάμος), John begins to shape the mapping to fit his rhetorical aims, because other lexical terms could be employed to describe marriage more generally. The verb συνοικέω ("to live with"), for example, can be used to describe married life (e.g., 1 Pet 3:7; Josephus, *A.J.* 7.3.84).[39] While συνοικέω might be used to describe a married couple's life together after the wedding, Revelation's use of γάμος focuses the audience's imagination on the *beginning* of the marriage. John especially emphasizes this sense of beginning and newness in chap. 21 when he describes the bride's descent within the context of a newly created heaven and earth (21:1).

4. CHRIST IS A LAMB; CHRIST IS A BRIDEGROOM

By introducing the image of the wedding of the Lamb, Revelation compels the reader to envision the Lamb, Revelation's vision of the risen Christ, as a bridegroom. The use of the WEDDING metadomain prompts the audience to read the characters in these verses in terms of the culturally designated participants, such as bridegroom and bride, in a wedding. That the Lamb should be aligned with the male gender role and not the female stems from the fact that the next phrase mentions the "woman," ostensibly the bride, who participates in the wedding. Thus, the text encourages the audience to envision the Lamb as a metaphorical bridegroom (THE LAMB IS A BRIDEGROOM).[40]

---

[39] Another example can be found in Romans, where the idiom "law of the husband" describes a woman's married state (Rom 7:2) (Nida, *Greek-English Lexicon*, 1:427).

[40] The image of the Lamb, the target domain described by the source domain BRIDEGROOM, is one of Revelation's central images and can be understood as a metaphorical blend. In Revelation the designation "lamb" is not simply a metaphorical designation for the risen Christ, because the text blends elements from both conceptual domains LAMB and CHRIST in constructing the image of the "Lamb." John draws on the source domain LAMB, highlighting the sacrificial function of lambs, and characterizes the Lamb as "slaughtered" (5:6). John also utilizes traditional messianic characteristics in depicting the character of the "Lamb." Immediately prior to the initial vision of the Lamb an angel introduces this character as "the Lion of the tribe of Judah, the root of David" (5:5), a messianic reference (Gen 49:9; Isa 11:10). It is this Lamb, a metaphorical image of the risen Christ as slaughtered Lamb and messianic Lion, that John here depicts as a bridegroom.

The description of the Lamb as bridegroom in Revelation 19 is terse, in spite of the richness of the first-century concepts of WEDDINGS and MARRIAGE. Analysis of marriage in the Greco-Roman milieu suggests that the culture was generally more interested in the characteristics of a bride than of a bridegroom.[41] Likewise, at this point in the narrative, the author of Revelation does not explicitly ascribe any characteristics to the bridegroom. The author does not, for instance, mention the sexual purity of the Lamb, which is something he ascribes to followers of the Lamb in chap. 14 (14:4).[42] Although the Lamb, as Christ, is one of the dominant images in the text of Revelation as a whole, the bridegroom gets short shrift in 19:7–8. These particular verses do not further guide the audience in understanding the metaphorical mapping CHRIST IS A BRIDEGROOM.

In spite of the text's failure to assign any specific characteristics to the bridegroom, the blended metadomain of a royal wedding implies that the Lamb is a royal bridegroom. While the primary image of Christ in Revelation is as the Lamb, John also describes Christ in kingly terms (1:5). The kingly image of Christ is developed most fully in the verses following Revelation's nuptial imagery (19:11ff.). These verses depict Christ wearing many crowns and a garment with the title "King of kings and Lord of lords" (19:12, 16).[43] Additionally, the kingly imagery in 19:11–16 is somewhat similar to that in Psalm 45, in which the Psalmist describes a king coming to his wedding.[44] Below we explore how Rev 19:11–16 might function as part of Revelation's nuptial imagery.

5. A COMMUNITY IS A WOMAN; A COMMUNITY IS A WIFE

As in Roman social discourse, Rev 19:7–8 emphasizes the feminine role in the wedding by quickly shifting focus from the Lamb to "his woman" or "his wife," ἡ γυνὴ αὐτοῦ. The lexical term ἡ γυνή implies both the general sense of "woman" and the more specific social role "wife," reflecting the first-century assumption that all women marry. Set within the context of the metadomain WEDDING, the term conveys both senses, as a woman who

[41] Susan Treggiari, *Roman Marriage: Iusti Coniuges from the Time of Cicero to the Time of Ulpian* (Oxford: Clarendon Press, 1991), 87.

[42] Sexual purity was not necessarily a characteristic that was valued in the first-century bridegroom. Plutarch, for instance, warns a new bridegroom not to come home smelling of another woman. Rather than arouse jealousy in his new wife, it is better to bathe before coming home! (*Advice* 144.44).

[43] The kingly description of Christ highlights the fact that at times in Revelation the boundary between God and Christ is somewhat unclear. For, while Christ is the King of kings, God is the one who sits on the throne (see above).

[44] Cothenet, "L'Église," 100. There are a number of parallels between the description of the king in Psalm 45 and the description of Christ in the subsequent verses of chap. 19, including the fact that both ride on horses and are characterized by truth (19:11; Ps. 45:4).

weds takes on the social role wife. For our purposes we will identify the domain to which ἡ γυνή refers as WIFE.

As we saw in chap. 4, the concept of WIFE communicates a variety of socially determined ideas, especially within a context in which social discourse about the *domus* is so prevalent. Within the first-century discourse about the family, the concept of WIFE suggests maintenance of the *domus*, concord or *harmonia* with one's husband, sexual fidelity, bearing and caring for children, etc. Revelation 19:7 potentially alludes to all of these interrelated ideas.

The use of "his," a pronoun referring to the Lamb, or Christ, to describe ἡ γυνή indicates that the term functions as a metaphorical focus. In this instance, the term is nonsensical if read as describing an actual woman or wife, since deities do not actually have human wives, and must be read as a metaphorical description of another concept. Even though John does not make an explicit metaphorical connection between this woman and another entity, the prevalence of marriage imagery as a metaphor for the relationship between a deity and a community (see above) suggests that this woman functions to describe a community: A COMMUNITY IS A WOMAN. Further, John makes this metaphorical mapping explicit in chap. 21 when he characterizes the new Jerusalem, a community that constitutes a city, as the Lamb's wife. Additionally, the description of the city of Babylon as a prostitute in chap. 17, specifically 17:18, introduces the related metaphorical mapping A CITY IS A WOMAN into the narrative.[45] The proximity of this imagery to 19:7 effectively casts the image of the bride as a community/city metaphor.

---

[45] A full elaboration of this metaphorical mapping would be a book in itself; as the imagery extends over two full chapters and is multilayered. In 17:1, one of the angels of the bowl plagues informs John that he will show him the judgment of the Great Prostitute. Immediately, John sees a woman sitting on a beast (v. 3), only to be informed by his angel guide that the woman, the prostitute, bears the name "Babylon"—the woman is a city (v. 5). Upon hearing this, John reacts with complete wonder (v. 6). The audience, however, is left wondering whether this reaction is on account of the woman's appearance or a reaction to the disparity between what he sees and what he hears. If it were not for a reference to Babylon as a city in 16:19, one might mistakenly assume that chap. 17 describes a woman who is simply named "Babylon." In fact, much of chap. 17 promotes such a reading, including references to the woman's clothing, drunkenness, and even to her illicit relationships with "the kings of the earth." As the description of this chapter progresses, however, the audience receives a few clues implying that the angel describes a metaphorical woman, not an actual woman: We begin to see that the vision is not *about* a woman or even women, for that matter. For instance, this woman sits upon seven mountains: "the seven heads [of the beast] are seven mountains on which the woman is seated . . ." (v. 9). If we put aside that the angel equates the seven heads of the beast with seven mountains, we see that the reference to the seven mountains and the phrase "is seated" signal to the audience that we are not to read the woman literally. Putting these phrases in relation to the image of a woman makes the expression nonsensical on a literal level and suggests that "woman" functions as a metaphorical focus. The focus, however, *is not* what the metaphor is ultimately about. Even though the woman's name suggests that

Below, when we address the nuptial imagery in chap. 21, we will examine how Revelation's image of the city, the new Jerusalem, functions as a community image as well. John clearly depicts a community of people, those faithful to God and the Lamb, as a city, the new Jerusalem (THE CHRISTIAN COMMUNITY IS THE NEW JERUSALEM). At this point, it is important to recognize that John, like his predecessors, uses metaphor to depict the community as an individual person.

John further qualifies the conceptual domain WIFE by placing it in the context of the metadomain WEDDING. By using ἡ γυνή in a wedding context, the text encourages the audience to envision this woman or wife, the community, specifically as a bride: THE CHRISTIAN COMMUNITY IS A BRIDE. Reflecting this and following the use of νύμφη in chap. 21, some ancient manuscripts replace γυνή with νύμφη, "bride," in 19:7.[46] The presence of ἡ γυνή in this wedding context, however, communicates the whole range of meanings associated with Greco-Roman feminine identity and weddings. The use of this broad term allows the audience to think of the woman as a bride and as a wife, the social role she is entering.

Our analysis in chap. 4 revealed some of the complexity inherent within the depiction of brides in the first century. In particular, Rev 19:8, which announces "and his wife has prepared herself" (ἡτοίμασεν ἑαυτήν), encourages the audience to envision any number of different activities that the bride performed in preparation for her wedding. The bride's pre-wedding toilette, depicted in visual and literary arts, was a meaning-laden event in the Greco-Roman context.[47] The bride's preparation involved her appropriating symbols of her new role as wife, including symbols of fidelity, fecundity, and domesticity. The bride's appropriation of these symbols, in her dress and through the objects she carries during the wedding, communicates her transitional nature. Within this milieu, the bride is a figure

---

she metaphorically represents a city, it is not until the end of this chapter (17:18) that the angel, actually using propositional language, blatantly reveals the metaphorical mapping A CITY IS A WOMAN: "And the woman which you saw *is* the great city. . . ."

[46] Aune suggests that this use of νύμφη is the result of assimilating this verse to Rev 21:2, 9; 22:17 (*Revelation*, 3:1017). This assimilation makes sense within the context of 19:7–9, since these verses use wedding imagery and suggest a bride and not a wife. Jan Fekkes tries to explain the use of ἡ γυνή, indicating that this hymn serves primarily as the wedding announcement, which implies that the actual marriage has not occurred; the word "woman" denotes the betrothed. This suggestion is problematic; this is not simply a wedding announcement, but an announcement that the wedding has occurred. See Jan Fekkes, "'His Bride Has Prepared Herself': Revelation 19–21 and Isaian Nuptial Imagery," *JBL* 109 (1990): 271 n. 4. Likewise, some modern English translations of Revelation render ἡ γυνή as "bride" (e.g., NIV, NIB, NAS). These translations reflect the way in which a conceptual domain represented by a single word, such as ἡ γυνή, can be narrowed simply by the context into which it is set.

[47] Treggiari, *Roman Marriage*, 163.

who is in the process of moving into a new role or identity. More specifically, within the Greco-Roman milieu a bride transitions into the identity for which supposedly she was born—that of wife, or woman. To depict a community as a bride implies that the community takes on this transitional, or bridal, role.

a. A BRIDE IS AN OBJECT

Revelation 19:8 qualifies the image of the Lamb's bride by depicting her in relationship to the bridegroom: ἡ γυνὴ αὐτοῦ ("his wife"). A basic characteristic of this woman is that she belongs to or is associated with the Lamb. This description of the bride contrasts completely with John's description of the Whore in chaps. 17 and 18. While Revelation characterizes the Great Prostitute by her relationships with multiple partners, namely, the kings of the earth (e.g., 18:3), Revelation 19 characterizes the wife of the Lamb by her relationship to only one masculine figure, namely, the Lamb.

The use of the possessive pronoun αὐτοῦ in the phrase "his wife" can be read as an expression of the metaphorical mapping A WIFE IS AN OBJECT. A wife is like an object that is possessed and controlled by her husband. This view would be in keeping with some of the traditional Greek ways of understanding the marriage relation, in which a wife's husband is lord (κύριος) over the wife. Likewise, this view is consistent with the Roman idea of guardianship, which dictated that a woman be under the control of her father, husband, or other male relative. In 21:2, however, when John views the new Jerusalem, he turns the phrase around: She appears as a bride adorned for *her* husband (τῷ ἀνδρὶ αὐτῆς). Perhaps this suggests that the husband is also an object controlled by his wife. More likely, however, is the suggestion that John can use the possessive pronoun to express a relationship between entities, rather than solely to express the concept of possession.

The idea that the Lamb's wife is controlled by outside forces is suggested in the next verse, which employs the passive form of δίδωμι ("to give"). John writes, "and it has *been given* (ἐδόθη) to her that she be clothed in fine linen . . ." (v. 8). Tina Pippin writes, "The Bride is woman as object, adorned and passive. . . ."[48] However, throughout Revelation this passive verbal form conveys a sense that one has been granted permission to do something, presumably by God (e.g., 6:8; 7:2; 9:3).[49] The use of the passive δίδωμι points to a major assumption undergirding Revelation—that all things, in heaven and on earth, are ultimately under the control and author-

[48] Pippin, *Death and Desire*, 72. Marla Selvidge also characterizes the bridal image as one of passivity ("Powerful and Powerless Women in the Apocalypse" *NeoT* 26 [1992]: 157–67).

[49] Aune, *Revelation*, 3:1017; Prigent, *L'Apocalypse*, 283

ity of the one who sits on the throne. The suggestion that the Lamb's wife has been allowed to adorn herself suggests that she too acts within the realm of God's control.[50] The use of the passive ἐδόθη, however, does not conceptually image the wife of the Lamb as an object (A WOMAN/WIFE IS AN OBJECT). Rather, the use ἐδόθη implies that God's permission or will is an object, like a crown (Rev 6:2) or rod (11:1), which can be given to another: PERMISSION IS AN OBJECT.

John further characterizes the Lamb's wife by suggesting that she "has prepared herself" (ἡτοίμασεν ἑαυτήν). The use of the active verb and the reflexive pronoun assumes the woman's agency—she prepares herself, rather than *is being prepared*.[51] While the woman/wife may be described as a possession of the Lamb, John also communicates that she participates in bringing about the wedding. Again, this mitigates the metaphorical mapping A WOMAN/WIFE IS AN OBJECT.

Thinking about the depiction of the Lamb's wife in relation to some of the biblical traditions that preceded it, it is striking that the use of adornment imagery in Revelation 19 *does not* make a metaphorical equation between the bride and an object. As we saw in chap. 3, the depiction of Jerusalem in Ezekiel 16, as in Revelation 19, emphasizes the theme of adornment. In so doing, this text depicts God clothing the city-woman: "I clothed you with embroidered cloth. . . . I bound you in fine linen and covered you with rich fabric" (16:10). Through the repetitive use of first-person verbs Ezekiel emphasizes God's action in clothing Jerusalem, who is imaged as a passive object. This emphasizes God's role in bringing Jerusalem out of shame into a place of honor. When Jerusalem does anything regarding her own garments in Ezekiel 16, she constructs a shrine to other deities: "You took some of your own garments, and made for yourself colorful shrines, and on them played the whore . . ." (16:16 NRSV). In so doing, Jerusalem brings shame on herself and on her husband, God.

Ezekiel's depiction of Jerusalem differs markedly from Revelation's depiction of the wife of the Lamb, even though both texts draw on similar metaphorical mappings (A CITY IS A WOMAN and A COMMUNITY IS A WOMAN, respectively) and both elaborate this mapping in terms of the woman's adornment. Ezekiel blends this mapping with another conventional mapping, A WOMAN IS AN OBJECT, in his depiction of a Jerusalem whom God clothes much like a mannequin.[52] In contrast, the text of Revelation builds on the COMMUNITY IS A WOMAN mapping by depicting the bride's act of clothing herself. This activity elicits praise among the inhab-

[50] Beale, *The Book of Revelation* 942–43.

[51] Prigent, *L'Apocalypse*, 283.

[52] Mary E. Shields, "Multiple Exposures: Body Rhetoric and Gender Characterization in Ezek 16," *JFSR* 14 (1998): 10.

itants of heaven, for it describes a community that actively adorns itself, just as a bride prepares herself for her wedding. Just as a bride takes on a costume indicating her new role, so this community takes on a costume indicative of its new role.

Additionally, while a popular rhetorical topos within the Greco-Roman milieu was the female's obsession with appearance, in Rev 19:7–8 the bride's active participation in creating her appearance is presented positively.

b. DEEDS/ACTIONS ARE A GARMENT

John describes the garment with which the bride adorns herself by employing an explicit metaphorical expression, "the fine linen is the righteous deeds of the saints." John clearly equates the actions of the saints with a fabric or garment. Since Revelation is not primarily concerned with the nature of fabric, the focus of this metaphorical expression is "fine linen" (τὸ βύσσινον), while the metaphor's referent is "righteous deeds" (τὰ δικαιώματα). Since linen describes a particular type of fabric or garment, we can deduce that the conceptual domain to which it refers is the more general concept of FABRIC or GARMENT. Likewise, since "righteous deeds" describes a set of actions of a specific character, we can assume that the more general domain is that of DEEDS or ACTIONS. The conceptual mapping is represented as DEEDS/ACTIONS ARE A GARMENT. The image created by this mapping is that of a group of actions, which actually are separate entities or events, constituting a unity, a whole piece of cloth.

The translation of the neuter plural noun phrase τὰ δικαιώματα τῶν ἁγίων, which describes the mapping's target domain, proves difficult. There are two issues in translating this phrase: (1) how to render τὰ δικαιώματα, which occurs only twice in Revelation; and (2) whether to read τῶν ἁγίων as a subjective or objective genitive. The other occurrence of τὰ δικαιώματα is found in the hymn in Rev 15:4: "and [the nations] will worship before you [God]; for your τὰ δικαιώματα have been revealed." The NRSV translates τὰ δικαιώματα as "judgments," reflecting the traditional understanding of the verb δικαιόω,"to show justice" or "to justify."[53] Translating τὰ δικαιώματα as "judgments" seems inappropriate in Revelation 19, if one assumes, translating τῶν ἁγίων as a subjective genitive, that these deeds are performed by the saints and not God: "the fine linen is the judgments of the saints." In Revelation, God alone judges and not the followers of God (e.g., 6:10). To attribute acts of judgments to the saints would be placing them in God's role. Thus, some interpreters argue that the genitive be read

[53] BAGD 197.

as an objective genitive, describing someone else's, namely, God's, actions on behalf of the saints.[54]

The phrase τὰ δικαιώματα may be also understood as actions that are just or right and not only acts that administer justice in a legal sense.[55] Interpreting the phrase in this way, the genitive τῶν ἁγίων makes most sense as a subjective genitive, describing the saints' actions. This rendering, "the fine linen is the righteous deeds of the saints," coheres best with the passage's imagery.[56] Since the saints, those who are faithful to God and the Lamb and who resist the power of the Beast (e.g., 11:18; 13:7, 10; 14:12), can be understood as the community that constitutes "the bride," it makes sense to imagine their actions as creating the bridal garment. In contrast to Beale, we read the genitive τῶν ἁγίων as a subjective genitive. This coheres to the image of the bride preparing *herself*, especially since Greek and Roman brides traditionally created their own bridal garments. As we noted in chap. 4, the first-century bride wove her own bridal costume, including the *tunica recta* which she adopted as a sign of becoming a woman. The bride's act of weaving her tunic suggested her ability to fulfill the role of a wife, which was ideally symbolized in spinning and weaving. Therefore, just as the first-century bride actively constructed a garment indicative of her new identity, so the community of the saints, which will become the new Jerusalem, creates its own bridal garment. Similarly, the saints' ability to create such a garment suggests the community's readiness to accept their future identity.

The image of the bride creating her own bridal garment is further supported by the grammatically awkward construction τὸ γὰρ βύσσινον τὰ δικαιώματα τῶν ἁγίων ἐστίν, which equates a plural participle (τὰ δικαιώματα) with a singular noun (τὸ βύσσινον).[57] This seemingly clumsy phrase encourages the audience to imagine that a set of actions or multiple actions comprise a single garment or fabric: DEEDS/ACTIONS ARE A GARMENT. The pure and just actions of the faithful constitute a unity.

---

[54] Gregory K. Beale addresses the translation of τὸ γὰρ βύσσινον τὰ δικαιώματα τῶν ἁγίων ἐστίν by arguing that τῶν ἁγίων should be understood as an objective genitive. Beale argues that this understanding conforms to clothing imagery found throughout Revelation. He writes, "Without exception receiving white clothes elsewhere in the Apocalypse precisely conveys the idea of *purity resulting from a text of persevering faith* . . . therefore, the white clothes here should be equated not with the 'righteous deeds' of perseverance . . . but with the reward or result of such deeds. In this light the final clause of v 8 could be interpretatively paraphrased as 'the fine linen is *the reward for (or result of)* the righteous deeds of the saints'" (*The Book of Revelation*, 936).

[55] Aune, *Revelation*, 3:1031.

[56] Ruiz notes that this translation functions as part of the contrast between the Bride and the Whore, as the latter is characterized as performing unclean or immoral deeds (*Ezekiel in the Apocalypse*, 502).

[57] Aune, *Revelation*, 3:1017.

John describes the nature of this garment using τὸ βύσσινον, which refers to a linen fabric of fine quality.[58] Although the term occurs infrequently in extant Greek texts, the Septuagint version of Ezekiel 16 employs the term to describe Zion's bridal attire (16:10). This linguistic similarity actually points to the difference between Ezekiel's description of God's bride and Revelation's depiction of the bride of the Lamb. While Ezekiel 16 presents Jerusalem as a passive recipient of God's fine linen (A WOMAN IS AN OBJECT), Revelation 19 presents the Christian community as an active participant in creating its bridal attire.

i. IMMORALITY IS DIRT.

John characterizes this bridal garment as "clean" (καθαρός). This description serves as a stark contrast to John's depiction of the Great Whore, who carries a cup full of unclean things related to her fornication (ἀκάθαρτα τῆς πορνείας αὐτῆς, 17:4; cf. 18:2). The text does not specify whether these "dirty things" are acts of prostitution or the results of prostitution. Despite this, the association between uncleanliness and fornication in this context reflects a metaphorical association between immoral actions and dirt: IMMORALITY IS DIRT. John draws on this metaphorical equation elsewhere in Revelation.[59] In 3:4–5, for instance, the risen Christ mentions those in Sardis who have not "stained" (μολύνω) their clothing. They maintain the cleanliness of their robes by "conquering," refusing to worship the beast and following the Lamb (cf. 15:2). Likewise, John describes 144,000 virgins who have not "stained" or "defiled" themselves through improper sexual activity (14:4).[60] In addition, their cleanliness (ἄμωμοι) relates to their unwillingness to lie (14:5). Particular actions, according to Revelation, are like dirt that "stains" one's garments. The bride has not participated in these actions, because her garment is without

---

[58] Josephus uses βύσσινος to describe the garments of the priests in the Jerusalem Temple (*A.J.* 3.7.2; *B.J.* 5.235).

[59] An interesting metaphorical mapping that relates to the theme of cleanliness is BLOOD IS A CLEANSING AGENT. In 7:4 John describes a great multitude who stand before the throne of God. They are robed in white, and an angel explains that their robes have been washed in blood. Similarly, a variant reading of Rev 1:5 describes blood as "cleansing" individuals from sin.

[60] This meaning of 14:4 is difficult to untangle, because it seems to equate sexual activity in general and not just fornication with uncleanliness: "These are those who have not defiled themselves with women, for they are virgins." The apparent reference to male virgins in itself is unusual. In fact, the term παρθένοι typically describes young women who have not married (Aune, *Revelation*, 2.811). In addition, virginity in men was not necessarily valued in the Greco-Roman milieu. See Peter Brown, *The Body and Society: Men, Women, and Sexual Renunciation in Early Christianity* (New York: Columbia University Press, 1988), 28. Celibacy or sexual abstinence was, however, occasionally seen as a mark of virtue. In first-century Judaism, sexual abstinence appears to have been seen as an important preparation for holy war. Thus, the community at Qumran emphasized celibacy (Aune, *Revelation*, 2:819).

stain. Furthermore, through this description of the bridal garment John establishes a connection between the Lamb and those who are faithful to God, such as the 144,000, and the bride.

ii. GOD IS A LIGHT SOURCE; SIMILARITY IS PROXIMITY

John also characterizes the bride's garment as "shining" (λαμπρός). This characterization suggests that the bridal garment functions as part of a metaphorical expression, since garments do not typically give off light. In fact, the adjective λαμπρός draws on an important theme throughout Revelation, in which Christ is characterized by "light" (φῶς). Early in the narrative, for example, John describes Christ amidst seven lamp-stands with a face shining like the sun (1:12–16). Revelation similarly uses light imagery in describing God upon the throne: Coming out of God's throne are lightening flashes or bursts of light and before the throne are seven burning torches (4:5). John later makes a more explicit metaphorical connection between God and light when he describes the new Jerusalem: "And there will no longer by any night and they will not need the light of a lamp nor the light of the sun; for the Lord God will shine upon them [the faithful] . . ." (22:5). Within this metaphorical expression the future tense verbal construction "will shine" (φωτίσει) functions as the metaphorical focus. Attributing the activity of shining to God signals the expression's metaphorical nature. In this case, the metaphorical referent is part of the frame, "the Lord God." By attributing the act of shining to God, even comparing this activity to a lamp or to the sun, the text suggests a metaphorical mapping GOD IS A LIGHT SOURCE.

Within the logic of the conceptual mapping GOD IS A LIGHT SOURCE, anything that is near God will shine or reflect God's light. Hence, the face of Christ shines (2:16) and the bride of the Lamb wears garments that are bright, supposedly reflecting the light of God. The shining nature of the bride's garments suggests that she is near God. This likely indicates that the bride's association with God reflects a metaphorical equation between nearness and similarity. Something that is near another shares at least some of the characteristics of the other:[61] SIMILARITY IS PROXIMITY.

iii. GARMENTS ARE CHARACTER; APPEARANCE IS ESSENCE

Revelation's language of adornment is not ultimately about the external appearance of the bride or the other characters in the text who are adorned in some way (e.g., those before the throne of God [7:13–14], the Great Whore [17:4], the armies of heaven [19:14]). Instead, as implied throughout our discussion of the bride, John employs the language of garment and adornment to represent qualities of character and religious com-

[61] Turner describes this in terms of lateral relations (*Death Is the Mother of Beauty: Mind, Metaphor, Criticism* (Chicago: University of Chicago Press, 1987), 33–37.

mitment. For example, those who stand before the throne are robed in white, which reflects the fact that they have followed the Lamb even to the point of death. As one of the twenty-four elders explains to John, "These are the ones who have come out of the great persecution and who have washed their robes, making them white in the blood of the Lamb" (7:13–14). The garments of the faithful, like the garments of the bride, metaphorically represent the character of those who wear them, suggesting that the text assumes the conceptual mapping GARMENTS ARE CHARACTER. This mapping reflects an even more basic metaphorical equation between the tangible appearance of a thing and its nature or essence: APPEARANCE IS ESSENCE.[62] The external appearance of the bride, including the appearance of her garments, metaphorically describes the essence of the bride—her faithfulness, purity, and closeness to God.

The connection between appearance and essence or character that Revelation assumes also points to the "bride's" role in constructing her own character. The deeds of the bride, the community of the saints, comprise her garments (DEEDS ARE A GARMENT). The outward appearance of this garment metaphorically indicates the bride's character (GARMENTS ARE CHARACTER; APPEARANCE IS ESSENCE), and suggests that the bride's actions exemplify her essence.

Excursus: Is Christ the Warrior Also Christ the Bridegroom?

Austin Farrer argues that the nuptial imagery of Revelation 19 extends past the beatitude of 19:9 into the description of Christ the warrior: "Then I saw heaven opened, and behold, a white horse! And the one sitting upon it is called Faithful and True, and in righteousness he judges and makes war" (19:11). Revelation 19:11–16 clearly blends the conceptual mappings CHRIST IS A KING and CHRIST IS A WARRIOR. Marc Brettler suggests that the metaphor YHWH IS A WARRIOR often functions as more specific form of YHWH IS A KING.[63] The image of this king on a horse echoes the imagery of Psalm 45, which depicts a king on his mount girded with his sword. Aune comments, "The view that Rev 19:11–16 presents Christ as the royal bridegroom, based on the royal wedding song in Ps 45 . . . is suggestive. Ps 45:7–8 is quoted in Heb 1:8–9 and given a christological interpretation."[64] In preparation for the king's wedding, the

---

[62] Lakoff and Turner, *More Than Cool Reason*, 148.

[63] In his analysis of warrior metaphors for God in the Psalms, Marc Brettler suggests that the metaphor YHWH IS A WARRIOR often functions as a more specific form of YHWH IS A KING ("Images of YHWH the Warrior in Psalms," *Semeia* 61 [1993]: 135–65). As early as Ireneaus, some interpreters read the first horseman of the seven seals, who rides on a white horse and who is given a crown (6:2), as an image of Christ as a kingly warrior (Aune, *Revelation,* 2:393). The image of Christ as a king is introduced in the beginning of Revelation (1:5) and culminates in the final chapters. After the warrior king imagery of chap. 19, Christ reigns (βασιλεύω) with the faithful on earth for a thousand years (20:4–6).

[64] Aune, *Revelation,* 3:1046–47.

author of the psalm lauds the king's prowess on the battlefield: "Gird your sword on your thigh, O mighty one, in your glory and majesty. In your majesty ride on victoriously for the cause of truth and to defend the right. . . . Your arrows are sharp in the heart of the king's enemies; the peoples fall under you" (Ps 45:3–5; NRSV). This parallel imagery raises the possibility that John similarly relates kingly wedding imagery with warrior imagery, especially given his dependence on traditions in the Hebrew Bible about a Davidic Messiah (e.g., 5:5).

In his reading of Revelation's war imagery, Stephen Moore suggests that a metaphorical connection exists between military imagery and masculine sexuality.[65] Moore notes the double entendre implicit in Revelation's claim that Christ will rule the nations with a "rod of iron," which uses a phallic image to describe Christ's coming reign (12:5; 19:15; cf. Ps 2:9).[66] The metaphorical connection between military prowess and masculine sexuality can be found in the Hebrew Bible, as well as in other ancient Near Eastern texts. Harry Hoffner comments, "The masculinity of the ancient was measured by two criteria: (1) his prowess in battle, and (2) his ability to sire children. . . . These two aspects of masculinity were frequently associated with each other. . . . Those symbols which primarily referred to his military exploits often served to remind him of his sexual ability as well."[67] In the ancient world, the concept of masculine sexuality, which was assumed to be an active role,[68] can be mapped on to the concept of military power or vice versa: SEX IS WAR and WAR IS SEX.

The metaphorical connection between masculine sexuality and military conquest or war also resides in Roman traditions. The popular Roman writer Ovid, for instance, often replaces the language of sexuality with the language of violence.[69] In *Ars Amatoria* Ovid recounts one of Rome's foundational myths, the abduction of the Sabine women by Romulus and his men, using marital

---

65 Stephen D. Moore, *God's Beauty Parlor and Other Queer Spaces in and around the Bible* (Stanford, Calif.: Stanford University Press, 2001), 180–81.

66 Moore, *God's Beauty Parlor*, 181. Interestingly, in the letter to Thyatira, which incorporates imagery of sexual violence with regard to the prophet Jezebel (2:22), the risen Christ promises that those who conquer will be given authority to rule over the nations with an iron rod (2:27).

67 Harry A. Hoffner, Jr., "Symbols for Masculinity and Femininity: Their Use in Ancient Near Eastern Sympathetic Magic Rituals," *JBL* 85 (1966): 327. This article is brought to light by Moore, who quotes this same passage (*God's Beauty Parlor*, 181–82).

68 Especially in the Roman milieu, masculine sexuality was understood as an active role. The masculine role in sexual intercourse was to penetrate and never to be penetrated; thus, males who were penetrated in homosexual intercourse would be described as "having a woman's experience" (*muliebria pati*). See Jonathan Walters, "Invading the Roman Body: Manliness and Impenetrability in Roman Thought," in *Roman Sexualities*, ed. Judith P. Hallett and Marilyn B. Skinner (Princeton: Princeton University Press, 1997), 29–43.

69 Pamela Gordon and Harold C. Washington, "Rape as a Military Metaphor in the Hebrew Bible," in *A Feminist Companion to the Latter Prophets*, ed. Athalya Brenner (Sheffield: Sheffield Academic Press, 1995), 312; Amy Richlin, "Reading Ovid's Rapes," *Pornography and Representation in Greece and Rome*, ed. Amy Richlin (New York: Oxford University Press, 1992), 168. See also Leslie Cahoon, "The Bed as Battlefield: Erotic Conquest and Military Metaphor in Ovid's Amores," *TAPA* 118 (1988): 293–307.

imagery to describe the Roman men's "conquest" over the women. The women, for instance, are described as "marital booty," and the men are described as soldiers receiving a bonus (Ovid, *Ars* 1.125–30). Richlin notes that this recounting of the myth reflects one of Ovid's favorite metaphors, *militat omnis amans* ("every lover is a soldier").[70] In his discussion of the Roman wedding, Plutarch wonders whether aspects of the Roman wedding allude to this foundation myth. Plutarch asks whether the tradition of carrying the bride over the threshold symbolizes that the first Roman wives were carried off by force (*Quaes. rom.* 29) and whether the wedding hymn "Talassio" refers to this event as well (*Ques. rom.* 31). Likewise, Plutarch suggests that the Roman tradition of parting the bride's hair with a spear may "symbolize the marriage of the first Roman wives by violence with attendant war" or it may teach the bride that she is about to be married to a "warlike" man (*Ques. rom.* 87). In making these connections, Plutarch suggests that underlying the Roman concept of marriage is an equation between bridegrooms and the warriors of Romulus.

In light of this commonplace metaphorical connection between masculine sexuality and military might, as well as the possible Roman tradition of depicting the bridegroom as a warrior, it seems little wonder that Revelation 19 moves so easily from the image of the Lamb as a bridegroom to the image of Christ as a royal warrior. The images are not necessarily incompatible, as a contemporary reader might assume. Rather, the image of the bridegroom, which at least implies the concept of masculine sexuality, might naturally give way to the image of the warrior. Perhaps underlying Revelation's shift from the wedding of the Lamb into the image of Christ the warrior is the conceptual mapping A BRIDEGROOM IS A WARRIOR.

On the surface, the nuptial imagery of Rev 19:7–8 appears quite simple. A closer look at the imagery, however, reveals the ways in which metaphorical mappings undergirding this imagistic language encourage Revelation's audience to think about the Lamb and the Christian community, as well as the relationship between these two, in very specific ways. This way of analyzing Revelation's imagery prevents us from falling into a propositional treatment of the language. It shows that as interpreters we do the imagery a disservice if we simply conclude that "the bride of the Lamb is the church" and proceed to the analysis of the next significant metaphorical image. Rather, our analysis demonstrates that the linguistic expressions in the text function as part of a larger conceptual framework entailing various interrelated mappings.

We must emphasize that Revelation's readers would not have necessarily differentiated the different mappings articulated in this presentation. Rather, a reader of this text experiences the cumulative effect of these mappings. The metaphorical expressions within the text lead the readers into

[70] Richlin, "Reading Ovid's Rapes," 168. For another version of the story of the Sabine women, see Livy 1.9.233. Livy's version of the story generally refrains from using the military imagery favored by Ovid.

the conceptual mappings, encouraging them to envision one thing in terms of another. In constructing this imagery John draws on conventional mappings from his symbolic world, but he casts them in new terms in order to address the communities of first-century Asia Minor. By bringing the mappings to the surface, we hope to illustrate how the imagery as a whole serves to encourage these audiences to think about the Christian community's relation to the Lamb.

An Invitation Is Extended: Revelation 19:9

Immediately following the hymn in 19:1–8, a "voice"[71] instructs John to write the following blessing: "Blessed are those who have been invited to the wedding banquet of the Lamb" (v. 9).[72] This declaration reintroduces the metadomain WEDDING and prompts the audience to imagine one aspect of this domain—the wedding banquet (τὸ δεῖπνον τοῦ γάμου), which is believed to have followed a wedding.[73] Mention of the banquet, therefore, could suggest the end of the wedding, the culmination and celebration of an important transitional event.

1. THE MESSIANIC AGE IS A WEDDING BANQUET

In a manner similar to 19:7, the use of "Lamb" in this declaration signals that τὸ δεῖπνον τοῦ γάμου describes something other than an actual wedding banquet. John again resists offering an explicit metaphorical expression, allowing his audience to think about the wedding banquet primarily in relation to the aforementioned wedding or in relation to some contextual knowledge.

Commentators often read this reference as a depiction of a messianic banquet as described in the Hebrew Bible prophets and subsequently

---

[71] The voice in this verse is probably that of the bowl angel who initially appears in 17:1 to show John the Great Whore. This angel also appears in chap. 21 to show John the descent of the new Jerusalem (21:9). The fact that the voice of 19:9 comes from an angel and not from God or Christ is suggested by the voice's response when John prostrates himself before the speaker: "I am your fellow slave . . . !" (Aune, *Revelation*, 3:1031; Prigent, *L'Apocalypse*, 284).

[72] This is one of seven beatitudes in Revelation. The others occur in 1:3; 14:13; 16:15; 20:6; 22:7, 14.

[73] Δεῖπνον, the word used for "feast" in 19:9, is also used in 19:17, when an angel calls the birds in midheaven to feast on the armies of the beast who have been destroyed by Christ and the armies of heaven. While this gruesome scene does depict an "eschatological feast," since it is offered to the birds, it is not likely that this is the same feast as the one described in 19:9. It does, however, seem to function as an ironic parody of the wedding feast. While the people of God will participate in the wedding feast of the Lamb, those who make war against God will also participate in a feast–and they will be the main course.

revised in the Gospels.[74] In Isaiah especially, banqueting imagery describes the abundance and blessing that God provides in a renewed Israel: "On this mountain the LORD of hosts will make for all peoples a feast of rich food, a feast of well-aged wines, of rich food filled with marrow, of well-aged wines strained clear" (Isa 25:6; cf. 55:1). In later centuries this imagery of abundance could be used to metaphorically describe an eschatological messianic age (e.g., *1 Enoch* 62:15; *2 Baruch* 29:1–8).[75] This usage reflects the conceptual mapping THE MESSIANIC AGE IS A BANQUET. Banquet imagery also appears in the Gospels, where it is often more explicitly depicted as wedding banquet imagery. For instance, two Matthean parables about the kingdom of God are often read as metaphorically describing the messianic banquet as a wedding feast (Matt 22:2ff.; 25:10ff.; cf. Luke 13:29f.).[76] Eugene Boring suggests that these parables combine the imagery of the messianic banquet with the prophetic marriage metaphor to create an image of the eschatological age, in which Christ "weds" his people, as a wedding banquet.[77] The conceptual metaphor YAHWEH (or his anointed one) IS THE BRIDEGROOM OF HIS PEOPLE is combined with the mapping THE MESSIANIC AGE IS A BANQUET to describe the eschatological age. The resulting metaphorical mapping can be represented as THE MESSIANIC AGE IS A WEDDING BANQUET.

Interpreters often read Rev 19:9 in relation to these traditions. Referring to Matthew 22 specifically, Schüssler Fiorenza writes, "Christians . . . will participate in eschatological well-being symbolized by the marriage feast. . . ."[78] In terms of conceptual metaphor theory, Schüssler Fiorenza assumes that Rev 19:9 reflects a metaphorical equation between the eschatological or messianic age and a wedding banquet (THE MESSIANIC AGE IS A WEDDING BANQUET). In so doing, Schüssler Fiorenza indicates that the well-being of one, a wedding feast, directly refers to the well-being of the other. This reading of the text reflects Aristotle's view that metaphor requires one to see similarities between unlike things (*Poetica* 22.17). Interestingly, however, while Rev 19:9 echoes the traditions that perceive this similarity, John does not exploit this connection.

---

[74] Aune, *Revelation*, 3:1033; Beale, *The Book of Revelation*, 945; Isbon T. Beckwith, *The Apocalypse of John* (New York: Macmillan, 1919), 728; Fekkes, *Isaiah and Prophetic Traditions in the Book of Revelation: Visionary Antecedents and Their Development* (Sheffield: JSOT Press, 1994), 232–33; Lohmeyer, *Die Offenbarung*, 156; Prigent, *L'Apocalypse*, 284.

[75] Dennis E. Smith, "Messianic Banquet," *ABD* 4:789–90.

[76] Louis Arther Vos, *The Synoptic Traditions in the Apocalypse* (Kampen: Kok, 1965), 163–74. Prigent also suggests a connection between Rev 19:9 and Luke 14:15, "Blessed is the one who will eat bread in the kingdom of God" (*L'Apocalypse*, 284).

[77] Eugene Boring, "Matthew: Introduction, Commentary, and Reflections," in *The New Interpreter's Bible* (Nashville: Abingdon Press, 2001), 6:235 n. 198.

[78] Schüssler Fiorenza, *The Book of Revelation*, 102.

2. THE FAITHFUL ARE WEDDING GUESTS

Although 19:9 continues to draw on the conceptual domain WEDDING, the verse shifts the focus away from the bridegroom and bride. This verse focuses on another set of participants culturally associated with the concept of a WEDDING—the guests, or "those who have been invited."[79] As Beale notes, "Verse 9 presents a different perspective on the wedding metaphor from vv 7–8. There the bride, the corporate church, was viewed as about to wed the Lamb, but now individual Christians are portrayed as guests at the marriage banquet."[80] Moreover, the use of the phrase "Blessed are those . . ." encourages the audience to imagine itself in the role of those invited to the wedding banquet.[81] The text asks the audience to conceptualize itself as a single entity, the personified wife of the Lamb, and then almost immediately asks the members of the audience to imagine themselves attending the wedding banquet: THE FAITHFUL ARE WEDDING GUESTS.

This conceptual shift, requiring the audience to shift from imagining themselves as a personified bride to imagining themselves as individual guests, leads some interpreters to question whether the image of the bride in vv. 7–8 describes the community. Rossing challenges, "In light of the macarism of Rev 19:9, scholars who argue that the bride is the church in this text are faced with the task of explaining how readers can be both bride and guests in the same scene."[82] The conceptual shift required by the text may seem abrupt when we analyze the logic of the text in a piecemeal fashion.[83] As we saw in our analysis of the Jewish literary traditions, such conceptual shifts are typical for imagistic language. In Isaiah 62, for example, the prophet shifts from a conceptual mapping depicting Zion as bride to Zion as mother. We can imagine that if an interpreter envisions the text's imagery as she reads the text, such a shift in conceptual imagery is not an obstacle to coherent interpretation.[84]

---

[79] Although καλέω is used seven times in Revelation, on no other occasion does it convey the sense of invitation; rather, it is used in reference to the nomenclature for particular characters or places (e.g., 1:9; 11:8).

[80] Beale, *The Book of Revelation*, 945.

[81] As Boring suggests, moreover, even though this macarism is primarily an indicative statement about those who have accepted the invitation of John, this blessing also functions as an invitation to those who have not yet accepted: "The first announcement of the wedding feast in 19:7 is an invitation to the hearer-reader, sealed by God himself, to share in the eschatological wedding party at the consummation of the ages" (*Revelation*, 193).

[82] Rossing includes this argument among her reasons against reading the bridal image as a community image (*The Choice between Two Cities*, 140).

[83] Aune suggests that the shift in imagery reflects an editorial seam in the text (*Revelation*, 3:1032).

[84] For a discussion of the ways in which humans can understand complex networks of conceptual mappings, see Gilles Fauconnier and Mark Turner, *The Way We Think: Conceptual*

The image of the wedding banquet draws on the same semantic domain as the preceding verses, WEDDING, although it requires the audience to view itself within different roles in the metaphorical construction. Contrary to Rossing's estimation, the fact that these verses employ two different ways of imagining the community suggests that Revelation's nuptial imagery is primarily concerned with the community's identity in relationship to the Lamb. By offering two different views of the community within one metaphorical construction, Rev 19:7–9 points to the complexity of the community's relationship to the risen Christ.

Deductio in domum mariti: Nuptial Imagery in Revelation 21

The conclusion of Revelation is dominated by John's vision of a celestial city, a new Jerusalem, that descends as part of a new heaven and a new earth. Revelation includes parallel descriptions of this city, both of which employ explicit nuptial imagery. In the first vision John writes:

> [1]And I saw a new heaven and a new earth, for the first heaven and first earth passed away and the sea was no longer. [2]And I saw the holy city, a new Jerusalem,[85] descending out of heaven from God, prepared as a bride (νύμφην) adorned for her husband (τῷ ἀνδρὶ αὐτῆς). [3]And I heard a great voice from the throne[86] saying, "Behold the dwelling place (ἡ σκηνή) of God with humanity! And [God] will dwell with them and they will be his peoples.[87] And God himself will dwell with them as their God." (21:1–3).

Revelation 21:9–11 presents another vision using nuptial imagery to describe Jerusalem:

> [9]And one of the seven angels, from the ones who had the seven bowls full[88] of the last plagues, came and spoke to me, saying, "Come, I will show you the

Blending and the Mind's Hidden Complexities (New York: Basic Books, 2002). They argue that the human mind is continually shifting from one conceptual blending to another.

[85] Some English translations, including the NRSV and the NIB, include the definite article before the adjective "new," rendering the text "*the* new Jerusalem." The Greek text does not include a definite article with either "Jerusalem" or "new."

[86] Although not identified as the voice of God, this voice presumably is that of God, because it comes from the throne. Throughout Revelation, God is identified with the throne (e.g., 4:2, 9; 5:1, 13; 7:10) (Bauckham, *The Theology of the Book of Revelation*, 31–32). Furthermore, in 21:5 the one who sits on the throne, God, speaks directly to John.

[87] The manuscript tradition includes both the plural λαοί and the singular λαός. I have chosen to render the text in terms of the former, since it is (1) the more difficult reading (Aune, *Revelation*, 3:1110), and (2) because the plural captures the communal nature of the new Jerusalem.

[88] The Greek τῶν γεμόντων presents a grammatical problem, because it doesn't agree with the case of its antecedent,τὰς ἑπτὰ φιάλας. As a result, the manuscript tradition includes variants that seek to correct the error.

> bride (νύμφην) the wife (γυναῖκα) of the Lamb." [10]And he took me up in the spirit to a great and high mountain and he showed me the holy city, Jerusalem, descending out of heaven from God, [11]having the glory of God. Its radiance is like a precious stone, like a stone of jasper, as crystal. . . .

Here Revelation offers parallel visions that look very similar. Scholars often attribute this "duplication" to an editorial error or as a mindless repetition.[89] In contrast, our analysis will demonstrate how two passages that look quite similar on the surface, since both employ city and nuptial imagery, function quite differently. We will see how these passages employ metaphorical mappings in different ways and for different functions.

1. A CITY IS A WOMAN

In Revelation 21:2 the image of the bride of the Lamb, introduced in chap. 19, is clearly a metaphor for a city and specifically for a new Jerusalem. John constructs the metaphorical expression as a similarity statement: "I saw the holy city, a new Jerusalem . . . prepared *as* a bride. . . ." The comparative particle ὡς ("as")[90] might lead some to argue that John uses a simile here and not a metaphor.[91] While this is true in terms of a linguistic understanding of metaphor (as described in chap. 2), a conceptual understanding of metaphor suggests that a grammatical expression's use of a comparative term, such as "like" or "as," still involves understanding one thing in terms of another. Similarity statements can compare like items (e.g., "encyclopedias are like dictionaries") or unlike items (e.g., "encyclopedias are like gold mines").[92] While the former is not a metaphor, since

[89] Lohmeyer tries to make sense of 21:6–22:6 by arguing that this unit is a different type of vision that consists of paraenesis addressed directly to the seer's present community (*Die Offenbarung*, 169–71). Aune argues that the second vision of the bride is an editorial insertion. He maintains that the content of 21:3–5 seems to flow naturally into 22:3–5, creating a poetic description of God's dwelling with humanity (*Revelation*, 3:1115). See also Heinrich Kraft, *Die Offenbarung des Johannes* (Handbuch zum Neuen Testament 16a; Tübingen: J. C. B. Mohr, 1974), 262–69. In contrast, Mathias Rissi, for instance, reads 21:1–8 as an interpretive prologue to the vision that begins in 21:9. The content of vv. 1–8 is primarily auditory and tells John how to understand the vision of the city, which he catches a glimpse of in v. 2, but is shown more fully starting in v. 9 (Rissi, *The Future of the World*, 54–57).

[90] For a discussion of the comparative particle, see Smyth §2772, §3002.

[91] Robert Gundry describes this possibility by answering a rhetorical question: "But what shall we make of elements in the text that seem to distinguish the New Jerusalem from the saints? The city cannot be the bride, the church, can it, because 21:2 *compares* the city to a bride . . . ? More accurately, however, 21:2 does not compare the city itself to a bride; it compares the *preparation* of the city to the adornment of a bride for her husband. This comparison leads naturally and without contradiction to an identification of the city itself with the bride, the Lamb's wife, several verses later (21:9)" ("The New Jerusalem: People as Place, Not Place for People," *NovT* 29 [1987]: 263).

[92] Raymond W. Gibbs, *The Poetics of Mind: Figurative Thought, Language, and Understanding* (Cambridge: Cambridge University Press, 1994), 218.

both terms are part of a common category (reference books), the latter is a metaphorical statement. Returning to Aristotle's understanding of metaphor, the latter example involves imagining one thing in terms of something unlike it. In the case of Rev 21:2 although John expresses his description of "the holy city, a new Jerusalem" as a simile, he still encourages his audience to envision this entity as something it is not—a bride. We can, therefore, represent the metaphorical expression as "the holy city, new Jerusalem *is* a bride."

Identifying the metaphorical expression in the verse enables us to identify the conceptual mapping that undergirds the expression. The focus of a metaphorical expression typically relates to the source domain of a conceptual mapping. The metaphorical focus in this expression, "bride," is one aspect of the more general concept WOMAN. "Bride" functions as a particular social role within this domain, as described in our discussion of 19:7–8. The source domain within the conceptual mapping, however, can be understood as WOMAN. The conceptual mapping's target domain relates to the expression's referent, "the holy city, new Jerusalem." This particular referent expresses both the general conceptual domain CITY and its more specific expression, Jerusalem or new Jerusalem. We can therefore represent the central conceptual mapping undergirding 21:2 as A CITY IS A WOMAN. Here John draws on the conventional metaphorical mapping also used within the Jewish literary traditions that inform so much of Revelation.

One of the ways that Revelation develops this conventional mapping is by characterizing Jerusalem as a holy city (τὴν πόλιν τὴν ἁγίαν).[93] Revelation often employs the adjective "holy" (ἅγιος) as a descriptor for those people who faithfully follow God and the Lamb, "the saints" (οἱ ἅγιοι). Revelation 14:12, for example, characterizes the saints as those who keep God's commands and hold to the faith of Jesus, and suggests that holiness results from a person's actions and commitments. Holiness, in other words, implies an ability to act and make decisions. Robert M. Royalty points out that in Greco-Roman discourse rhetoricians sometimes attribute moral qualities to cities.[94] Aristotle, in fact, notes that an encomium speech, a speech praising a person's virtue, can be extended beyond praising humans and gods to praise "even inanimate things" (Aristotle, *Rhetorica* 1.9.9). This practice draws on a metaphorical equation between cities and humans and their ability to act morally or immorally: A CITY IS AN ACTOR or HUMAN. By depicting the new Jerusalem as a woman, Revelation encourages the audience to assume that this city acts as an individual

---

[93] "Holy city" often functions as a designation for the city of Jerusalem, according to Aune (*Revelation*, 3:1121). See, for instance, Isa 52:1.

[94] Royalty, *The Streets of Heaven*, 217.

entity and, in this case, acts in accordance with God's commands.[95] This is in contrast to those who read the image as depicting holy individuals or righteous "members."[96]

Furthermore, in describing this city as "holy," John contrasts it to the other city that predominates throughout Revelation—Babylon. John attributes to Babylon acts of fornication (e.g., 17:2), implying that Babylon is like a human who can make moral decisions. Whereas Revelation characterizes Babylon's actions as beyond redemption, leading to the city's destruction (19:2), this new Jerusalem is characterized as acting in a way worthy of God and the Lamb (e.g., 3:7; 4:8).

a. THE CHRISTIAN COMMUNITY IS A RENEWED ISRAEL; THE CHRISTIAN COMMUNITY IS A NEW JERUSALEM

John narrows the target domain CITY by suggesting that the city he views is not just any city, but a city bearing the significations of the historical city of Jerusalem. "Jerusalem" functions as an important part of the Jewish cultural imagination of Diaspora Jews and those who aligned themselves with the Jewish messianic movement of early Christianity. Even within the Diaspora the city functioned as the spiritual heart of the Jewish people.[97] Consequently, Revelation's appropriation of the image of Jerusalem conjures a variety of possible meanings and entailments, including memories of the Temple's greatness (e.g., Josephus, *J.W.* 5.11.6) and prophetic traditions about a rebuilt Jerusalem (e.g., Isa 65:17–25). For some early Christians, the designation "Jerusalem" might also suggest the place where "their Lord was crucified" (Rev 11:8). Additionally, within the Jewish liter-

---

[95] *Contra* Gundry, who argues that the holiness of the new Jerusalem stems from the fact that the city excludes those who are unholy (Rev 21:8) ("The New Jerusalem," 258).

[96] Kevin E. Miller, "The Nuptial Eschatology of Revelation 19–22," *CBQ* 60 (1998): 301–19.

[97] For a discussion of the significance of Jerusalem to Jews living in the Mediterranean Diaspora, see John M. G. Barclay, *Jews in the Mediterranean Diaspora: From Alexander to Trajan (323 BCE–117 CE)* (Edinburgh: T & T Clark, 1996), 418–24. For a discussion of various implications in the image of Jerusalem in OT and noncanonical Jewish sources, see Rissi, *The Future of the World*, 41–51. Rissi's analysis of Revelation's Jerusalem in relation to these traditions tends toward a supercessionism, which is problematic. At times it becomes difficult to determine where Rissi's reading of Revelation ends and his own opinions about Israel begin. See especially Rissi, *The Future of the World*, 64–65. While Revelation's harsh language suggests fierce intercommunity disagreements (e.g., "the synagogue of Satan" in 2:10), the text also exhibits a need to "sound" like Jewish tradition (e.g., the abundant use of prophetic texts and themes) and to position itself within this tradition. See Schüssler Fiorenza, "Visionary Rhetoric and Social Political Situation," in *The Book of Revelation: Justice and Judgment*, 2nd ed. (Minneapolis: Fortress Press, 1998), 195; see also Klaus Wengst, "Babylon the Great and the New Jerusalem: The Visionary View of Political Reality in the Revelation of John," in *Politics and Theopolitics in the Bible and Postbiblical Literature*, ed. Henning Graf Reventlow, Yair Hoffman, and Benjamin Uffenheimer (Sheffield: JSOT, 1994), 202.

ary traditions that depict Jerusalem as a woman the concept of "Jerusalem" communicates multiple meanings. As we saw in chap. 3, Jerusalem can be a place, a religious center, a gathering place for exiles, a participant in a covenant with God.

In Rev 21:2, the textual frame around "Jerusalem" signals that it is not to be understood literally, that it functions as a metaphorical focus. First, the text describes this as a *new* Jerusalem, in contrast to the current city of Jerusalem, implying that it is not referring to the actual city.[98] Second, by characterizing this city as "descending out of heaven," the text suggests that we are not dealing with an actual, historical city. "Jerusalem" describes another entity, something other than the historical city Jerusalem.

The metaphorical referent to which Jerusalem relates can be determined through attention to the narrative of Revelation. (This is a *co-textual implicit* referent, to return to the language articulated in chap. 2.) Throughout the narrative, John describes the ideal Christian community, those who remain faithful to the witness of Christ (7:14), as a renewed Israel. Already in the first chapter John employs imagery traditionally associated with the faithful people of Israel to describe the Christian community, praising Christ for making "us to be a kingdom, priests of God . . ." (1:6; 5:9–10; cf. Exod 19:6).[99] This verse suggests that the Christian community is being formed into the future identity promised to the people of Israel in Exodus. Further, Revelation 7 dramatically connects those who are faithful to the Lamb with the people of Israel, for John "hears the number" of those who are "sealed" from the twelve tribes of Israel (7:4). After hearing that 144,000 Israelites are selected and sealed, he looks and sees these 144,000 as a great crowd composed of people from every nation and from every tongue (7:9). These are the people who stand before the throne of God and before the Lamb.[100] An elder in heaven then clarifies the identity of this group for John (and for John's audience), explaining, "These are the ones who have come out of the great ordeal and washed their robes and made them white in the blood of the Lamb" (7:13). Here John blends the image of an ideal Israel with the image of the Christian faithful from every

[98] Beale suggests that the use of the term "new" to describe this Jerusalem alludes to Isa 62:1–2 which promises that Jerusalem will be called by a new name, *The Book of Revelation*, 1044.

[99] Schüssler Fiorenza, "Redemption as Liberation (Rev 1:5–6 and 5:9–10)," in *The Book of Revelation: Justice and Judgment*, 2nd ed. (Minneapolis: Fortress Press, 1998), 72.

[100] Not all scholars agree that the 144,000 and the great crowd described in 7:9 constitute the same group of people. For a discussion of these two groups as distinct, see Schüssler Fiorenza, *Revelation*, 66ff. In crucial places in the narrative John employs this same rhetorical technique in which an entity is identified as one thing but appears as another. For instance, in Revelation 5, an elder informs John that he will see the Lion of Judah open the seals, yet John sees the Lamb (5:5–6). Likewise, in chap. 17 an angel takes John to see the destruction of the Whore, yet John sees a city (17:1–6).

nation,[101] suggesting the conceptual mapping THE CHRISTIAN COMMUNITY IS A RENEWED ISRAEL. The 144,000 will appear again in the narrative, where they are linked with a crowd standing by a sea of glass and singing the Song of Moses. This is a clear allusion to the Exodus, again indicating that the 144,000 are a refashioned Israel (14:1–5; 15:1–5).[102]

The city of Jerusalem, the cultural and religious heart of Israel, can function as a metonym for the nation and the people of Israel, as we noted in chap. 3.[103] Such is the case in Revelation's depiction of the renewed Israel. After John's vision of the 144,000, the elder further informs John that "God will wipe away every tear from their eyes" (7:17), a clear allusion to Isaiah's vision of a restored Zion/Jerusalem (Isa 25:8) and a proleptic reference to Revelation's vision of a new Jerusalem (21:4). The elder implies that the community of the Christian faithful, the renewed Israel, will comprise a future Jerusalem. When John's audience encounters his vision of a new Jerusalem they are ready to view it as a vision of the faithful: THE CHRISTIAN COMMUNITY IS A NEW JERUSALEM.[104]

---

[101] Boring, *Revelation,* 204; Caird, *The Revelation of Saint John*, 94; Rissi, *The Future of the World*, 56.

[102] For a discussion of the faithful as a new Israel, see Bauckham, *The Theology of the Book of Revelation*, 98ff.; Beale, *The Book of Revelation*, 1045; Böcher, "Israel und die Kirche," 37–40.

[103] Beckwith, *The Apocalypse of John*, 588–90.

[104] In a subsection entitled "City or Community?" in his book *The Streets of Heaven,* Robert M. Royalty argues against reading the Jerusalem image as a metaphor for the Christian community (*The Streets of Heaven*, 215). Even though he acknowledges the historical precedence for reading Revelation's Jerusalem image as a community image, Royalty dismisses it as contrary to how the original interpreters would have heard it. He suggests that the Jerusalem image must be read as describing *either* a city, specifically a location, *or* a community. This claim assumes that words can mean only one thing at a time, which is a claim that fails to recognize the richness of language in general and figurative language in particular. In bolstering his claim, Royalty argues that an "allegorical" reading of Jerusalem demands an allegorical reading of Babylon as well (*The Streets of Heaven*, 217). Revelation's image of Babylon *does*, however, include more than topographical elements. For example, Revelation 18 includes a series of laments that depict various inhabitants of Babylon, sailors, business people, kings, mourning the city's destruction. The image of Babylon clearly includes a social or communal element, as well as topographical; and this points to the rich nature of imagistic language. In Revelation, Babylon is a place, a social organization, and a political entity. Another one of Royalty's arguments against reading Jerusalem as a metaphor for the Christian community is that the OT traditions that John employs in his description of this new Jerusalem refer to "real" cities such as Tyre and Babylon, and not allegorical cities (*The Streets of Heaven*, 217). Royalty's use of "real" and "allegorical" here is confusing, since his complaint seems to be with assuming that literary references to cities describe a community of people instead of or in addition to a locale. In this way, Royalty apparently confuses "real" with "topographical" and "allegorical" with "communal" and thereby fails to recognize that references to "real" or historical cities can include a variety of interrelated ideas, including the city's location, population, political structures, etc.

Revelation's first reference to this new Jerusalem sheds some light on John's use of the image. In Rev 3:12 the risen Christ promises "those who conquer," those who remain faithful to him and his teaching, that they will be inscribed with the name of God and "the name of the city of my God, the new Jerusalem that descends out of heaven. . . ." In this promise, as Robert H. Gundry observes, "Christ identifies the New Jerusalem with the person who overcomes. . . ."[105] The individual person is labeled as part of or being in relation to this future city. This close association between the faithful individual and the new Jerusalem suggests that Revelation's city imagery functions as an image of the faithful community.[106] The conceptual mapping THE CHRISTIAN COMMUNITY IS A NEW JERUSALEM encourages Revelation's audience to envision the faithful, those inscribed with the name "new Jerusalem," as a single, unified entity.

b. THE NEW JERUSALEM IS A DWELLING PLACE

In Revelation 21:3–4 a voice from the throne, presumably God, describes the specific nature of the new Jerusalem as a place as well. These verses employ language drawn from the history of Israel to narrow the concept NEW JERUSALEM. Echoing Hebrew Bible literary traditions (Ezek 37:27; Lev 26:11–12; Zech 8:8; cf. 2 Cor 6:16–18),[107] the voice identifies this city as the place where God dwells with humanity: "Behold the dwelling place (ἡ σκηνή) of God with humanity! And [God] will dwell with them and they will be his people. And God himself will dwell with them as their God" (21:3). The Christian community as the new Jerusalem exists, according to these verses, as the dwelling place of God and humanity: THE NEW JERUSALEM IS A DWELLING PLACE.

2. THE CHRISTIAN COMMUNITY IS A NEW JERUSALEM IS A WOMAN

As we saw in Ezekiel and Isaiah, sometimes the boundaries between mappings are blurred and sometimes an author seems to layer mappings one on top of another. Such is the case in Rev 21:2. At the most basic level, this verse envisions a city as a woman (A CITY IS A WOMAN). As we have shown,

[105] Gundry, "The New Jerusalem," 256.

[106] Rissi writes, "But however detailed the seer's description of the form of the city, his real interest does not lie in places or things. His real concern is with *men*, the people of God, who will participate in the benefits of salvation. . . . The holy Jerusalem points to the new situation which God's people will occupy in the reality of the new creation" (*The Future of the World*, 56–57).

[107] Prigent, *L'Apocalypse*, 327–28; Schüssler Fiorenza, *Priester für Gott: Studien zum Herrschafts- und Priestermotiv in der Apokalypse* (Münster: Verlag Aschendorff, 1972), 351.

the domain CITY is narrowed by the adjective "holy" and the designation "new Jerusalem." The latter reflects another metaphorical mapping developed in Revelation's narrative, THE CHRISTIAN COMMUNITY IS A NEW JERUSALEM. In this way, in 21:2 the conceptual domain CITY is augmented by and includes the concept of the CHRISTIAN COMMUNITY. It is this qualified CITY domain that is compared to a bride, suggesting THE CHRISTIAN COMMUNITY IS A NEW JERUSALEM IS A WOMAN.

As in Revelation 19, the nuptial imagery of chap. 21 mentions the idea of adornment in depicting the bride. The city has been "prepared as a bride adorned for her husband" (21:2). Again, among all the possible ideas culturally associated with the conceptual domain BRIDE, the text emphasizes the bride's adornment and appearance. The repeated mention of adornment further encourages the audience to imagine the bride primarily in these terms, limiting the imagery's potential meanings. The repetition of this theme, highlighted by the repetition of the word ἑτοιμάζω (19:7), also connects this bride with the wife of the Lamb of the earlier hymn. One is reminded of the image of the community creating the bridal garment through their deeds, fashioning their identity through their just actions. Through the allusion to Rev 19:7, the text alludes to the earlier metaphorical mapping APPEARANCE IS ESSENCE.

John expands on the image of the bride's adornment through use of the term κοσμέω, which I have rendered as "adorn." This term primarily connotes a sense of external preparation (see Matt 12:44; 23:29).[108] In contrast to the hymn of chap. 19, the vision of the bride in Revelation 21 seemingly resists explicit conceptual mappings linking the bride's appearance to her character or essence. There are, for instance, no descriptions of the bride's adornment in relation to her deeds (19:8); rather, the text allows the image of the bride's *external preparation* to predominate. The text allows the audience's imagination to remain focused upon the physical act of adornment.

3. A WOMAN IS A CITY

The only other time the verb κοσμέω occurs in Revelation is within the conclusion to the second vision of the new Jerusalem: "The foundations of the wall of the city *are adorned* (κεκοσμημένοι) with every precious stone: the first jasper, the second sapphire, the third agate . . ." (21:19). This verse reveals a shift in Revelation's nuptial imagery, as the concept of the BRIDE

---

[108] BAGD 445. The term κοσμέω is used, for example, of Aseneth in the pseudepigraphal work *Joseph and Aseneth* (ca. first century B.C.E.–second century C.E.). After she dresses herself in her finest attire, including a linen robe, a golden girdle, and abundant jewels, Aseneth is described as "adorned like a bride of God" (*Jos. Asen.* 4.1).

or WOMAN begins to function as the target domain described by the source domain CITY (THE BRIDE IS A CITY). Perhaps the text's reticence to describe adornment in relation to essence in 21:2 prepares the audience for the shift toward viewing the city and its ornate physical construction.

The parallel vision of the bride in 21:9–11 involves shifting the audience's focus by shifting the conceptual mappings undergirding the text. In this second vision Revelation encourages the audience to envision the bride as a city (A BRIDE IS A CITY), rather than envisioning the city as a bride (A CITY IS A BRIDE), as in the first vision. This turns the audience's view toward the city of the new Jerusalem, while effectively blurring the boundaries between the different concepts at play in these visions—the community, the new Jerusalem, the bride, the city.

The text accomplishes this conceptual shift through a short narrative unit. An angel informs John that "I will *show* (δείξω) to you the bride, the wife of the Lamb" (v. 9).[109] The angel explicitly uses vision language to coach John and, therefore, John's audience to envision a woman. When John describes the "bride," he sees, however, that she is actually a city: "And he took me up in the spirit . . . and he showed to me the holy city, Jerusalem, descending out of heaven from God" (21:10). In the tradition of Aristotle's view of metaphor, which involves setting something before the eyes, Revelation's audience is prompted to see one thing (WOMAN), which is then defined as something else (CITY). In this way the text sets up the conceptual mapping A BRIDE, or A WOMAN, IS A CITY.

The woman that the audience is instructed to envision in 21:10 is described as both bride (νύμφη) and wife (γυνή).[110] As we noted earlier, γυνή describes a woman in general or a wife in particular. This reflects the ancient assumption that all women were wives. By describing the new Jerusalem as a bride and as a woman/wife, the text captures the fact that the Greco-Roman bride symbolically embodied her role as wife. Here the text prompts the audience to envision the new Jerusalem in this transitional role, taking on the new social role of "wife of the Lamb."[111]

By shifting from one conceptual mapping (A CITY IS A WOMAN) to an inverse of the same mapping (A WOMAN IS A CITY), these two visions blur the boundaries between the conceptual domains involved in the nuptial

[109] Commentators note the similarity between this verse and 17:1–3, in which an angel shows John the Great Whore. The similarity of these verses suggests that the Whore, who is Babylon, functions as a parallel image of the Bride, who is Jerusalem. See Aune, *Revelation*, 3:1146; Beale, *The Book of Revelation*, 1063–64; Prigent, *L'Apocalypse*, 336.

[110] Two ancient manuscripts, 2053 and 2062, include only γυνή. Beale suggests that this was likely the result of a copying error (*The Book of Revelation*, 1065).

[111] *Contra* Prigent, who suggests that the language used here suggests that the bride has already become a wife. He writes, "Le mariage est regardé comme accomplí: Jérusalem est nommée non seulement 'fiancée' . . . mais 'femme, épouse'" (*L'Apocalypse*, 336).

imagery. The city, which is the Christian community as a new Jerusalem, is a bride, and this bride is a city. Max Black's interactionist view of metaphor probably provides the best explanation of this metaphorical circularity. As described in chap. 2, Black maintains that the two terms within a metaphorical construction, the focus and the subject, necessarily interact to create meaning.[112] While Black's view addresses metaphor primarily as a linguistic phenomenon, his point seems applicable to conceptual metaphors as well. The city can be envisioned as bride and the bride can be envisioned as a city; for John, both mappings are essential.

As the second vision progresses, the text clearly moves into an elaboration of how this bride, the Christian community who has adorned itself in righteousness (19:8), is a city. Entailments from the source domain CITY, including architectural features, predominate as John begins to envision the bride as a city. In particular, as Fekkes points out, John describes how this bride is "adorned" (κεκοσμημένοι) with precious jewels of every kind (21:19).[113]

a. A CITY IS A CONTAINER

As discussed in chap. 3, the metaphorical depiction of cities as women (A CITY IS A WOMAN) reflects the ancient view of both cities and women as containers.[114] The physical construction of ancient cities, which were walled, encourages the conceptual mapping A CITY IS A CONTAINER. Likewise, the physiological make-up of women, who typically possess wombs, gives rise to the conceptual mapping A WOMAN IS A CONTAINER. John clearly describes the new Jerusalem, as a city, in terms reminiscent of a container. The city possesses a high wall with gates through which one can, presumably, enter and exit (21:12; cf. 21:24–27). Like a container, the city also has contents, including the river of the water of life and the tree of life (22:1–2).

b. A WOMAN IS A CONTAINER

Although John blends the imagery of the bride and the city (A CITY IS A WOMAN), John resists describing the new Jerusalem, as a woman or bride, as a container. John does not exploit the metaphorical connection between containers and women in his description of the new Jerusalem. One of his female interpreters, the medieval visionary Hildegard of Bingen,

[112] Black, *Models*, 41.

[113] Fekkes, "'His Bride Has Prepared Herself,'" 283. Fekkes suggests that Rev 21:9–21 is modeled after Isa 54:11–12 with regard to the blending of architectural and feminine imagery.

[114] For a discussion of the ancient depiction of women in relation to vases, see Page Du Bois, *Sowing the Body: Psychoanalysis and Ancient Representations of Women* (Chicago: University of Chicago Press, 1988), 47–49.

does, however, extend Revelation's imagery in this way, providing a fascinating comparison to John's depiction of the new Jerusalem:[115]

> After this I saw the image of a woman as large as a great city, with a wonderful crown on her head and arms from a splendor hung like sleeves, shining from Heaven to earth. Her womb was pierced like a net with many openings, with a huge multitude of people running in and out. She had no legs or feet, but stood balanced on her womb in front of the altar that stands before the eyes of God, embracing it with her outstretched hands and gazing sharply with her eyes throughout all of Heaven. (Hildegard, *Scivias* 2.3.vision [Hart])

This woman, whom Hildegard characterizes as a city and later identifies as the bride of Christ (*Scivias* 2.3.1), consists almost entirely of a womb, a container. Further emphasizing the image of a woman as a container, Hildegard describes the church's womb as netlike, allowing for a continual stream of souls to enter and exit. As a container, the church possesses clear, although permeable, boundaries. So Hildegard can speak of those whom Ecclesia expels on account of unbelief (*Scivias* 2.3.1). Hildegard's emphasis on the church's womb corresponds to her focus on the procreative aspect of the church. Hildegard explains that the woman of the vision "is always pregnant and procreating children by the true ablution, and offering them devoutly to God" (*Scivias* 2.3.6). For Hildegard, the church *must* be imagined in terms of feminine gender since one of its primary functions is to birth the souls that will create a new heavenly kingdom and thereby repair the fall (*Scivias* 2.3.4).

Interestingly, Hildegard emphasizes the procreative aspect of the bridal imagery, although Revelation seemingly avoids the issue. Revelation avoids alluding to the possibility of the bride's maternal role, in spite of the fact that this theme was prominent in first-century discussions of weddings and marriage (see chap. 4). Hildegard's reading demonstrates how Revelation's language both shapes thought and evokes new meanings. Hildegard exploits Revelation's use of the container mapping (A CITY IS A CONTAINER) and allows that imagery to suggest an idea not expressly articulated in the text (A WOMAN IS A CONTAINER).

4. CHANGE OF STATE IS CHANGE OF LOCATION

In both visions of this new Jerusalem, John describes the city as a bride descending: "And I saw the holy city, a new Jerusalem, descending

---

[115] Living and writing during the eleventh century, Hildegard's visions often echo the imagery of Revelation. Revelation's image of the city-bride provides Hildegard with a valuable vehicle for addressing the need for church reform and church unity. See Barbara Newman, *Sister of Wisdom: St. Hildegard's Theology of the Feminine* (Berkeley, Calif.: University of California Press, 1987), 11.

(καταβαίνουσαν) out of heaven from God, prepared as a bride for her husband" (21:2; cf. 21:10; 3:12). The fact that this action is attributed to a city indicates that "descending" functions as a metaphorical focus. This action metaphorically alludes to something other than physical movement from one place to another.

The use of the present participle καταβαίνουσαν communicates a sense of movement.[116] Augustine's reading of Rev 21:2 exploits this sense of action, as he writes, "This City has been coming down from heaven since its beginning" (Augustine, *Civ.* 20.17). Likewise, Caird suggests that "descent from heaven is . . . a permanent characteristic of this city."[117] Revelation persuades its audience to envision the city-bride existing in a state of movement from one place (out of heaven) to another. The destination for the city remains unstated, although the reference to the "new earth" in v. 1 introduces the possibility that the city is destined to be a part of this new creation.[118] Set within a context marked by radical change, the passing away of the first heaven and earth and the creation of a new heaven and earth (21:2),[119] the descent of the new Jerusalem connotes the change or transition of the Christian community. In this way Revelation's vision of the descending city draws on the conceptual mapping CHANGE OF STATE IS CHANGE OF LOCATION.[120] The vision of this new Jerusalem coming out of heaven suggests that it exists in a state of transition into the new creation.

a. A COMMUNITY'S TRANSITION IS A WEDDING (*DEDUCTIO*)

As we have stated a number of times, the image of the bride within the Greco-Roman milieu is one of transition from one social role to another. Indicative of this transitional identity was the *deductio*, the central wedding event which entailed the bride's procession from the home of her father to the home of her new bridegroom; it was the central event of the wedding. As the legal writer Pomponius noted, the *deductio* was a necessary element of the wedding, although the bridegroom need not be physically present![121] The bride's procession to her new home indicated *her* transition into her new role. The act of physical movement from one place to another metaphorically represents her transition from one role to another. This action reflects the conceptual mapping A CHANGE IN STATE IS A CHANGE IN LOCATION.

[116] McKay, *A New Syntax*, 29–30.
[117] Caird, *The Revelation of St. John*, 267.
[118] Rissi, *The Future of the World*, 55.
[119] Caird, *The Revelation of St. John*, 266.
[120] Lakoff and Turner, *More Than Cool Reason*, 8
[121] Pomponius, *Digest* 23.2.5, as quoted in Treggiari, *Roman Marriage*, 167.

The bride's "descent" from heaven in Rev 21:2, 10 recalls, intentionally or unintentionally, the *deductio* in the Greco-Roman wedding. The culmination of this procession was at the home of the bridegroom, although in some cases this could have been the home of the bridegroom's father.[122] The culmination traditionally included rituals in which the bride acknowledged this new *domus* as her own (e.g., Plutarch, *Quaest. rom.* 1, 29, 31).[123] It is interesting that within this context, Revelation's bride does not just enter into her new *domus*, but she *becomes* the new *domus* (see above).[124] The voice from the throne proclaims of the new Jerusalem, the bride: "Behold the dwelling of God with humanity! And [God] will dwell with them and they will be his peoples" (21:3). The bride, the new Jerusalem, embodies the new dwelling place which is God's dwelling place with God's people. This reconfiguration of traditional wedding imagery points to the fluidity of Revelation's imagistic language.

In contrast to chap. 19, which does not specify the identity of the bride, chap. 21 fails to identify the groom in the first nuptial vision. Whereas 19:7 mentions only the "wife/woman of the Lamb," 21:2 mentions only the bride's "husband/man" (ἀνήρ). Since the text identifies the bridegroom as the Lamb in chap. 19 it seems appropriate to assume that chap. 21 continues to make this connection, especially in light of 21:9. In the second nuptial vision, the role of the Lamb within the wedding scenario is made explicit, as the bride is described as the wife of the Lamb (21:9). In 21:3, however, the roles are blurred, for the text describes God dwelling within the new Jerusalem.

In the Greco-Roman milieu the bride's arrival into her new home also included a sexual element, the consummation of the new marriage (see Plutarch, *Quaest. rom.* 65).[125] While Revelation's nuptial imagery certainly could include this interpretive possibility, John resists elaborating on the theme. Some of Revelation's later interpreters do, however, take Revelation's nuptial imagery in this direction. For example, Mechthild of Magdeburg, a Beguine from the thirteenth century, expands on the nuptial imagery's erotic potential. After describing the wedding banquet of the Lamb, which she reads as a reference to the Eucharist, Mechthild imagines "the intimate sweetness and intense oneness" the brides (individual souls) will experience with the Lamb.[126]

---

[122] Treggiari, *Roman Marriage*, 410.

[123] Ibid., 168.

[124] Even though I am using the Latin term *domus* here, the Vulgate's translation of 21:3 maintains the Greek text's allusion to OT traditions by translating σκηνή as *tabernaculum*.

[125] Treggiari, *Roman Marriage*, 168.

[126] Mechthild of Magdeburg, *The Flowing Light of the Godhead*, trans. Frank Tobin (New York: Paulist Press, 1998), 3.1. For a discussions of Mechthild, see Amy Hollywood, *The Soul as Virgin Wife: Mechthild of Magdeburg, Marguerite Porete, and Meister Eckhart* (Notre Dame, Ind.:

5. THE UNION BETWEEN THE CHRISTIAN COMMUNITY AND CHRIST/GOD IS A MARRIAGE

Undergirding the descriptions of the bride's descent and the new life shared by the bride and God is the conceptual equation of a human relationship with the relationship between the divine and the faithful community. As we saw in chap. 3, this metaphorical mapping undergirds prophetic depictions of the relationship between God and Jerusalem. In Revelation this mapping takes a decidedly Christian tone and can be represented as THE UNION BETWEEN THE CHRISTIAN COMMUNITY AND CHRIST/GOD IS A MARRIAGE.

The text characterizes this "marriage" as one of togetherness: God will be with his people and God's people will be with him. While this communicates a sense of unity, it does not diminish the identity and roles of either partner: "And they will be his peoples and God himself will be with them as their God" (21:3).[127] God remains God and the community remains as such, living within a new relationship. The Greco-Roman concept of *harmonia* or *concordia* in marriage resonates with this image. This brings us back to the image of the imperial couple in the traditional pose of marital harmony, the *dextrarum iunctio*.

Revelation 21 presents two visions that build on the conventional mapping A CITY IS WOMAN in constructing a nuptial image. While these visions sound quite similar, they each employ the A CITY IS WOMAN in different ways. The latter vision, 21:9–11, reverses the traditional mapping, using city imagery to describe the bride (A WOMAN IS A CITY). This effectively blurs the boundaries between the CITY and the WOMAN domains as John constructs his image of the Christian community. Drawing on and reformulating mappings from within the Jewish literary traditions, John encourages his audience to view themselves as the new Israel, the new Jerusalem, and the *new* bride of the Lamb.

Revelation 22:17: "The Spirit and the Bride Say, 'Come!'"

The final lexical reference to nuptial imagery occurs within the liturgical conclusion to the text as a whole (22:8–21).[128] Revelation 22:17 begins, "The

University of Notre Dame Press, 2001); and Barbara Newman, "*La mystique courtoise*: Thirteenth-Century Beguines and the Art of Love," in *From Virile Woman to WomanChrist: Studies in Medieval Religion and Literature* (Philadelphia: University of Pennsylvania Press, 1995), 137–67.

[127] The text of 21:3 is notoriously difficult to translate. Pointing to its grammatical awkwardness, various manuscripts have deleted different portions of the phrase. For a discussion of these variants, see Aune, *Revelation*, 3:1110–11. Generally, the phrase seems to be communicating that God himself (the intensive use of αὐτός) will be among the community and will be their God.

[128] Ugo Vanni, "Liturgical Dialogue as a Literary Form in the Book of Revelation," *NTS* 37 (1991): 359.

spirit and the bride say, 'Come!' And let everyone who hears say, 'Come.'" Through this liturgical dialogue, as Ugo Vanni describes it, the audience is asked to be part of the Christian community that is a new Jerusalem. As Revelation assumes a context of performance (1:3), the command extends beyond the bounds of the text, encouraging the audience to enter into a new Jerusalem.[129] In some sense, this imperative encourages the audience to transition into the new way of being suggested by the new Jerusalem imagery, reflecting the mapping A CHANGE IN STATE IS A CHANGE OF LOCATION. The text uses the language of physical movement to encourage the audience to "move" into a new state of existence—the new Jerusalem, which is the Lamb's bride. The audience is beckoned to become the city and the bride.

At the culmination of his narrative vision, John sets before his audience's eyes a vision of a wedding with a bride that is eventually identified as a city, as a new Jerusalem. In this chapter, I have set out to explore the metaphorical mappings that provide the conceptual foundation for this imagery. This sort of analysis, which draws on conceptual metaphor theory, allows us to see the ways that John uses imagistic language to compel his audience to think about things in particular ways. In particular, the analysis of Revelation's nuptial imagery reveals how John uses the image of the Lamb's wedding, which functions as a counter image to imperial familial imagery, as a way of molding his audience's view of its union with the risen Christ and God. As argued above, Revelation's image of the Lamb's bride or wife serves to shape the community's view of its own identity in relation to the Lamb. Drawing upon prophetic depictions of cities as women, Revelation's bridal imagery prompts the audience to imagine itself, as a community, in the bridal role.

The identity that Revelation offers its audience, the community, draws on Greek and Roman bridal and wedding traditions. In so doing, the audience is encouraged to envision itself as embodying a state of transition. This bride actively prepares her own bridal garment, as did brides of the day, although she does so by performing righteous deeds rather than by spinning pure wool. The righteous deeds of the community, the saints, indicate the bride's identity and her character, as one of faithfulness and purity. In addition, this community, which is a bride and which is also a city, is envisioned as becoming a home—the dwelling place of God and community. John plays on the Greek and Roman wedding traditions that involve the bride's procession into her new home by depicting this bride as becoming her new home. We are reminded that Revelation's imagery is amazingly fluid and unwilling to be bound by the rules of literal language.

Finally, my description of the text's efforts to "prompt," "persuade," and "compel" is an attempt at capturing how conceptual metaphor func-

[129] Vanni, "Liturgical Dialogue," 360.

tions: Conceptual metaphorical mappings often work at a level beneath the language of a text, making unspoken equations between different conceptual domains, as a means of persuasion. The power of metaphor comes from its ability to make an audience view one thing in terms of another, which necessarily shapes how the first thing is understood, without forcing the connection. For instance, by not slavishly spelling out "the community is the Lamb's bride," by assuming the metaphorical mapping instead, John obliges his audience to think similarly. In this way, by assuming metaphorical connections, John uses wedding imagery and the image of the bride to shape, in a way that some might characterize as deceptive and others might characterize as artful, his audience's identity.

CONCLUSION

"Like a Bride Adorned": Reading Metaphor in Revelation

The phrase "like a bride adorned," which functions as part of this book's title, is one of the ways that John describes the new Jerusalem that descends from heaven. This phrase can also be read as describing one of the ways interpreters have understood the relationship between Revelation and its imagistic language. Many interpreters approach Revelation's imagistic language as though it is adornment. In chap. 2 we noted the prevalence of this view of metaphorical language in general.[1] This approach to metaphorical language has had considerable influence upon Revelation scholars and still influences readings of this highly imagistic text.

In this view, the message of a text such as Revelation lies underneath the fantastic images and complicated figures. An interpreter must push past the layers of adornment to find the text's true meaning, the "body" of the text. The message of a particular text is found by stripping it of its metaphorical language. Once the meaning of the text has been seen, then it is possible to "decode" the various pieces of imagery in light of this meaning.[2] For instance, once an interpreter has realized that Revelation's nuptial imagery draws on the prophetic tradition of describing Jerusalem as the wife of God, she can return to Revelation and read all references to the bride as code for the church, the supposed Christian equivalent to the image of Jerusalem. This book demonstrates that this is not the only approach to Revelation's imagistic language. Moreover, we have shown that approaching Revelation's imagistic language as adornment fails to do justice to the persuasive power of the text.

Metaphor and Revelation

Contemporary theories of metaphor, particularly conceptual metaphor theory, demonstrate that metaphor provides us with one of the primary

---

[1] As expressed in the writings of Thomas Hobbes and John Locke, this understanding of metaphor gained popularity during the Enlightenment. See Ted Cohen, "Metaphor and the Cultivation of Intimacy," in *On Metaphor*, ed. Sheldon Sacks (Chicago: University of Chicago Press, 1978), 3.

[2] Judith Kovacs and Christopher Rowland, *Revelation* (Blackwell Bible Commentaries; Malden, Mass.: Blackwell, 2004), 8.

ways of understanding abstract and complex ideas.[3] Far from simple adornment, metaphor allows humans to use their experience and understanding of the concrete to understand and express the abstract. Metaphor entails employing the ideas and structures of one concept, referred to as a source domain, to understand another concept, referred to as a target domain. By mapping a source domain on to a target domain, a metaphor necessarily highlights some aspects of the target domain and downplays others. Thus, metaphorical mappings are necessarily interpretive and not expressions of reality. Metaphorical language or expressions reflect underlying metaphorical mappings which an audience is prompted to assume as they listen to or read along with a text. Conceptual metaphor theory suggests that much of metaphor's persuasive power lies beneath the surface of a text, because a text's metaphorical mappings prompt the audience to understand particular concepts in interpretive ways. For example, by employing the A CITY IS A WOMAN mapping, a text encourages an audience to envision a collective as an individual entity, which then acts as an individual. This necessarily downplays aspects of the concept CITY that do not fit this mapping and so persuades the audience to think about this concept in very specific ways.

Conceptual metaphor theory actually draws on a much older understanding of metaphorical language, as articulated by Aristotle in *Poetics* and *On Rhetoric*.[4] As we have noted throughout this book, Aristotle understands metaphor as one way a speaker or author "sets something before the eyes" of his or her audience. Drawing on perceived similarities between different things (*Poetica* 22.17), an author helps his audience to envision one thing as something else. This helps the audience to understand the more difficult concept or thing and lends persuasive power to a text. Even though this understanding of metaphor becomes obscured in the later Latin rhetorical traditions, such as in the *Rhetorica ad Herennium*, and in the medieval grammars, some of the most influential interpreters of Revelation naturally approach Revelation's images in this way. Joachim of Fiore, as

---

[3] Eva F. Kittay, *Metaphor: Its Cognitive Force and Linguistic Structure* (Oxford: Clarendon Press, 1987); George Lakoff, "The Contemporary Theory of Metaphor," in *Metaphor and Thought*, ed. Andrew Ortony; 2nd ed. (Cambridge: Cambridge University Press, 1993); George Lakoff and Mark Johnson, *Metaphors We Live By* (Chicago: University of Chicago Press, 1980); George Lakoff and Mark Turner, *More Than Cool Reason: A Field Guide to Poetic Metaphor* (Chicago: University of Chicago Press, 1989); Mark Turner, *Death Is the Mother of Beauty: Mind, Metaphor, Criticism* (Chicago: University of Chicago Press, 1987); and idem, *The Literary Mind* (New York: Oxford University Press, 1996).

[4] Gilles Fauconnier and Mark Turner, *The Way We Think: Conceptual Blending and the Mind's Hidden Complexities* (New York: Basic Books, 2002), 8–9, 36–37. For a discussion of reading Aristotle's view of metaphor, see James Edwin, "Getting Your Sources Right: What Aristotle *Didn't* Say," in *Researching and Applying Metaphor*, ed. Lynne Cameron and Graham Low (Cambridge: Cambridge University Press, 1999), 69–80.

described in chap. 1, read the visions of Revelation with the "eyes of the mind" (*oculi mentis*).[5] A visionary himself, Joachim envisioned Revelation's images along with the text or along with John. Joachim found new ways of understanding the text's figures because he allowed the images to resonate with his knowledge of other scriptural texts and with his experience of the world around him. Joachim allowed the images of Revelation to create new meanings by elaborating on aspects of the images only implied in John's visions.

Judith Kovacs and Christopher Rowland describe the type of interpretive process employed by Joachim as "actualizing" the text. They contrast this approach to the view that Revelation's metaphorical language functions as adornment or as a code to be cracked: "Decoding involves presenting the meaning of the text in another, less allusive form, showing what the text *really* means, with great attention to the details. Actualizing means reading the Apocalypse in relation to new circumstances, seeking to convey the spirit of the text. . . ."[6] Interpreters such as Joachim allow the structures of Revelation's images to lead them into new meanings and new interpretations. Interpreters such as Joachim testify to the persuasive power of the metaphors undergirding Revelation's imagistic language.

Using the insights of conceptual metaphor theory to read Revelation provides interpreters with a method to see what interpreters such as Joachim see as they envision the images of the text. By using Revelation's metaphorical expressions to identify the conceptual mappings within the text, we bring to light some of the ways that Revelation's metaphorical language encourages an audience to imagine along with the text. We do not assume that a reader of Revelation automatically differentiates the conceptual mappings, as has been done in this book. Instead, an audience experiences the cumulative effect of these mappings, as the text leads its readers from one understanding of reality to another. Differentiating these mappings serves as a tool for helping the interpreter identify the various conceptual moves that a text requires of an audience. In this way, using conceptual metaphor theory as a method to guide the analysis of Revelation allows one to discover the text's persuasive power.

---

[5] Marjorie Reeves and Beatrice Hirsch-Reich, *The Figurae of Joachim of Fiore* (Oxford: Clarendon Press, 1972), 20.

[6] Kovacs and Rowland complete this sentence with the phrase, "rather than being preoccupied with the plethora of detail" (*Revelation*, 8). I disagree with this characterization, because many of the interpreters who can be understood as "actualizing the text," including Joachim of Fiore, Hildegard of Bingen, and other medieval figures, are very interested in the details of the text. However, they read these details differently from those who decode the text, because they do not necessarily assign to each detail a singular meaning. The details in Revelation's images function in conjunction with the larger image to which they belong, which can be extended and elaborated to create new meanings. See, for instance, my discussion in chap. 1 of Joachim's illustration of the seven-headed dragon.

Revelation's Nuptial Imagery

Our analysis focused on Revelation's nuptial imagery, positioned at the culmination of the narrative, since this imagery provides one of the final ways John characterizes the Christian community and since this imagery has not often been the subject of focused analysis. As we noted earlier, the history of interpretation reveals an interest in the city aspect of Revelation's nuptial imagery,[7] which draws on the conventional equation of cities and women. Contemporary discussions of Revelation's city-bride imagery tend to emphasize the prophetic source for the text's nuptial imagery, concluding that the imagery functions in the same or a similar manner.[8] To return to the metaphor employed above, the nuptial imagery functions as an adornment to the text's main interest, the city of the new Jerusalem.

In contrast to readings that approach Revelation's nuptial imagery as the text's adornment, conceptual metaphor theory provides us with tools for exploring how this imagery functions to shape thought. In our analysis we have seen that undergirding Revelation's nuptial imagery is a framework of overlapping metaphorical mappings. This imagery draws on the conventional A CITY IS A WOMAN mapping, employed in various Jewish literary traditions. As we saw in chap. 3, these traditions creatively appropriate this traditional metaphorical association to depict Jerusalem as God's bride and wife: THE RELATIONSHIP BETWEEN GOD AND JERUSALEM IS A MARRIAGE. Like his prophetic predecessors, John elaborates on the conventional mapping in ways that reflect his own rhetorical situation and intentions.[9] In Rev 19:6–8, for instance, John shapes the conventional mapping, especially the prophetic tradition of depicting the relationship between a deity and a community as a marriage or wedding, to depict a royal wedding. In a cultural milieu dominated by discourse that includes wedding and marriage imagery to portray the imperial family as the ideal family, John presents an alternative vision of the ideal family—the Christian community's relationship to the Lamb and to God. Through his appro-

---

[7] J. A. DuRand, "The Imagery of the Heavenly Jerusalem (Revelation 21:9–22:5)," *Neot* 22 (1988): 65–86.

[8] Celia Deutsch, "Transformation of Symbols: The New Jerusalem in Rv 21.1–22.5," *ZNW* 78 (1987): 106–26. See also Jan Fekkes, "'His Bride Has Prepared Herself': Revelation 19–21 and Isaian Nuptial Imagery," *JBL* 109 (1990): 269–87.

[9] The use of conceptual theory in analyzing biblical metaphors underscores the importance of bringing the biblical texts into conversation with their symbolic worlds, including literary and nonliterary manifestations. This view of approaching the text is articulated in the work of Vernon K. Robbins, who employs the metaphor of a tapestry to describe the various threads of tradition and allusion within biblical texts. The ideas presented by Robbins shape some of the assumptions behind this book. See Robbins, *Exploring the Texture of Texts: A Guide to Socio-Rhetorical Interpretation* (Valley Forge, Pa: Trinity Press, 1996); and idem, *The Tapestry of Early Christian Discourse: Rhetoric, Society, and Ideology* (London: Routledge, 1996).

priation of the traditional A CITY IS A WOMAN mapping, John counters and challenges an important element of imperial discourse. This coheres with one of Revelation's overall rhetorical aims—challenging the imperial powers that seemingly challenge the authority and reign of God.[10]

In Rev 19:6–8, John further draws on the traditional understanding of brides and weddings within his milieu to depict the bride of the Lamb as an individual who actively constructs her own identity. In so doing John highlights an aspect of the bridal metaphor (JERUSALEM IS A BRIDE) also used in prophetic texts—adornment. John employs the concept of adornment in a manner coherent with Greco-Roman traditions about brides, namely, that they create their own bridal garment as a symbol of their transition into their new role. This understanding of the wedding garments reflects a metaphorical equation of an individual's status or identity and a garment (IDENTITY IS A GARMENT). This encourages John's audience to think about "putting on" an identity characterized by morality and connection to God, created through deeds of justice and righteousness. By formulating the traditional marriage metaphor, as articulated in the Jewish literary traditions, for his cultural context, which includes this understanding of the bridal garments, John encourages his audience to envision the Christian community as an individual within this state of transition, actively constructing "her" own identity.

Our analysis of the nuptial imagery in Revelation 21 similarly highlights the issue of the Christian community's identity, as John presents the community as a renewed Jerusalem that descends out of heaven to become the dwelling place of God and God's people. For John, this state of existence can be described only through the nuptial imagery which echoes the language of the prophets. John encourages his audience to envision the Christian community's transition into its new role as a wedding: A COMMUNITY'S TRANSITION IS A WEDDING. Revelation 21:1–4 prompts the audience to conceive of the goal of this "wedding," like the Greco-Roman wedding, as a new home, which is part of God's new creation.

Furthermore, by analyzing the conceptual mappings employed in the parallel visions of a new Jerusalem, we begin to see the complexity of the conceptual framework beneath Revelation 21. This text leads the audience through a number of related, yet shifting, metaphorical mappings that highlight different aspects of the community's existence as a new Jerusalem. Although these visions both employ nuptial imagery, they draw on different or inverted metaphorical mappings. The first vision encourages the audience to imagine the Christian community as a city, specifically a new Jerusalem, which is a bride (A CITY IS A BRIDE). Through the use of bridal imagery, John highlights the community's transition into its new role as a

[10] Steven J. Friesen, *Imperial Cults and the Apocalypse of John: Reading Revelation in the Ruins* (Oxford: Oxford University Press, 2001).

dwelling place for and with God. The second vision of a new Jerusalem inverts the basic conceptual mapping undergirding the text to describe this bride, the wife of the Lamb, as a city (A BRIDE IS A CITY). In so doing, John pushes the audience to think about the city as a structure and as a container that holds what is good and pure.

Overall, our analysis of Revelation's nuptial imagery demonstrates why and how this imagery cannot be reduced to a simple statement. Rather, interpreters must begin to think about how the text leads its audience through the imagery by encouraging them to envision through metaphor.

John describes his text as an *apokalypsis*, an "unveiling." He brings to sight things that have never been seen before, things heretofore shrouded. It is interesting that at the end of his text, John presents for his audience an *anakalypsis*, the unveiling of a bride at her wedding. John reveals to his audience the bride of the Lamb: a vision of the Christian community constructing its identity as it transitions into its new role in relation to God and the Lamb, a vision of a holy new Jerusalem becoming God's dwelling place. By exploring Revelation's nuptial imagery with the insights of conceptual metaphor theory, this book seeks to be an *anakalypsis* as well, by uncovering ways in which John constructs his bridal imagery to shape his audience's thought. This unveiling of the text, moreover, has broader implications as we gain insight into how Revelation employs metaphorical language as a tool for persuasion and begin to see why and how Revelation's images have been able to capture the imagination of interpreters throughout history.

APPENDIX

Babylon—A City without a Bride: Revelation 18:23

The nuptial reference in 18:23 functions as part of a larger unit of text (18:21–24) that echoes pronouncements of judgment found in the prophetic traditions of the Hebrew Bible. After casting a millstone into the sea, a prophetic sign-act symbolizing the fate of "Babylon," an angel offers an interpretation of this act:[1]

> And a mighty angel lifted up a stone, like a great millstone, and cast it into the sea, saying, "With such great violence[2] Babylon the great city will be thrown down, and will be found no more;[3] and the sound of harpists and musicians and flutists and trumpeters will be heard in you no more; and an artisan of any trade will be found in you no more; and the sound of the millstone will be heard in you no more; and the light of a lamp will shine in you no more; and

---

[1] The image of an angel casting the millstone into the sea reflects John's reworking of the prophetic traditions found in the Hebrew Bible. As a number of scholars point out, 18:21 echoes the command given in Jer 51:63–64: "When you finish reading this scroll [which describes the destruction of Babylon], tie a stone to it, and throw it into the middle of the Euphrates, and say, 'Thus shall Babylon sink, to rise no more, because of the disasters that I am bringing on her"; see G. B. Caird, *The Revelation of St. John* (BNTC 19; Peabody, Mass.: Hendrickson, 1966), 231; R. H. Charles, *A Critical and Exegetical Commentary on the Revelation of St. John* (ICC; Edinburgh: T. & T. Clark, 1920), 2:107; Eduard Lohse, *Die Offenbarung des Johannes: Übersetzt und Erklärt* (Göttingen: Vandenhoeck & Ruprecht, 1935; repr. Göttingen: Vandenhoeck & Ruprecht, 1988), 100; Robert H. Mounce, *The Book of Revelation*, rev. ed. (NICNT; Grand Rapids, Mich.: Eerdmans, 1998), 337; Jean-Pierre Ruiz, *Ezekiel in the Apocalypse: The Transformation of Prophetic Language in Revelation 16,17–19,10* (Frankfurt am Main: Peter Lang, 1989), 464. Although John's depiction differs from the text of Jeremiah in a number of ways, especially by substituting an angel for a prophet, the allusion to a prophetic sign-act is clear. Likewise, the description of an abandoned Babylon, following the casting of the stone, draws on prophetic texts in which the fate of a destroyed city is pronounced (Adela Yarbro Collins, *Crisis and Catharsis: The Power of the Apocalypse* [Philadelphia: Westminster Press, 1984], 120).

[2] As Charles notes, the word ὅρμημα is somewhat unclear, as it is not used elsewhere in the NT, *A Critical and Exegetical Commentary*, 2:107.

[3] The text underscores the absence of these things through the repetitive use of an emphatic negative formula (David E. Aune, *Revelation* [WBC 52; Dallas: Word, 1998], 3:972). Barbara Rossing explains that this formula is characteristic of "city laments" found in the Hebrew Bible and in Mesopotamian traditions (*The Choice between Two Cities: Whore, Bride, and Empire in the Apocalypse* [Harrisburg, Pa.: Trinity Press, 1999], 104–5).

> the voice[4] of a bridegroom and a bride will be heard in you no more. . . ." (18:21–23)

In this context, the voice or sound of the bridegroom and the bride could simply be one of the many things that will no longer be present in Babylon; however, the position of the nuptial reference at the end of this list, a position of emphasis, suggests its possible importance.[5] Further, knowing the relative proximity of Revelation's subsequent nuptial imagery (19:1–10), one assumes that this reference, albeit brief, points to the coming imagery of the Lamb's wedding.[6]

Revelation's reference to the absent voice of the bridegroom and bride does not specifically function as a metaphorical expression. Even though the voice of the bridal couple may function as a metonymical indicator of joy and hopefulness (see below), the text resists depicting the voice or sound (the Greek word φωνή indicates either voice or sound) of the bridal couple as anything other than a sound.[7] Similarly, in the text cited above (18:21–23) there are no linguistic markers suggesting that we read the bridegroom and bride as metaphorical terms. Consequently, interpreters generally read this clause as a literal statement, as the cessation of a basic human activity and event in the great city Babylon.[8]

The mapping A CITY IS A WOMAN, specifically the source domain WOMAN, recedes into the background as the text describes the fallen *city* of Babylon in 18:1ff.[9] The mapping (A CITY IS A WOMAN), however, resur-

[4] In some manuscripts, including some Syriac translations, another "sound" or "voice" (φωνή in the Greek) is included: "and the voice of a bridegroom and the voice of a bride will be heard in you no more." Most likely this is an assimilation to traditions in Jeremiah that describe the voice of the bridegroom and the voice of the bride (e.g., Jer 16:9) (Aune, *Revelation*, 3:973).

[5] Ruben Zimmerman, *Geschlechtermetaphorik und Gottesverhältnis: Traditionsgeschichte und Theologie eines Bildfelds in Urchristentum und antiker Umwelt* (Tübingen: Mohr Siebeck, 2001), 412.

[6] Many scholars fail to explore a possible connection between the specific reference to the sound of the bridegroom and bride in 18:23 and the rest of Revelation's nuptial imagery. See, for instance, Caird, *The Revelation of Saint John*, 231–32; and Mounce, *The Book of Revelation*, 338–39. Two notable exceptions include Rossing, *The Choice between Two Cities*, 102–11; and Zimmermann, *Geschlechtermetaphorik*, 412.

[7] Metonymy occurs when one entity describes something related to it. One piece of a whole, for instance, can be used to describe the whole. In this case, the sound of the bridal couple represents the reason for the sound—joy, happiness, etc. For a discussion of metonymy, see George Lakoff and Mark Johnson, *Metaphors We Live By* (Chicago: University of Chicago Press, 1980), 35–40.

[8] Many scholars note that the text shifts from feminine imagery to city imagery in chap. 18. See Charles, *A Critical and Exegetical Commentary*, 2:110–11; Mounce, *The Book of Revelation*, 339; Pierre Prigent, *L'Apocalypse de Saint Jean*, 2nd ed. (Commentaire du Nouveau Testament; Geneva: Labor et Fides, 1988), 274–75.

[9] Ruiz, *Ezekiel in the Apocalypse*, 379.

faces when the angel in 18:21 uses the second person singular, "in you," to describe and address Babylon. The angel addresses Babylon using this pronoun no less than six times in two verses![10] The text's use of the singular form, rather than the plural (which would be expected if the text were addressing the kings, merchants, and magnates described throughout chap. 18), suggests a personal form of address. An uncharitable reader might suggest that John "slips" by using this pronoun, as he has clearly been emphasizing the CITY domain of the mapping A CITY IS A WOMAN; however, a more generous reading understands this use of the pronoun as effectively bringing the WOMAN domain back into the audience's sight. The text seems subtly to remind its audience that this Babylon, the fallen city, is the Great Whore described earlier.

The text couples the pronoun "you" with the preposition "in" five times in 18:22–23. Functioning as part of a larger linguistic pattern ("'x' will no longer be found *in you*"), the use of the pronoun "in" alludes again to the container metaphor described above. Through this language the text metaphorically images Babylon as a container. Whether city or woman, Babylon still functions as a container *in* which things can be found or, in this case, not found (A CITY/WOMAN IS A CONTAINER). More importantly, the "contents" of this container or the absence of certain contents tells the audience something about the nature of the container itself.

In describing the deficits of Babylon in 18:21–24, Revelation draws on traditional language of prophetic judgment. Specifically, this passage reworks proclamations in which the prophet Jeremiah announces the fate of Jerusalem on account of Judah's disobedience (e.g., Jer 7:34; 16:9; 25:10).[11] Among other things, in a number of these proclamations, Jeremiah, as Revelation will do later, predicts that a city judged by God will no longer possess the sound of a bridal couple. In these instances, Jeremiah explicitly associates the voice of the bridegroom and bride with mirth and gladness: "For thus says the Lord of hosts, the God of Israel: I am going to banish from this place, in your days and before your eyes, the voice of mirth and the voice of gladness, the voice of the bridegroom and the voice of the bride" (Jer 16:9); and "I will banish from them the sound of mirth and the sound of gladness, the voice of the bridegroom and the voice of the bride . . ." (Jer 25:10; see also Jer 7:34; 33:11). Aune further notes that the association between mirth and gladness and the voice of a bridal couple occurs in rabbinic literature, including in this blessing by Rabbi Judah: "Speedily, O Lord our God, may be heard in the cities of Judah, and in the streets of Jerusalem, the voice of joy and the voice of gladness, the voice of the bride-

---

[10] In one instance the pronoun is a genitive and not a dative.

[11] For a brief discussion of the use of Jeremiah in Revelation 18, see Aune, *Revelation*, 3:983–84.

groom and the voice of the bride. . . ."[12] Aune suggests that in some contexts, the connection between the "the voice" of the bridegroom and bride and joy connotes a sense of sexual enjoyment.[13] Whether or not this is the case, the absence of this voice seems to indicate a lack of gladness and joy in the fallen Babylon.

Within a first-century context, the reference to the voice of the bridegroom and bride communicates even more than the sense of mirth and gladness, especially given the cultural importance of weddings in this milieu. As discussed in the previous chapter, weddings, including wedding songs, traditionally highlight the importance of procreation in marriage. Bearing children in marriage was, in fact, encouraged by the legal statutes and rhetoric of the Roman Empire. Thus, the absence of the bridegroom and bride's voice conveys, among other things, a sense of hopelessness for the future of Babylon, since theoretically no marriage results in no children. Within a cultural context that promotes a connection between bearing children and the stability of the empire, Rev 18:23 suggests the complete destruction of the city and society called "Babylon." Not only does the reference to the bridal couple's silence recall the prophetic threats of Jeremiah, but it simultaneously alludes to a whole network of ideas and assumptions about the significance of marriage and weddings.

The absence of the bridegroom and bride's voice metonymically points to innumerable absences or deficits within Babylon: a lack of joy, gladness, sexual enjoyment, procreation, family, hope, etc. In light of this, conceptual metaphor theory underscores the importance of asking how the underlying metaphorical mapping functions to shape these references. That is, the reference to the bridal couple's voice possibly alludes to a number of different things. Our goal is not to enumerate them all or even to find the most likely referent (whether that is the one the author intended, the one most likely heard by the original audience, the one most in line with our interpretive predilections, or a reference meeting some other criteria). Rather, we ask how the conceptual mappings at play in this text organize these multiple references. Recognizing the text's use of the container metaphor (A CITY/WOMAN IS A CONTAINER), it becomes clear that the important fact is that these things no longer exist *within* Babylon. These realities, especially those positive characteristics associated with the sound of the bride and bridegroom, are no longer contained within Babylon. In addition, the fact that Babylon no longer contains the voice of the bridegroom and bride points to the disparity between Babylon, the Great Whore, and the upcoming image of the bride. Babylon completely lacks the gladness of a wedding and marriage, which is the primary way in which the city of God, the new Jerusalem, will be characterized.

---

[12] *B. Ketub.* 8a, as quoted in Aune, *Revelation*, 3:1009.

[13] Aune, *Revelation*, 3:1009.

Furthermore, following the "logic" of the metaphorical mapping, one might ask where the former "contents" of Babylon exist now that they are no longer housed within Babylon. If Babylon is a container that metaphorically holds a number of different entities, including all that the voice of the bridegroom and bride imply, then these realities are all metaphorically contents (e.g., JOY IS AN OBJECT; HOPE IS AN OBJECT). With the destruction of Babylon there comes a need for a new location for these contents. No longer within the confines and, consequently, control of Babylon, what becomes of all that was once part of Babylon?[14] Thus, we might ask, is it any coincidence that the following chapters of Revelation introduce another city-woman?

[14] One of the traditional entailments of container metaphors is that, "Containment also limits and restricts forces within the container" (Mark Johnson, *The Body in the Mind: The Bodily Basis of Meaning, Imagination, and Reason* [Chicago: University of Chicago Press, 1987], 22).

BIBLIOGRAPHY

1. Ancient and Medieval Primary Texts

Alberic of Monte Cassino. *Flores Rhetorici*. Pages 131–61 in *Readings in Medieval Rhetoric*. Edited by Joseph M. Miller et al. Translated by Joseph M. Miller. Bloomington: Indiana University Press, 1973.

Aristotle. *The "Art" of Rhetoric*. Translated by John Henry Freese. Loeb Classical Library. Cambridge, Mass.: Harvard University Press, 1926.

——. *On Rhetoric: A Theory of Civic Discourse*. Edited and translated by George A. Kennedy. New York: Oxford University Press, 1991.

Augustine. *On Christian Doctrine*. Translated by D. W. Robertson. Upper Saddle River, N. J.: Prentice Hall, 1958.

——. *The City of God against the Pagans*. Translated by William Chase Greene. 7 vols. Loeb Classical Library. Cambridge, Mass.: Harvard University Press, 1960.

——. *Concerning the City of God against the Pagans*. Translated by Henry Bettenson. London: Penguin Books, 1972.

——. The *Confessions* and *Letters of St. Augustine*. In vol. 7 of The Nicene and Post-Nicene Fathers, Series 1. Edited by Philip Schaff. 1886–1889. Repr. Peabody, Mass.: Hendrickson, 1994.

——. *Literal Interpretation of Genesis*. Pages 143–88 in *Saint Augustine: On Genesis*. Translated by Roland J. Teske. The Fathers of the Church 84. Washington, D.C.: Catholic University of America Press, 1991.

Bede. *Concerning Figures and Tropes*. Pages 96–122 in *Readings in Medieval Rhetoric*. Edited by Joseph M. Miller et al. Translated by Gussie Hecht Tannenhaus. Bloomington: Indiana University Press, 1973.

——. *De schematibus et tropis*. Pages 142–17 in *Bedae Venerabilis Opera: Opera Didascalica I*. Corpus Christianorum: Series latina. Turnhout: Brepols, 1975.

Bernard of Clairvaux. *On Loving God*. Edited and translated by Emero Stiegman. 4 vols. Cistercian Fathers Series 13b. Kalamazoo, Mich.: Cistercian Publications, 1995.

——. *On the Song of Songs*. Translated by Kilian Walsh. Cistercian Fathers Series 7. Kalamazoo, Mich.: Cistercian Publications, 1976.

Biblia Hebraica Stuttgartensia. Edited by K. Elliger and W. Rudolph. 5th ed. Stuttgart: Deutsche Bibelgesellschaft, 1997.

Biblia Sacra Iuxta Vulgatam Versionem. Edited by B. Fischer et al. Deutsche Bibelgesellschaft, 1994.

Catullus. Translated by Francis Warre Cornish. Loeb Classical Library. Cambridge, Mass.: Harvard University Press, 1962.

Cicero, *De inventione*. Translated by H. M. Hubbell. Loeb Classical Library. Cambridge, Mass.: Harvard University Press, 1949.

——. *De oratore*. Translated by H. Rackham. Loeb Classical Library. Cambridge, Mass.: Harvard University Press, 1942.

[Cicero]. *Ad Herennium*. Translated by Harry Caplan. Loeb Classical Library. Cambridge, Mass.: Harvard University Press, 1954.

Columella. *On Agriculture*. Translated by Harrison Boyd Ash. Loeb Classical Library. Cambridge, Mass.: Harvard University Press, 1941.

Cyprian. *To Quirinius: Testimonies against the Jews*. In vol. 5 of *The Ante-Nicene Fathers*. Edited by Alexander Roberts and James Donaldson. 1886. 10 vols. Repr. Peabody, Mass: Hendrickson, 1995.

Dio Cassius. *Roman History*. Translated by Earnest Cary. 9 vols. Loeb Classical Library. Cambridge, Mass.: Harvard University Press, 1914.

Diogenes Laertius. *Lives of the Eminent Philosophers*. Translated by R. D. Hicks. 2 vols. Loeb Classical Library. Cambridge, Mass.: Harvard University Press, 1979.

Eusebius. *The Ecclesiastical History*. Translated by Kirsopp Lake. 2 vols. Loeb Classical Library. Cambridge, Mass.: Harvard University Press, 1980.

Hildegard of Bingen. *Sanctae Hildegardis abbastissae Opera omnia*. In vol. 197 of Patrologiae Latina. Edited by J.-P. Migne. Paris: 1855.

——. *Scivias*. Edited and translated by Mother Columba Hart and Jane Bishop. The Classics of Western Spirituality. New York: Paulist Press, 1990.

Horace. *Odes and Epodes*. Translated by C. E. Bennet. Loeb Classical Library. Cambridge, Mass.: Harvard University Press, 1914.

Hugh of St. Victor. *The Didascalicon of Hugh of St. Victor: A Medieval Guide to the Arts*. Translated by Jerome Taylor. New York: Columbia University Press, 1961.

Irenaeus. *Against Heresies*. In vol. 1 of *The Ante-Nicene Fathers*. Edited by Alexander Roberts and James Donaldson. 1885. 10 vols. Repr. Peabody, Mass: Hendrickson, 1995.

Jerome. *Select Letters of Jerome*. Translated by F. A. Wright. Loeb Classical Library. Cambridge, Mass.: Harvard University Press, 1933.

Joachim von Fiore. *Expositio in Apocalypsim*. 1527. Frankfurt am Main: Minerva, 1964.

Josephus. Translated by H. St. J. Thackeray et al. 10 vols. Loeb Classical Library. Cambridge, Mass.: Harvard University Press, 1926–65.

Juvenal and Persius. Translated by G. G. Ramsay. Loeb Classical Library. Cambridge, Mass.: Harvard University Press, 1918.

Livy. Translated by B. O. Foster. 14 vols. Loeb Classical Library. Cambridge, Mass.: Harvard University Press, 1919.

Lucian. Translated by A. M. Harmon. Loeb Classical Library. Cambridge, Mass.: Harvard University Press, 1915.

Martial. *Epigrams*. Translated by Walter C. A. Ker. 2 vols. Rev. ed. Loeb Classical Library. Cambridge, Mass.: Harvard University Press, 1978–79.

Mechthild of Magdeburg. *The Flowing Light of the Godhead*. Translated by Frank Tobin. The Classics of Western Spirituality. New York: Paulist Press, 1998.

Neusner, Jacob. *Mekhilta according to Rabbi Ishmael: An Analytical Translation*. 2 vols. Brown Judaic Studies. Atlanta: Scholars Press, 1988.

Michalowski, Piotr. *Lamentations over the Destruction of Sumer and Ur*. Winona Lake, Ind.: Eisenbrauns, 1989.

Musonius Rufus. "That Women Too Should Study Philosophy" and "Should Daughters Receive the Same Education as Sons?" Translated by Cora E. Lutz in "Musonius Rufus: the Roman Socrates." *Yale Classical Studies* 10 (1947): 3–147.

Novum Testamentum Graece. Edited by Kurt Aland, et al. 27th ed. Stuttgart: Deutsche Bibelgesellschaft, 1993.

Origen. *On First Principles*. Translated by G. W. Butterworth. Harper & Row, 1966. Repr. Gloucester: Peter Smith, 1973.

Ovid. *Art of Love, and Other Poems*. Translated by J. H. Mobley. Loeb Classical Library. Cambridge, Mass.: Harvard University Press, 1979.

——. *Fasti*. Translated by Sir James George Frazer. 2nd rev. ed. Edited by G. P. Goold. Loeb Classical Library. Cambridge, Mass.: Harvard University Press, 1989.

Pliny. *Letters*. Translated by William Melmoth. 2 vols. Revised by W. M. L. Hutchinson. Loeb Classical Library. Cambridge, Mass.: Harvard University Press, 1915.

——. *Natural History*. Translated by H. Rackham. 10 vols. Loeb Classical Library. Cambridge, Mass.: Harvard University Press, 1945.

Plutarch. *Advice to the Bride and Groom*. Pages 5–13 in *Plutarch's Advice to the Bride and Groom and A Consolation to His Wife: English Translations, Commentary, Interpretive Essays, and Bibliography*. Translated by Donald Russell. Edited by Sarah B. Pomeroy. New York: Oxford University Press, 1999.

——. *Lives*. Translated by Bernadotte Perrin. 11 vols. Loeb Classical Library. Cambridge, Mass.: Harvard University Press, 1914.

——. *Moralia*. Translated by Frank Cole Babbitt. 14 vols. Loeb Classical Library. Cambridge, Mass.: Harvard University Press, 1927.

Quintilian. *Institutio oratoria*. Translated by H. E. Butler. 4 vols. Loeb Classical Library. Cambridge, Mass.: Harvard University Press, 1921.

Seneca. *Ad Lucilium epistulae morales*. Translated by Richard M. Gummere. 3 vols. Loeb Classical Library. Cambridge, Mass.: Harvard University Press, 1917–25.

Septuaginta. Id est Vetus Testamentum graece iuxta LXX interpetes. Edited by Alfred Rahlfs. 2 vols. Stuttgart: Deutsche Bibelgesellschaft, 1979.

Sherk, Robert K. *The "Res Gestae" of Augustus* in *The Roman Empire: Augustus to Hadrian*. Cambridge: Cambridge University Press, 1988.

Strabo. *The Geography of Strabo*. Translated by Horace Leonard Jones. 8 vols. Loeb Classical Library. Cambridge, Mass.: Harvard University Press, 1917–32.

Suetonius. *Lives of the Caesars*. Translated by J. C. Rolfe. 2 vols. Loeb Classical Library. Cambridge, Mass.: Harvard University Press, 1913.

Tacitus. *The Annals*. Translated by John Jackson. 2 vols. Loeb Classical Library. Cambridge, Mass.: Harvard University Press, 1937.

——. *Dialogus de ortoribus*. Translated by W. Peterson and revised by M. Winterbottom. Loeb Classical Library. Cambridge, Mass.: Harvard University Press, 1970.

Tertullian. *On the Resurrection of the Flesh*. In vol. 3 of *The Ante-Nicene Fathers*. Edited by Alexander Roberts and James Donaldson. 1885. Peabody, Mass: Hendrickson, 1995.

Ulpian. Translated by Tony Honoré. Oxford: Clarendon Press, 1982.

Xenophon. *Oeconomicus*. Translated by E. C. Marchant. Loeb Classical Library. Cambridge, Mass.: Harvard University Press, 1923.

2. Reference and Grammatical Works

Bauer, Walter. *A Greek-English Lexicon of the New Testament and Other Early Christian Literature*. Translated by William Arndt and F. Wilbur Gingrich and revised by Frederick W. Danker and F. Wilbur Gingrich. 2nd rev. ed. Chicago: University of Chicago Press, 1979.

Brown, Francis, S. R. Driver, Charles A. Briggs. *The New Brown-Driver-Briggs-Gesenius Hebrew and English Lexicon.* Peabody, Mass.: Hendrickson, 1979.

Fanning, Buist M. *Verbal Aspect in New Testament Greek.* Oxford: Clarendon Press, 1990.

Liddell, Henry George, Robert Scott, Henry Stuart Jones, and Roderick McKenzie. *A Greek-English Lexicon.* Oxford: Clarendon, 1968.

Louw, J. P. *Semantics of New Testament Greek.* Atlanta: Scholars Press, 1982.

——, and Eugene A. Nida. *Greek-English Lexicon of the New Testament Based on Semantic Domains.* 2nd ed. 2 vols. New York: United Bible Societies, 1988.

McKay, K. L. *A New Syntax of the Verb in New Testament Greek: An Aspectual Approach.* Studies in Biblical Greek 5. New York: Peter Lang, 1994.

Smith, Sir William, and Sir John Lockwood. *Chambers Murray Latin-English Dictionary.* Edinburgh: Chambers, 1976.

Smyth, Herbert Weir. *Greek Grammar.* Rev. ed. Cambridge, Mass.: Harvard University Press, 1984.

3. Commentaries on the Book of Revelation

Allo, E.-B. *L'Apocalypse.* 4th ed. Études Bibliques. Paris: J. Gabalda, 1933.

Aune, David E. *Revelation.* 3 vols. Word Biblical Commentary 52A-B. Dallas: Word, 1997–1998.

Barr, David L. *Tales of the End: A Narrative Commentary on the Book of Revelation.* Santa Rosa, Calif.: Polebridge Press, 1998.

Beale, Gregory K. *The Book of Revelation: A Commentary on the Greek Text.* New International Greek Testament Commentary. Grand Rapids: Mich: Eerdmans, 1999.

Beasley-Murray, G. R. *The Book of Revelation.* Rev. ed. New Century Bible Commentary. Grand Rapids, Mich.: Eerdmans, 1983.

Beckwith, Isbon T. *The Apocalypse of John.* New York: Macmillan, 1919.

Bleek, Friedrich. *Vorlesungen über die Apokalypse.* Berlin: Georg Reimer, 1862.

Boismard, M.-E. *L'Apocalypse.* 3rd ed. La Sainte Bible. Paris: Les Éditions du Cerf, 1959.

Boring, Eugene M. *Revelation.* Interpretation. Louisville, Ky.: John Knox Press, 1989.

Bousset, Wilhelm. *Die Offenbarung Johannis.* 2nd ed. Göttingen: Vandenhoeck & Ruprecht, 1906.

Caird, G. B. *The Revelation of St. John.* Black's New Testament Commentaries 19. Peabody, Mass.: Hendrickson, 1966.

Cerfaux, Lucien, and Jules Cambier. *L'Apocalypse de Saint Jean lue aux Chrétiens.* Lectio Divina 17. Paris: Les Éditions du Cerf, 1964.

Charles, R. H. *A Critical and Exegetical Commentary on the Revelation of St. John.* 2 vols. The International Critical Commentary. Edinburgh: T. & T. Clark, 1920.

Elull, Jacques. *Apocalypse: The Book of Revelation.* Translated by George W. Schreiner. New York: Seabury Press, 1977.

Farrer, Austin. *A Rebirth of Images: The Making of St. John's Apocalypse.* Boston: Beacon Press, 1949.

Feuillet, André. *The Apocalypse.* Translated by Thomas E. Crane. Staten Island: Society of St. Paul, 1965.

Kovacs, Judith, and Christopher Rowland. *Revelation.* Blackwell Bible Commentaries. Malden, Mass.: Blackwell, 2004.

Kraft, Heinrich. *Die Offenbarung des Johannes.* Handbuch zum Neuen Testament 16a. Tübingen: J. C. B. Mohr, 1974.

Lohse, Eduard. *Die Offenbarung des Johannes: Übersetzt und Erklärt.* Göttingen: Vandenhoeck & Ruprecht, 1935. Repr. Göttingen: Vandenhoeck & Ruprecht, 1988.

Loisy, Alfred. *L'Apocalypse de Jean.* Paris: Emile Nourry, 1923.

Lücke, Friedrich. *Versuch einer Vollständigen Einleitung in die Offenbarung des Johannes oder Allgemeine Untersuchungen über die apokalyptische Litteratur überhaupt und die Apocalypse des Johannes insbesondere.* 2nd ed. Bonn: Eduard Weber, 1852.

Massyngberde Ford, J. *Revelation.* Anchor Bible 38. Garden City, N.Y.: Doubleday, 1975.

Minear, Paul S. *I Saw a New Earth: An Introduction to the Visions of the Apocalypse.* Washington, D.C.: Corpus, 1968.

Mounce, Robert H. *The Book of Revelation.* Rev. ed. New International Commentary on the New Testament. Grand Rapids, Mich.: Eerdmans, 1998.

Murphy, Frederick J. *Fallen is Babylon: The Revelation to John.* The New Testament in Context. Harrisburg, Pa.: Trinity Press, 1998.

Prigent, Pierre. *L'Apocalypse de Saint Jean.* 2nd ed. Commentaire du Nouveau Testament. Geneva: Labor et Fides, 1988.

Rowland, Christopher C. *The Book of Revelation.* Pages 503–743 in vol. 12 of *The New Interpreter's Bible.* Edited by Leander Keck et al. Nashville: Abingdon Press, 1998.

Schüssler Fiorenza, Elisabeth. *Revelation: Vision of a Just World.* Proclamation Commentaries. Minneapolis: Fortress Press, 1991.

Thompson, Leonard L. *Revelation.* Abingdon New Testament Commentaries. Nashville: Abingdon Press, 1998.

Zahn, Theodor. *Die Offenbarung des Johannes.* R. Brockhaus Verlag Wuppertal, 1986.

4. Articles, Essays, and Monographs Pertaining to Revelation

Baril, Gilberte. *The Feminine Face of the People of God: Biblical Symbols of the Church as Bride and Mother*. Translated by Florestine Audette. Collegeville, Minn.: Liturgical Press, 1991.

Barr, David. "The Apocalypse as a Symbolic Transformation of the World: A Literary Analysis." *Interpretation* 38 (1984): 39–50.

——. "Blessed Are Those Who Hear: John's Apocalypse as Present Experience." Pages 87–103 in *Biblical and Humane: A Festschrift for John Priest*. Edited by Linda Bennett Elder, David L. Barr, and Elizabeth Struthers Malbon. Atlanta: Scholars Press, 1996.

Batey, Richard A. *New Testament Nuptial Imagery*. Leiden: E. J. Brill, 1971.

Bauckham, Richard. "The *Figurae* of John of Patmos." Pages 107–25 in *Prophecy and Millenarianism: Essays in Honor of Marjorie Reeves*. Essex: Longman, 1980.

——. *The Theology of the Book of Revelation*. New Testament Theology. Cambridge: Cambridge University Press, 1993.

Böcher, Otto. "Bürger der Gottesstadt: Kirche in Zeit und Endzeit nach Apk 21f." Pages 157–67 in *Kirche in Zeit und Endzeit: Aufsätze zur Offenbarung des Johannes*. Neukirchen: Neukirchener Verlag, 1983.

——. "Israel und die Kirche in der Johannesapokalypse." Pages 28–57 in *Kirche in Zeit und Endzeit: Aufsätze zur Offenbarung des Johannes*. Neukirchen: Neukirchener Verlag, 1983.

——. *Die Johannesapokalypse*. Erträge der Forschung. Darmstadt: Wissenschaftliche Buchgesellschaft, 1975.

Bogaert, P.-M. "Les Apocalypses contemporaines de Baruch, d'Esdras et de Jean." Pages 47–68 in *L'Apocalypse johannique et l'Apocalyptique dans le Nouveau Testament*. Edited by Jan Lambrecht. Leuven: Leuven University Press, 1980.

Boismard, M.-E. "'L'Apocalypse' ou 'Les Apocalypses' de St. Jean." *Revue Biblique* 56 (1949): 507–41.

——. "Notes sur l'Apocalypse." *Revue Biblique* 59 (1952): 161–81.

Boring, Eugene. "The Theology of Revelation: 'The Lord Our God the Almighty Reigns.'" *Interpretation* 40 (1986): 257–69.

Bousset, Wilhelm. *The Antichrist Legend: A Chapter in Christian and Jewish Folklore*. Translated by A. H. Keane. Atlanta: Scholars Press, 1999.

Charles, R. H. *Studies in the Apocalypse*. 2nd ed. Edinburgh: T & T Clark, 1915.

Comblin, J. "La liturgie de la nouvelle Jérusalem." *Ephemerides Theologicae Lovanienses* 29 (1953): 5–40.

Cothenet, Édouard. "L'Église, Épouse du Christ (Éph 5; Apoc 19 et 21)." Pages 81–106 in *L'Église dans la liturgie*. Edited by Achille M. Triacca and A. Pistoia. Rome: Edizioni Liturgiche, 1980.

Court, J. C. *Myth and History in the Book of Revelation*. Atlanta: John Knox Press, 1979.

Deutsch, Celia. "Transformation of Symbols: The New Jerusalem in Rv 21.1–22.5." *Zeitschrift für die Neutestamentliche Wissenschaft* 78 (1987): 106–26.

Du Rand, J. A. "The Imagery of the Heavenly Jerusalem (Revelation 21:9–22:5)." *Neotestamentica* 22 (1988): 65–86.

Fekkes, Jan. "'His Bride Has Prepared Herself': Revelation 19–21 and Isaian Nuptial Imagery." *Journal of Biblical Literature* 109 (1990): 269–87.

——. *Isaiah and Prophetic Traditions in the Book of Revelation: Visionary Antecedents and Their Development*. Sheffield: JSOT Press, 1994.

Feuillet, André. *L'Apocalypse*. Studia Neotestamentica 3. Paris: Desclée de Brouwer, 1963.

Friesen, Steven J. *Imperial Cults and the Apocalypse of John: Reading Revelation in the Ruins*. Oxford: Oxford University Press, 2001.

Gager, J. *Kingdom and Community: The Social World of Early Christianity*. Englewood Cliffs, N.J.: Prentice-Hall, 1975.

Garrett, Susan R. "Revelation." Pages 377–82 in *The Women's Bible Commentary*. Edited by Carol A. Newsom and Sharon H. Ringe. Louisville, Ky.: Westminster John Knox Press, 1992.

Georgi, Dieter. "Die Visionen vom himmlischen Jerusalem in Apk 21 und 22." Pages 351–72 in *Kirche: Festschrift für Günther Bornkamm zum 75. Geburtstag*. Edited by Dieter Lührmann and Georg Strecker. Tübingen: J. C. B. Mohr, 1980.

Giblin, Charles H. "Recapitulation and the Literary Coherence of John's Apocalypse." *Catholic Biblical Quarterly* 56 (1994): 81–96.

——. "Structural and Thematic Correlations in the Theology of Revelation 16–22." *Biblica* 55 (1974): 487–504.

Giesen, Heinz. "Symbole und mythische Aussagen in der Johannesapokalypse und ihre theologische Bedeutung." Pages 255–77 in *Metaphorik und Mythos im Neuen Testament*. Edited by Karl Kertelge. Quaestiones Disputatae 126. Freiburg: Herder, 1990.

Glonner, Georg. *Zur Bildersprache des Johannes von Patmos: Untersuchung der Johannesapokalypse anhand einer um Elemente der Bildinterpretation erweiterten historisch-kritischen Method*. Munster: Aschendorff, 1999.

Gundry, Robert H. "The New Jerusalem: People as Place, Not Place for People." *Novum Testamentum* 29 (1987): 254–64.

Gunkel, Hermann. *Schöpfung und Chaos in Urzeit und Endzeit: Eine religionsgeschichtliche Untersuchung über Gen 1 und Ap Joh 12*. 2nd rev. ed. Göttingen: Vandenhoeck & Ruprecht, 1921.

Hemer, Colin J. *The Letters to the Seven Churches of Asia in Their Local Setting*. 2nd ed. Grand Rapids, Mich.: William B. Eerdmans, 2001.

Hill, David, *New Testament Prophecy*. Atlanta: John Knox, 1979.

Howard-Brook, Wes, and Anthony Gwyther. *Unveiling Empire: Reading Revelation Then and Now*. Maryknoll, N.Y.: Orbis Books, 1999.

Humphrey, Edith McEwan. *The Ladies and the Cities: Transformation and Apocalyptic Identity in Joseph and Aseneth, 4 Ezra, the Apocalypse and the Shepherd of Hermas*. Journal for the Study of the Pseudepigrapha. Sheffield: Sheffield Academic Press, 1995.

Kim, Jean K. "'Uncovering Her Wickedness': An Inter(con)textual Reading of Revelation from a Postcolonial Feminist Perspective." *Journal for the Study of the New Testament* 73 (1999): 61–81.

Kraft, Heinrich. *Die Bilder der Offenbarung des Johannes*. Frankfurt am Main: Peter Lang, 1994.

Lambrecht, Jan. "A Structuration of Revelation 4,1–22,5." Pages 77–104 in *L'Apocalypse johannique et l'Apocalyptique dans le Nouveau Tesament*. Edited by Jan Lambrecht. Leuven: Leuven University Press, 1980.

Malina, Bruce J. "Does *Porneia* Mean Fornication?" *Novum Testamentum* 14 (1972): 10–17.

———. *The New Jerusalem in the Revelation of John: The City as Symbol of Life with God*. Collegeville, Minn.: Liturgical Press, 2000.

Minear, Paul S. "Ontology and Ecclesiology in the Apocalypse." *New Testament Studies* 13 (1967): 89–105.

Miller, Kevin E. "The Nuptial Eschatology of Revelation 19–22." *Catholic Biblical Quarterly* 60 (1998): 301–19.

Moore, Stephen D. "The Beatific Vision as a Posing Exhibition: Revelation's Hypermasculine Deity." *Journal for the Study of the New Testament* 60 (1995): 27–55.

———. *God's Beauty Parlor and Other Queer Spaces in and around the Bible*. Stanford, Calif.: Stanford University Press, 2001.

Müller-Fieberg, Rita. *Das "Neue Jerusalem"—Vision für Alle Herzen und Alle Zeiten? Eine Auslegung von Offb 21,1–22,5 im Kontext von alttestamentlich-frühjüdischer Tradition und literarischer Rezeption*. Bonner Biblische Beiträge; Berlin: Philo, 2003.

Murphy, Frederick J. "The Book of Revelation." *Currents in Research: Biblical Studies* 2 (1994): 181–225.

O'Leary, Stephen D. *Arguing the Apocalypse: A Theory of Millennial Rhetoric*. New York: Oxford University Press, 1994.

O'Rourke, John J. "The Hymns of the Apocalypse." *Catholic Biblical Quarterly* 30 (1968): 399–409.

Pippin, Tina. *Death and Desire: The Rhetoric of Gender in the Apocalypse of John*. Literary Currents in Biblical Interpretation. Louisville, Ky.: Westminster John Knox Press, 1992.

———. "Eros and the End: Reading for Gender in the Apocalypse of John." *Semeia* 59 (1992): 193–210.

———. "The Heroine and the Whore: Fantasy and the Female in the Apocalypse of John." *Semeia* 60 (1992): 67–82.

Prigent, Pierre. *Apocalypse 12: Histoire de l'exégèse*. Tübingen: J. C. B. Mohr and Siebeck, 1959.

Provan, Iain. "Foul Spirits, Fornication and Finance: Revelation 18 from an Old Testament Perspective." *Journal for the Study of the New Testament* 64 (1996): 81–100.

Rehmann, Luzia Sutter. *Geh, frage die Gebärenin! Feministisch-befreiungstheologische Untersuchungen zum Gebärmotiv in der Apokalyptik*. Gütersloh: Chr. Kaiser/ Gütersloher Verlag, 1995.

Rissi, Mathias. *The Future of the World: An Exegetical Study of Revelation 19:11–22:15*. Studies in Biblical Theology 23. Naperville, Ill.: Alec R. Allenson, 1972.

Rossing, Barbara R. *The Choice between Two Cities: Whore, Bride, and Empire in the Apocalypse*. Harrisburg, Pa.: Trinity Press, 1999.

Royalty, Robert M., Jr. *The Streets of Heaven: The Ideology of Wealth in the Apocalypse of John*. Macon, Ga.: Mercer University Press, 1998.

Ruiz, Jean-Pierre. "Betwixt and Between on the Lord's Day: Liturgy and Apocalypse." Pages 654–72 in *SBL Seminar Papers, 1992*. Society of Biblical Literature Seminar Papers 31. Atlanta: Scholars Press, 1992.

———. *Ezekiel in the Apocalypse: The Transformation of Prophetic Language in Revelation 16,17–19,10*. Frankfurt am Main: Peter Lang, 1989.

———. "The Politics of Praise: A Reading of Revelation 19:1–10." Pages 374–93 in *SBL Seminar Papers, 1997*. Society of Biblical Literature Seminar Papers 36. Atlanta: Scholars Press, 1997.

Schaberg, Jane. "Response to Tina Pippin, 'Eros and the End.'" *Semeia* 59 (1992): 219–26.

Schüssler Fiorenza, Elisabeth. *The Book of Revelation: Justice and Judgment*. 2nd ed. Minneapolis: Fortress Press, 1998.

———. "The Composition and Structure of Revelation." Pages 159–80 in *The Book of Revelation: Justice and Judgment*. 2nd ed. Minneapolis: Fortress Press, 1998.

———. "Epilogue: The Rhetoricality of Apocalypse and the Politics of Interpretation." Pages 205–36 in *The Book of Revelation: Justice and Judgment*. 2nd ed. Minneapolis: Fortress Press, 1998.

———. "History and Eschatology in Revelation." Pages 35–67 in *The Book of Revelation: Justice and Judgment*. 2nd ed. Minneapolis: Fortress Press, 1998.

———. "Introduction: Research Perspectives on the Book of Revelation." Pages 12–32 in *The Book of Revelation: Justice and Judgment*. 2nd ed. Minneapolis: Fortress Press, 1998.

———. *Priester für Gott: Studien zum Herrschafts- und Priestermotiv in der Apokalypse*. Münster: Verlag Aschendorff, 1972.

———. "Redemption as Liberation (Rev. 1:5–6 and 5:9–10)." Pages 68–81 in *The Book of Revelation: Justice and Judgment*. 2nd ed. Minneapolis: Fortress Press, 1998.

———. "Visionary Rhetoric and Social Political Situation." Pages 181–203 in *The Book of Revelation: Justice and Judgment*. 2nd ed. Minneapolis: Fortress Press, 1998.

Selvidge, Marla J. "Powerful and Powerless Women in the Apocalypse." *Neotestamentica* 26 (1992): 157–67.

Sim, Unyong. *Das himmlische Jerusalem in Apk 21,1–22,5 im Kontext biblisch-jüdischer Tradition und antiken Städtbaus*. Trier: Wissenschaftlicher Verlag Trier, 1996.

Stevenson, Gregory M. "Conceptual Background to Golden Crown Imagery in the Apocalypse of John (4:4, 10; 14:14)." *Journal of Biblical Literature* 114 (1995): 257–72.

Thompson, Leonard L. *The Book of Revelation: Apocalypse and Empire*. New York: Oxford University Press, 1990.

———. "Cult and Eschatology in the Apocalypse of John." *Journal of Religion* 49 (1969): 330–50.

Trummer, Peter. "Einige Aspekte zur Bildersprache der Johannesapokalypse." Pages 278–90 in *Metaphorik und Mythos im Neuen Testament*. Edited by Karl Kertelge. Quaestiones Disputatae 126. Freiburg: Herder, 1990.

Vanni, Ugo. "The Ecclesial Assembly 'Interpreting Subject' of the Apocalypse." *Religious Studies Bulletin* 4 (1984): 79–85.

———. "Liturgical Dialogue as a Literary Form in the Book of Revelation." *New Testament Studies* 37 (1991): 348–72.

Visser, Derk. *Apocalypse as Utopian Expectation (800–1500): The Apocalypse Commentary of Berengaudus of Ferrières and the Relationship between Exegesis, Liturgy and Iconography*. Studies in the History of Christian Thought. Leiden: E. J. Brill, 1996.

Vogelsgesang, Jeffrey. "The Interpretation of Ezekiel in the Book of Revelation." Ph.D. diss., Harvard University, 1985.

Vos, Louis Arthur. *The Synoptic Traditions in the Apocalypse*. Kampen: Kok, 1965.

Wainwright, Arthur W. *Mysterious Apocalypse: Interpreting the Book of Revelation*. Nashville: Abingdon Press, 1993.

Wengst, Klaus. "Babylon the Great and the New Jerusalem: The Visionary View of Political Reality in the Revelation of John." Pages 189–202 in *Politics and Theopolitics in the Bible and Postbiblical Literature*. Edited by Henning Graf Reventlow, Yair Hoffman, and Benjamin Uffenheimer. Sheffield: JSOT Press, 1994.

Yarbro Collins, Adela. *The Combat Myth in the Book of Revelation*. Missoula, Mont.: Scholars Press, 1976.

——. *Crisis and Catharsis: The Power of the Apocalypse.* Philadelphia: Westminster Press, 1984.

——. "Feminine Symbolism in the Book of Revelation." *Biblical Interpretation* 1 (1993): 20–33.

——. "Revelation 18: Taunt-Song or Dirge?" Pages 185–204 in *L'Apocalypse johannique et l'Apocalyptique dans le Nouveau Testament.* Edited by J. Lambrecht. Leuven: Leuven University Press, 1980.

Zimmermann, Ruben. *Geschlechtermetaphorik und Gottesverhältnis: Traditionsgeschichte und Theologie eines Bildfelds in Urchristentum und antiker Umwelt.* Göttingen: Mohr Siebeck, 2001.

——. "Die Virginitäts-Metapher in Apk 14:4–5 im Horizont von Befleckung, Loskauf und Erstlingsfrucht." *Novum Testamentum* 45 (2003): 45–71.

5. Other Works on Biblical Traditions and Interpretation

Ackerman, Susan. "Isaiah." *The Women's Bible Commentary.* Edited by Carol A. Newsom and Sharon H. Ringe. Louisville, Ky: Westminster, 1992.

——. "The Personal Is Political: Covenantal and Affectionate Love (*'ĀHĀB, 'AHĀBÂ*) in the Hebrew Bible." *Vetus Testamentum* 52 (1002): 437–58.

Adler, Elaine. "The Background for the Metaphor of the Covenant as Marriage in the Hebrew Bible." Ph.D. diss., University of California, Berkeley, 1990.

Ambra, R. *Bonds of Love: Methodic Studies of Prophetic Texts with Marriage Imagery (Isaiah 50:1–3 and 54:1–10, Hosea 1–3, Jeremiah 2–3).* Assen: Van Gorcum, 1999.

Bechtel, Lyn M. "Shame as a Sanction of Social Control in Biblical Israel: Judicial, Political, and Social Shaming." *Journal for the Study of the Old Testament* 49 (1991): 47–76.

Biddle, Mark E. "The Figure of Lady Jerusalem: Identification, Deification and Personification of Cities in the Ancient Near East." Pages 173–94 in *The Biblical Canon in Comparative Perspective.* Edited by K. Lawson Younger, William W. Hallo, Bernard F. Batto. Lewiston, N.Y.: Edwin Mellen Press, 1991.

Bird, Phyllis A. "'To Play the Harlot:' An Inquiry into an Old Testament Metaphor." Pages 219–36 in *Missing Persons and Mistaken Identities: Women and Gender in Ancient Israel.* Minneapolis: Fortress Press, 1997. Repr. from pp. 75–94 of *Gender and Difference in Ancient Israel.* Minneapolis: Fortress Press, 1989.

——. "Women (Old Testament)." Pages 52–66 in *Missing Persons and Mistaken Identities: Women and Gender in Ancient Israel.* Minneapolis: Fortress Press, 1997.

Blenkinsopp, Joseph. *Ezekiel.* Louisville, Ky: John Knox, 1990.

Boring, Eugene "Matthew: Introduction, Commentary, and Reflection." Pages 89–505 in vol. 6 of *The New Interpreter's Bible.* Nashville: Abingdon Press, 2001.

Brenner, Althalya. *The Song of Songs*. Sheffield: Sheffflield Academic Press, 1989.

———, and Fokkelien van Dijk-Hemmes. *On Gendering Texts: Female and Male Voices in the Hebrew Bible*. Leiden: E. J. Brill, 1993.

Brettler, Marc. "Images of YHWH the Warrior in Psalms." *Semeia* 61 (1993): 135-65.

Brueggemann, Walter. "At the Mercy of Babylon: A Subversive Rereading of the Empire." *Journal of Biblical Literature* 110 (1991): 3–22.

Carr, David. "Gender and the Shaping of Desire in the Song of Songs and Its Interpretation." *Journal of Biblical Literature* 119 (2000): 233–48.

———. "Reaching for Unity in Isaiah." *Journal for the Study of the Old Testament* 57 (1993): 61–80.

Childs, Brevard. *Isaiah*. The Old Testament Library. Louisville, Ky.: Westminster John Knox, 2001.

Day, Linda. "Rhetoric and Domestic Violence in Ezekiel 16." *Biblical Interpretation* 8 (2000): 205–30.

Day, Peggy L. "The Bitch Had It Coming to Her: Rhetoric and Interpretation in Ezekiel 16." *Biblical Interpretation* 8 (2000): 231–54.

Dijk Hemmes, Fokkelien. "The Imagination of Power and the Power of Imagination: An Intertextual Analysis of Two Biblical Love Songs: The Song of Songs and Hosea 2." *Journal for the Study of the Old Testament* 44 (1989): 75–88.

———. "The Metaphorization of Woman in Prophetic Speech: An Analysis of Ezekiel XXIII," *Vetus Testamentum* 43 (1993): 162–70.

Dobbs-Allsopp, F. W. *Weep, O Daughter of Zion: A Study of the City-Lament Genre in the Hebrew Bible*. Biblica et Orientalia. Rome: Biblical Institute Press, 1993.

Exum, Cheryl J. "'Mother in Israel': A Familiar Figure Reconsidered." Pages 73–85 in *Feminist Interpretation of the Bible*. Edited by Letty M. Russell. Philadelphia: Westminster Press, 1985.

Finkelstein, Louis. "The Origin of the Hallel." *Hebrew Union College Annual* 23 (1950–51): 319–37.

Fitzgerald, Aloysius. "*BTWLT* and *BT* as Titles for Capital Cities." *Catholic Biblical Quarterly* 37 (1975): 167–83.

———. "The Mythological Background for the Presentation of Jerusalem as a Queen and False Worship as Adultery in the OT." *Catholic Biblical Quarterly* 34 (1972): 403–16.

Frymer-Kensky, Tikva. *In the Wake of the Goddesses: Women, Culture and the Biblical Transformation of Pagan Myth*. New York: Fawcett Columbine, 1992.

Galambush, Julie. *Jerusalem in the Book of Ezekiel: The City as Yahweh's Wife*. Society of Biblical Literature Dissertation Series 130. Atlanta: Scholars Press, 1992.

Gordon Pamela, and Harold C. Washington. "Rape as a Military Metaphor in the Hebrew Bible." Pages 308–25 in *A Feminist Companion to the Latter Prophets*. Edited by Athalya Brenner. Sheffield: Sheffield Academic Press, 1995.

Greenberg, Moshe. *Ezechiel 1–20*. Herders Theologischer Kommentar zum Alten Testament. Freiburg im Breisgau: Herder, 2001.

——. *Ezekiel 1–20*. Anchor Bible 22. Garden City, N.Y.: Doubleday, 1983.

Halpern, Baruch. "The New Names of Isaiah 62:4: Jeremiah's Reception in the Restoration and the Politics of 'Third Isaiah.'" *Journal of Biblical Literature* 117 (1998): 623–43.

Johnson, E. Elizabeth. "Ephesians." Pages 338–42 in *The Women's Bible Commentary*. Edited by Carol A. Newsom and Sharon H. Ringe. Louisville, Ky.: Westminster John Knox Press, 1992.

Kaiser, Barbara Bakke. "Poet as 'Female Impersonator': The Image of Daughter Zion as Speaker in Biblical Poems of Suffering." *Journal of Religion* 67 (1987): 164–82.

Kümmel, Werner Georg. *The New Testament: The History of the Investigation of Its Problems*. Translated by S. McLean Lilmour and Howard C. Kee. Nashville: Abingdon Press, 1972.

Lapsley, Jacqueline E. "Shame and Self-Knowledge: The Positive Role of Shame in Ezekiel's View of the Moral Self." Pages 143–73 in *The Book of Ezekiel: Theological and Anthropological Perspectives*. Edited by Margaret S. Odell and John T. Strong. Atlanta: Society of Biblical Literature, 2000.

Macky, Peter W. *The Centrality of Metaphors to Biblical Thought: A Method for Interpreting the Bible*. Studies in the Bible and Early Christianity 19. Lewiston, N.Y.: Edwin Mellen Press, 1990.

Munro, Jill M. *Spikenard and Saffron: A Study in the Poetic Language of the Song of Songs*. Sheffield: Sheffield Academic Press, 1995.

Murphy, Roland E. *The Song of Songs: A Commentary on the Book of Canticles or the Song of Songs*. Hermeneia. Minneapolis: Fortress Press, 1990.

Newsom, Carol A. "A Maker of Metaphors: Ezekiel's Oracles against Tyre." Pages 188–99 in *Interpreting the Prophets*. Edited by James Luther Mays and Paul J. Achtemeier. Philadelphia: Fortress Press, 1987.

——. "Response to Norman K. Gottwald, 'Social Class and Ideology in Isaiah 40–55.'" *Semeia* 59 (1992): 73–78.

——. "Woman and the Discourse of Patriarchal Wisdom." Pages 116–31 in *Reading Bibles, Writing Bodies: Identity and the Book*. Edited by Timothy K. Beale and David M. Gunn. London: Routledge, 1997.

O'Connor, Kathleen M. "'Speak Tenderly to Jerusalem': Second Isaiah's Reception and Use of Daughter Zion." *Princeton Seminary Bulletin* 20, no. 3 (1999): 281–94.

Oswalt, John N. *The Book of Isaiah: Chapters 40–66*. New International Commentary on the Old Testament. Grand Rapids, Mich.: William B. Eerdmans, 1998.

Paine, Thomas. *The Age of Reason*. 6th ed. Worcester, Mass.: Isaiah Thomas, 1794.

Patton, Corrine. "'I Myself Gave Them Laws That Were Not Good': Ezekiel 20 and the Exodus Traditions." *Journal for the Study of the Old Testament* 69 (1996): 73–90.

Pfisterer Darr, Katheryn. "Ezekiel." Pages 183–94 in *The Women's Bible Commentary*. Edited by Carol A. Newsom and Sharon H. Ringe. Louisville, Ky.: Westminster John Knox, 1992.

——. "Ezekiel among the Critics." *Currents in Research* 2 (1994): 9–24.

——. "Ezekiel: Introduction, Commentary, and Reflections." Pages 1221–25 in vol. 6 of *The New Interpreter's Bible*. Nashville: Abingdon Press, 2001.

——. "Ezekiel's Justifications of God: Teaching Troubling Texts." *Journal for the Study of the Old Testament* 55 (1992): 97–115.

——. *Isaiah's Vision and the Family of God*. Louisville, Ky.: Westminster, 1994.

Raitt, Thomas M. *A Theology of Exile: Judgement/Deliverance in Jeremiah and Ezekiel*. Philadelphia: Fortress Press, 1977.

Robbins, Vernon K. *Exploring the Texture of Texts: A Guide to Socio-Rhetorical Interpretation*. Valley Forge, Pa: Trinity Press, 1996.

——. *The Tapestry of Early Christian Discourse: Rhetoric, Society, and Ideology*. London: Routledge, 1996.

Sawyer, John F. A. "Daughter of Zion and Servant of the Lord in Isaiah: A Comparison." *Journal for the Study of the Old Testament* 44 (1989): 89–107.

Schmitt, John J. "The Gender of Ancient Israel." *Journal for the Study of the Old Testament* 26 (1983): 115–25.

——. "The Motherhood of God and Zion as Mother." *Revue Biblique* 92 (1985): 557–69.

——. "The Wife of God in Hosea 2." *Biblical Research* 34 (1989): 5–18.

Seitz, Christopher R. "The Book of Isaiah 40–66: Introduction, Commentary, and Reflections." Pages 309–552 in vol. 6 of *The New Interpreter's Bible*. Nashville: Abingdon Press, 2001.

Setel, T. Dorah. "Prophets and Pornography: Female Sexual Imagery in Hosea." Pages 86–95 in *Feminist Interpretation of the Bible*. Edited by Letty M. Russell. Philadelphia: Westminster Press, 1985.

Shields, Mary E. "Multiple Exposures: Body Rhetoric and Gender Characterization in Ezekiel 16." *Journal of Feminist Studies in Religion* 14 (1998): 5–18.

Smith, Dennis E. "Messianic Banquet." Pages 788–91 in vol. 4 of *The Anchor Bible Dictionary*. Edited by David Noel Freedman. 6 vols. New York: Doubleday, 1992.

Stone, Ken, ed. *Queer Commentary and the Hebrew Bible*. Cleveland: Pilgrim Press, 2001.

Törnkvist, Rut. *The Use and Abuse of Female Sexual Imagery in the Book of Hosea: A Feminist Critical Approach to Hos 1–3*. Uppsala, 1998.

Watts, John D. W. *Isaiah 1–33*. Word Bible Commentary. Waco, Tex.; Word, 1985.

Webb, Barry G. "Zion in Transformation: A Literary Approach to Isaiah." Pages 69–71 in *The Bible in Three Dimensions: Essays in Celebration of Forty Years of Biblical Studies at the University of Sheffield*. Edited by David J. A. Clines, Stephen Fowl, and Stanley Porter. Sheffield: JSOT Press, 1990.

Wegner, Judith Romney. *Chattel or Person? The Status of Women in the Mishnah*. New York: Oxford University Press, 1988.

Weems, Renita J. *Battered Love: Marriage, Sex, and Violence in the Hebrew Prophets*. Minneapolis: Fortress Press, 1995.

Wilson, Robert. "Ezekiel." Pages 652–94 in *Harper's Bible Commentary*. Edited by James L. Mays. San Francisco: HarperCollins, 1988.

6. Works on the Ancient World

Barclay, John M. G. *Jews in the Mediterranean Diaspora: From Alexander to Trajan (323 BCE–117 CE)*. Edinburgh: T & T Clark, 1996.

Boatwright, Mary T. "The City Gate of Plancia Magna in Perge." Pages 189–207 in *Roman Art in Context: An Anthology*. Edited by Eve D'Ambra. Upper Saddle River, N.J.: Prentice Hall, 1993.

——. "The Imperial Women of the Early Second Century A.C." *American Journal of Philology* 112 (1991): 513–40.

Botha, P. J. J. "The Historical Domitian–Illustrating Some Problems of Historiography." *Neotestamentica* 23 (1989): 45–59.

Bullough, Vern, and Bonnie Bullough. *Women and Prostitution: A Social History*. Buffalo, N.Y.: Prometheus Books, 1987.

Bowersock, G. W. *Augustus and the Greek World*. Oxford: Clarendon Press, 1965.

Braund, Susanna H. "Juvenal–Misogynist or Misogamist?" *Journal of Roman Studies* 82 (1992): 71–86.

Brooten, Bernadette J. *Love between Women: Early Christian Responses to Female Homoeroticism*. Chicago: University of Chicago Press, 1996.

Brown, Peter. *The Body and Society: Men, Women, and Sexual Renunciation in Early Christianity*. New York: Columbia University Press, 1988.

Cahoon, Leslie. "The Bed as Battlefield: Erotic Conquest and Military Metaphor in Ovid's Amores." *Transactions of the American Philological Association* 118 (1988): 293–307.

Cantarella, Eva. "Marriage and Sexuality in Republican Rome: A Roman Conjugal Love Story." Pages 269–82 in *The Sleep of Reason: Erotic Experience and Sexual Ethics in Ancient Greece and Rome*. Edited by Martha C. Nussbaum and Julia Sihovola. Chicago: University of Chicago Press, 2002.

Clark, Gillian. "Roman Women." *Greece and Rome* 28 (1981) 193–212.

Cohen, David. "The Augustan Law on Adultery: The Social and Cultural Context." Pages 109–27 in *The Family in Italy from Antiquity to the Present*. Edited by David I. Kertzer and Richard P. Saller. New Haven: Yale University Press, 1991.

Croom, A. T. *Roman Clothing and Fashion*. Charleston, S.C.: Tempus, 2000.

D'Ambra, Eve. "The Cult of Virtues and the Funerary Relief of Ulpia Epigone." Pages 104–14 in *Roman Art in Context: An Anthology*. Edited by Eve D'Ambra. Upper Saddle River, N.J.: Prentice Hall, 1993.

———. *Private Lives, Imperial Virtues: The Frieze of the Forum Transitorium in Rome*. Princeton: Princeton University Press, 1993.

Davies, Glenys. "The Significance of the Handshake Motif in Classical Funerary Art." *American Journal of Archaeology* 89 (1985): 627–40

Dixon, Suzanne. *Reading Roman Women: Sources, Genres and Real Life*. London: Duckworth, 2001.

———. *The Roman Family*. Baltimore: Johns Hopkins University Press, 1992.

———. "The Sentimental Ideal of the Roman Family." Pages 99–113 in *Marriage, Divorce, and Children in Ancient Rome*. Edited by Beryl Rawson. Oxford: Clarendon Press, 1991.

Du Bois, Page. *Sowing the Body: Psychoanalysis and Ancient Representations of Women*. Chicago: University of Chicago Press, 1988.

Edwards, Catherine. "Unspeakable Professions: Public Performance and Prostitution in Ancient Rome." Pages 66–95 in *Roman Sexualities*. Edited by Judith P. Hallett and Marilyn B. Skinner. Princeton: Princeton University Press, 1997.

Fantham, Elaine, Helene Peet Foley, Natalie Boymel Kampen, Sarah B. Pomeroy, and H. Alan Shapiro. *Women in the Classical World: Image and Text*. New York: Oxford University Press, 1994.

Ferguson, John. *The Religions of the Roman Empire*. Ithaca, N.Y.: Cornell University Press, 1970.

Fischler, Susan. "Social Stereotypes and Historical Analysis: The Case of the Imperial Women at Rome." Pages 115–33 in *Women in Ancient Societies: An Illusion of the Night*. Edited by Léonie J. Archer, Susan Fischler, and Maria Wyke. Basingstoke: Macmillan, 1994.

Flory, Marleen B. "The Deification of Roman Women." *Ancient History Bulletin* 9 (1995): 127–34.

Friesen, Steven J. "The Cult of the Roman Emperors in Ephesos: Temple Wardens, City Titles, and the Interpretation of the Revelation of John." Pages 229–50 in *Ephesos: Metropolis of Asia: An Interdisciplinary Approach to its Archaeology, Religion, and Culture*. Edited by Helmut Koester. Valley Forge, Pa.: Trinity Press, 1995.

——. *Twice Neokoros: Ephesus, Asia and the Cult of the Flavian Imperial Family*. Leiden: E. J. Brill, 1993.

Fullerton, Mark D. "The *Domus Augusti* in Imperial Iconography of 13–12 B. C." *American Journal of Archaeology* 89 (1985): 473–83.

Gardner, Jane. *Women in Roman Law and Society*. London: Croom Helm, 1986.

Gardner, Percy. "Countries and Cities in Ancient Art." *Journal of Hellenic Studies* 9 (1888): 47–81.

Grubbs, Judith Evans. *Law and Family in Late Antiquity: The Emperor Constantine's Marriage Legislation*. Oxford: Oxford University Press, 1995.

Jones, Brian W. *The Emperor Domitian*. London: Routledge, 1992.

Joshel, Sandra R. "Female Desire and the Discourse of Empire: Tacitus's Messalina." Pages 221–54 in *Roman Sexualities*. Edited by Judith P. Hallett and Marilyn B. Skinner. Princeton: Princeton University Press, 1997.

Kampen, Natalie Boymel. "Biographical Narration and Roman Funerary Art." *American Journal of Archaeology* 85 (1981): 47–58.

Kirchhoff, Renate. *Die Sünde gegen den eigenen Leib: Studien zu πορνή und πορνεία in 1 Kor 6,12–20 und dem sozio-kulturellen Kontext der paulinischen Adressaten*. Göttingen: Vandenhoeck & Ruprecht, 1994.

Kleiner, Diana E. E. *Roman Imperial Funerary Altars with Portraits*. Rome: Bretschneider, 1987.

——. *Roman Sculpture*. New Haven: Yale University Press, 1992.

——. "Women and Family Life on Roman Imperial Funerary Altars." *Latomus* 46 (1987): 545–54.

Kramer, Samuel. "The Weeping Goddess: Sumerian Prototypes of the Mater Dolorosa." *Biblical Archeologist* 46 (1983): 69–80.

La Follette, Laetitia. "The Costume of the Roman Bride." Pages 54–64 in *The World of Roman Costume*. Edited by Judith Lynn Sebesta and Larissa Bonfante. Madison, Wis.: University of Wisconsin Press, 1994.

Lintott, Andrew. *Imperium Romanum: Politics and Administration*. London: Routledge, 1993.

Martin, Dale B. "The Construction of the Ancient Family: Methodological Considerations." *Journal of Roman Studies* 86 (1996): 40–60.

McGinn, Thomas A. J. *Prostitution, Sexuality, and the Law in Ancient Rome*. New York: Oxford University Press, 1998.

Mellor, Ronald. "The Goddess Roma." *Aufstieg und Niedergang der römischen Welt* 17.2:950–1030. Part 2, *Principat* 17.2. Edited by H. Temporini and W. Haase. New York: de Gruyter, 1981.

Mueller, Hans-Friedrich. "*Vita, Pudicitia, Libertus*: Juno, Gender, and Religious Politics in Valerius Maximus." *Transactions of the American Philological Association* 128 (1998): 221-63.

Myerowitz, Molly. "The Domestication of Desire: Ovid's *Parva Tabella* and the Theater of Love." Pages 131–57 in *Pornography and Representation in Greece and Rome*. Edited by Amy Richlin. New York: Oxford University Press, 1992.

Pomeroy, Sarah B. *Goddesses, Whores, Wives, and Slaves: Women in Classical Antiquity*. New York: Shocken Books, 1975.

——. "Reflections on Plutarch, *Advice to the Bride and Groom*: Something Old, Something New, Something Borrowed." Pages 33–42 in *Plutarch's Advice to the Bride and Groom and A Consolation to His Wife: English Translations, Commentary, Interpretive Essays, and Bibliography*. Edited by Sarah B. Pomeroy. New York: Oxford University Press, 1999.

——. "The Study of Women in Antiquity: Past, Present, and Future." *American Journal of Philology* 112 (1991): 263–68.

Price, S. R. F. "God and Emperors: The Greek Language of the Roman Imperial Cult." *Journal of Hellenic Studies* 104 (1984): 79–95.

——. *Rituals and Power: The Roman Imperial Cult in Asia Minor*. Cambridge: Cambridge University Press, 1984.

Radista, Leo Ferrero. "Augustus' Legislation Concerning Marriage, Procreation, Love Affairs and Adultery." *Aufstieg und Niedergang der römischen Welt* 2.13:278–339. Edited by H. Temporini and W. Haase. New York: de Gruyter, 1980.

Rawson, Beryl. "From 'Daily Life' to 'Demography.'" Pages 1–20 in *Women in Antiquity: New Assessments*. Edited by Richard Hawley and Barbara Levick. London: Routledge, 1995.

——. "The Roman Family." Pages 1–57 in *The Family in Ancient Rome: New Perspectives*. Edited by Beryl Rawson. Ithaca, N.Y.: Cornell University Press, 1986.

Reekmans, Louis. "La 'Dextrarum Iunctio' dans l'iconographie romaine et paléochrétienne." *Bulletin de l'Institut historique Belge à Rom* 31 (1958): 23–95.

Richlin, Amy. "Reading Ovid's Rapes." Pages 158–79 in *Pornography and Representation in Greece and Rome*. Edited by Amy Richlin. New York: Oxford University Press, 1992.

Rowlandson, Jane, ed. *Women and Society in Greek and Roman Egypt: A Sourcebook*. Cambridge: Cambridge University Press, 1998.

Saller, Richard P., and Brent D. Shaw. "Tombstones and Roman Family Relations in the Principate: Civilians, Soldiers, and Slaves." *Journal of Roman Studies* 74 (1984): 124–56.

Sebesta, Judith Lynn. "Symbolism in the Costume of the Roman Woman." Pages 46–53 in *The World of Roman Costume*. Edited by Judith Lynn Sebesta and Larissa Bonfante. Madison, Wis.: University of Wisconsin, 1994.

———. "Women's Costume and Feminine Civic Morality in Augustan Rome." Pages 105–17 in *Gender and Body in the Ancient Mediterranean*. Edited by Maria Wyke. Malden, Mass.: Blackwell, 1998.

Sherk, Robert A. *The Roman Empire: Augustus to Hadrian*. Cambridge: Cambridge University Press, 1988.

Sissa, Giulia. *Greek Virginity*. Translated by Arthur Goldhammer. Cambridge, Mass.: Harvard University Press, 1990.

Smith, R. R. R. "*Simulacra Gentium:* The Ethne from the Sebasteion at Aphrodisias." *Journal of Roman Studies* 78 (1988): 50–77.

Swain, Simon. "Plutarch's Moral Program." Pages 85–96 in *Plutarch's Advice to the Bride and Groom and A Consolation to His Wife: English Translations, Commentary, Interpretive Essays, and Bibliography*. Edited by Sarah B. Pomeroy. New York: Oxford University Press, 1999.

Treggiari, Susan. *Roman Marriage: Iusti Coniuges from the Time of Cicero to the Time of Ulpian*. Oxford: Clarendon Press, 1991.

Thomsen, Ole. *Ritual and Desire: Catullus 61 and 62*. Aarhus: Aarhus University Press, 1992.

Van Bremen, Riet. *The Limits of Participation: Women and Civic Life in the Hellenistic and Roman Periods*. Amsterdam: J. C. Gieben, 1996.

Varner, Eric R. "Domitia Longina and the Politics of Portraiture." *American Journal of Archaeology* 99 (1995): 187–206.

Walters, Jonathan. "Invading the Roman Body: Manliness and Impenetrability in Roman Thought." Pages 29–43 in *Roman Sexualities*. Edited by Judith P. Hallett and Marilyn B. Skinner. Princeton: Princeton University Press, 1997.

Wood, Susan. "Alcestis on Roman Sarcophagi." *American Journal of Archeology* 82 (1978): 499–510.

Wyke, Maria. "Woman in the Mirror: The Rhetoric of Adornment in the Roman World." Pages 134–51 in *Women in Ancient Societies: An Illusion of the Night*. Edited by Léonie J. Archer, Susan Fischler, and Maria Wyke. Basingstoke: Macmillan, 1994.

Zanker, Paul. *The Power of Images in the Age of Augustus*. Translated by Alan Shapiro. Ann Arbor, Mich.: University of Michigan Press, 1988.

7. Works on Ancient and Medieval Interpreters and Biblical Interpretation

Camille, Michael. "Visionary Perception and Images of the Apocalypse in the Later Middle Ages." Pages 276–89 in *The Apocalypse in the Middle Ages*. Edited by

Richard K. Emmerson and Bernard McGinn. Ithaca, N.Y.: Cornell University Press, 1992.

Emmerson, Richard K. "Introduction: The Apocalypse in Medieval Culture." Pages 293–334 in *The Apocalypse in the Middle Ages*. Edited by Richard K. Emmerson and Bernard McGinn. Ithaca, N.Y.: Cornell University Press, 1992.

———, and Ronald B. Herzmann. *The Apocalyptic Imagination in the Middle Ages*. Philadelphia: University of Pennsylvania Press, 1992.

Hamburger, Jeffrey F. *The Rothschild Canticles: Art and Mysticism in Flanders and the Rhineland Circa 1300*. New Haven: Yale University Press, 1990.

———. "The Visual and the Visionary: The Image in Late Medieval Monastic Devotions." *Viator* 20 (1989): 161–82.

Harrison, Carol. *Beauty and Revelation in the Thought of Saint Augustine*. Oxford: Clarendon Press, 1992.

Hollywood, Amy. *The Soul as Virgin Wife: Mechthild of Magdeburg, Marguerite Porete, and Meister Eckhart*. Notre Dame, Ind.: University of Notre Dame Press, 2001.

Jones, Ch. W. "Preface." Pages v–xvi in *Bedae Venerabilis Opera: Opera Didascalica I*. Corpus Christianorum: Series latina. Turnhout: Brepols, 1975.

Kennedy, George A. *A New History of Classical Rhetoric*. Princeton: Princeton University Press, 1994.

Lewis, Suzanne. *Reading Images: Narrative Discourse and Reception in the Thirteenth-Century Illuminated Apocalypse*. Cambridge: Cambridge University Press, 1995.

Lubac, Henri de. *Medieval Exegesis*. Translated by E. M. Macierowski. 2 vols. Grand Rapids, Mich.: William B. Eerdmans, 2000.

Markus, R. A. "St. Augustine on Signs." Pages 61–91 in *Augustine: A Collection of Critical Essays*. Edited by R. A. Markus. Garden City, N.Y.: Anchor Books, 1972.

McGinn, Bernard, ed. *Apocalyptic Spirituality: Treatises and Letters of Lactantius, Adso of Montier-En-Der, Joachim of Fiore, The Franciscan Spirituals, Savonarola*. The Classics of Western Spirituality. Mahwah, N.J.: Paulist Press, 1979.

———. "Apocalyptic Traditions and Spiritual Identity in Thirteenth-Century Religious Life." Pages 1–26 in *The Roots of the Modern Christian Tradition*. Edited by Rozanne Elder. Kalamazoo, Mich.: Cistercian Publications, 1984.

———. "Apocalypticism in the Middle Ages: An Historiographical Sketch." *Medieval Studies* 37 (1975): 252–86.

———. "Awaiting an End: Research in Medieval Apocalypticism." *Mediaevalia et Humanistica* 11 (1982): 267–78.

———. *The Calabrian Abbot: Joachim of Fiore in the History of Western Thought*. New York: Macmillan, 1985.

——. "Introduction: John's Apocalypse and the Apocalyptic Mentality." Pages 3–19 in *The Apocalypse in the Middle Ages*. Edited by Richard K. Emmerson and Bernard McGinn. Ithaca, N.Y.: Cornell University Press, 1992.

——. "Symbolism in the Thought of Joachim of Fiore." Pages 145–64 in *Prophecy and Millenarianism: Essays in Honour of Marjorie Reeves*. Edited by Ann Williams. Essex: Longman, 1980.

——. "Symbols of the Apocalypse in Medieval Culture." *Michigan Quarterly Review* 22 (1983): 265–83.

——. *Visions of the End: Apocalyptic Traditions in the Middle Ages*. 2nd ed. New York: Columbia University Press, 1998.

Murphy, James J. *Rhetoric in the Middle Ages: A History of Rhetorical Theory from St. Augustine to the Renaissance*. Berkeley: University of California Press, 1974.

Newman, Barbara. "*La mystique courtoise*: Thirteenth-Century Beguines and the Art of Love." Pages 137–67 in *From Virile Woman to WomanChrist: Studies in Medieval Religion and Literature*. Philadelphia: University of Pennsylvania Press, 1995.

Reeves, Marjorie. "The Development of Apocalyptic Thought: Medieval Attitudes." Pages 40–72 in *The Apocalypse in English Renaissance Thought and Literature*. Edited by C. A. Patrides and Joseph Wittreich. Manchester: Manchester University Press, 1984.

——. *Joachim of Fiore and the Prophetic Future: Medieval Study in Historical Thinking*. Rev. ed. Gloucestershire: Sutton, 1999.

——. "The Originality and Influence of Joachim of Fiore." *Tradition: Studies in Ancient and Medieval History, Thought, and Religion* 36 (1980): 269–316.

——, and Beatrice Hirsch-Reich. *The Figurae of Joachim of Fiore*. Oxford: Clarendon Press, 1972.

Rist, John M. *Augustine: Ancient Thought Baptized*. Cambridge: Cambridge University Press, 1994.

Smalley, Beryl. *The Study of the Bible in the Middle Ages*. 3rd ed. Oxford: Basil Blackwell, 1984.

Turner, Denys. *Eros and Allegory: Medieval Exegesis of the Song of Songs*. Cistercian Studies 156. Kalamazoo, Mich.: Cistercian Publications, 1995.

West, Delno C. "Introduction." Pages i–xv in *Joachim of Fiore in Christian Thought: Essays on the Influence of the Calabrian Prophet*. New York: Burt Franklin, 1975.

Wright, David F. "Augustine: His Exegesis and Hermeneutics." Pages 701–30 in *Hebrew Bible/Old Testament: The History of Its Interpretation*. Part 1: Antiquity. Edited by Magne Saebo. Göttingen: Vandenhoeck & Ruprecht, 1996.

8. Works on Metaphor and Theory

Bal, Mieke. "Metaphors He Lives By." *Semeia* 61 (1993): 185–207.

Black, Max. "Metaphor." Pages 273–94 in *Proceedings of the Aristotelian Society*. Vol. 55. London: Harrison and Sons, 1955.

——. *Models and Metaphors*. Ithaca, N.Y.: Cornell University Press, 1962.

——. "More About Metaphor." Pages 19–41 in *Metaphor and Thought*. 2nd ed. Edited by Andrew Ortony. Cambridge: Cambridge University Press, 1993.

Booth, Wayne C. "Metaphors as Rhetoric: The Problem of Evaluation." Pages 47–70 in *On Metaphor*. Edited by Sheldon Sacks. Chicago: University of Chicago Press, 1979.

Cameron, Lynne. "Operationalising 'Metaphor' for Applied Linguistic Research." Pages 3–28 in *Researching and Applying Metaphor*. Edited by Lynne Cameron and Graham Low. Cambridge: Cambridge University Press, 1999.

Camp, Claudia V. "Metaphor in Feminist Biblical Interpretation: Theoretical Perspectives." *Semeia* 61 (1993): 3–36.

Cienki, Alan. "Metaphoric Gestures and Some of Their Relations to Verbal Metaphoric Expressions." Pages 189–204 in *Discourse and Cognition: Bridging the Gap*. Edited by Jean-Pierre Koenig. Stanford: CSLI, 1998.

Clover, Carol J. "Her Body, Himself: Gender in the Slasher Film." Pages 235–50 in *Feminist Film Theory: A Reader*. Edited by Sue Thornham. Edinburgh: Edinburgh University Press, 1999. Repr. of pages 91–133 in *Fantasy and the Cinema*. Edited by J. Donald. London: BFI, 1989.

Cohen, Ted. "Metaphor and the Cultivation of Intimacy." Pages 1–10 in *On Metaphor*. Edited by Sheldon Sacks. Chicago: University of Chicago Press, 1978.

Crisp, Peter. "Metaphorical Propositions: A Rationale." *Language and Literature* 11, no. 1 (2002): 7–16.

Croft, William. "The Role of Domains in the Interpretation of Metaphors and Metonymies." *Cognitive Linguistics* 4 (1993): 335–70.

Eco, Umberto. "Denotation." Pages 43–77 in *On the Medieval Theory of Signs*. Edited by Umberto Eco and Costantino Marmo. Amsterdam: John Benjamins, 1989.

Fauconnier, Gilles. *Mappings in Thought and Language*. Cambridge: Cambridge University Press, 1997.

——, and Mark Turner. *The Way We Think: Conceptual Blending and the Mind's Hidden Complexities*. New York: Basic Books, 2002.

Frye, Northup. *The Great Code: The Bible and Literature*. San Diego: Harcourt Brace, 1981.

Gibbs, Raymond W. *The Poetics of Mind: Figurative Thought, Language, and Understanding.* Cambridge: Cambridge University Press, 1994.

Johnson, Mark. *The Body in the Mind: The Bodily Basis of Meaning, Imagination, and Reason.* Chicago: University of Chicago Press, 1987.

Kittay, Eva F. *Metaphor: Its Cognitive Force and Linguistic Structure.* Oxford: Clarendon Press, 1987.

Lacocque, Andre. "Apocalyptic Symbolism: A Ricoeurian Hermeneutical Approach." *Biblical Research* 26 (1981): 6–15.

Lakoff, George. "The Contemporary Theory of Metaphor." Pages 202–51 in *Metaphor and Thought.* 2nd ed. Edited by Andrew Ortony. Cambridge: Cambridge University Press, 1993.

———. "The Meanings of Literal." *Metaphor and Symbolic Activity* 1 (1986): 291–96.

———. *Women, Fire and Dangerous Things: What Categories Reveal about the Mind.* Chicago: University of Chicago Press, 1987.

Lakoff, George, and Mark Johnson. *Metaphors We Live By.* Chicago: University of Chicago Press, 1980.

———, and Mark Turner. *More Than Cool Reason: A Field Guide to Poetic Metaphor.* Chicago: University of Chicago Press, 1989.

Mahon, James Edwin. "Getting Your Sources Right: What Aristotle *Didn't* Say." Pages 69–80 in *Researching and Applying Metaphor.* Edited Lynne Cameron and Graham Low. Cambridge: Cambridge University Press, 1999.

Miller, George A. "Images and Models, Similes and Metaphors." Pages 357–400 in *Metaphor and Thought.* 2nd ed. Edited by Andrew Ortony. Cambridge: Cambridge University Press, 1993.

Ortony, Andrew. "Metaphor, Language, and Thought." Pages 1–16 in *Metaphor and Thought.* 2nd ed. Edited by Andrew Ortony. Cambridge: Cambridge University Press, 1993.

Quinn, Naomi. "The Cultural Basis of Metaphor." Pages 56–93 in *Beyond Metaphor: The Theory of Tropes in Anthropology.* Edited by J. Fernandez. Stanford, Calif.: Stanford University Press, 1991.

Ricoeur, Paul. *Interpretation Theory: Discourse and the Surplus of Meaning.* Fort Worth, Tex.: Texas Christian University Press, 1976.

———. "Metaphor and the Main Problems of Hermeneutics." Pages 303–19 in *A Ricoeur Reader: Reflection and Imagination.* Edited by Mario J. Valdés. Toronto: University of Toronto Press, 1991.

———. "The Metaphorical Process as Cognition, Imagination and Feeling." Pages 228–47 in *Philosophical Perspectives on Metaphor.* Edited by Mark Johnson. Minneapolis: University of Minnesota Press, 1981.

———. "Mimesis and Representation." Pages 137–55 in *A Ricoeur Reader: Reflection and Imagination*. Edited by Mario J. Valdés. Toronto: University of Toronto Press, 1991.

——. *The Rule of Metaphor: Multi-disciplinary Studies of the Creation of Meaning in Language*. Translated by R. Czerny with K. McLaughlin and J. Costello. Toronto: University of Toronto Press, 1977.

——. "Word, Polysemy, Metaphor: Creativity in Language." Pages 65–85 in *A Ricoeur Reader: Reflection and Imagination*. Edited by Mario J. Valdés. Toronto: University of Toronto Press, 1991.

Said, Edward W. "Criticism between Culture and System." Pages 178–225 in *The World, the Text, and the Critic*. Cambridge, Mass.: Harvard University Press, 1983.

——. "Introduction: Secular Criticism." Pages 1–30 in *The World, the Text, and the Critic*. Cambridge, Mass.: Harvard University Press, 1983.

——. "The World, the Text, and the Critic." Pages 31–53 in *The World, the Text, and the Critic*. Cambridge, Mass.: Harvard University Press, 1983.

Schön, Donald A. "Generative Metaphor: A Perspective on Problem-Setting in Social Policy." Pages 137–63 in *Metaphor and Thought*. 2nd ed. Edited by Andrew Ortony. Cambridge: Cambridge University Press, 1993.

Searle, John R. "Metaphor." Pages 83–111 in *Metaphor and Thought*. 2nd ed. Edited by Andrew Ortony. Cambridge: Cambridge University Press, 1993.

Soskice, Janet Martin. *Metaphor and Religious Language*. Oxford: Clarendon Press, 1985.

Steen, Gerard. "From a Linguistic to Conceptual Metaphor in Five Steps." Pages 57–77 in *Metaphor in Cognitive Linguistics: Selected Papers from the Fifth International Cognitive Linguistics Conference*. Edited by Raymond Gibbs and Gerard Steen. Amsterdam: John Benjamins, 1999.

——. "Metaphor and Discourse: Towards a Linguistic Checklist for Metaphor Analysis." Pages 81–104 in *Research and Applying Metaphor*. Edited by Lynne Cameron and Graham Low. Cambridge: Cambridge University Press, 1999.

——. "A Rhetoric of Metaphor: Conceptual and Linguistic Metaphor and the Psychology of Literature." Pages 145–63 in *The Psychology and Sociology of Literature: In Honor of Elrud Ibsch*. Edited by Dick Schram and Gerard Steen. Amsterdam: John Benjamins, 2001.

——. *Understanding Metaphor in Literature: An Empirical Approach*. London: Longman, 1994

Strauss, Claudia, and Naomi Quinn. *A Cognitive Theory of Cultural Meaning*. Cambridge: Cambridge University Press, 1997.

Turner, Mark. *Death Is the Mother of Beauty: Mind, Metaphor, Criticism*. Chicago: University of Chicago Press, 1987.

——. *The Literary Mind*. New York: Oxford University Press, 1996.

INDEX OF BIBLICAL AND EXTRABIBLICAL REFERENCES

INDEX OF AUTHORS